Dear Donald

Dear Donald

– Letters from Argo –
By Lars G. Kindem

About apples and life,
And provocative miscellany
Of mid-20th century Americana,
Growing up below the "Hill"
In Northfield, Minnesota

Compiled and edited by
B. Wayne Quist ("Hoz")

Copyright © 2019 by B. Wayne Quist (aka "Hoz")
All rights reserved.
Custodian of the "Argo" Letters for Fubar and the Kindem Family,
With roots in Northfield, Minnesota and Manitou Heights.
ISBN-13: 978-1505250022
ISBN-10: 1505250021

For Argo & Hobo

*And the Fubar rantipoles brought together by Argo
at the St. Olaf "Popstand" many years ago —
fiercely independent mavericks
in search of meaning, truth and new adventure;
unified with a mutual passion for eccentric action;
recognizing and embracing
the existential and the absurd,
while transcending traditional human behavior.*

- B. Wayne Quist ("Hoz")

"The Hill" at St. Olaf College in Northfield, MN
- Photo and logo on page 47 courtesy of St. Olaf College Archives

Contents

Preface	xiii

Letters

The Letter	3
Lincoln Street, 1940	7
Kids hangin' out at 'Olaf	11
"Sing it to your mother, Lars"	15
The Bells of Northfield	17
Amerikabrev	21
Fruits of my labors	25
"Strudel"	29
"Dub Dub" Dooley	33
A deed? Indeed: Thoughts on our plots	37
Code Name: "Cynthia"	39
The Lion, Rampant	47
Writing to Disk	51
Vacuum Cleaning on Sunday	53
Telephone Tricks	55
Telephone Tricks, II	57
Flagpole Sitting	59
Muus Hunt – Gjengangere (Ghosts)	63
Role Models	67
Apple Run	75
Boys Will Be Boys	81
Grandparents	85
Angel Arianna	89
Many Glacier Hotel	93
"La Biche" – The Doe	99
TZXCCVBNM6969 (Security)	105
Predictions	109

The Past Is Prologue	111
Options	115
Oddfellows' Home	117
Not All the Vikings Are Dead	121
Pop Hill and the Popstand	125
Pride	131
Relativity	133
Reputation	135
San Francisco Beckons	137
The First Pick: Pluck & Pack	141
The Fortune Cookie	145
The Pour	147
The Price of Tea	153
The Rookie	157
The Screen	159
The Shade	163
The Minnesota State Fair	167
The Visit	173
Too Easy	175
War on 'Coons	177
Wednesay night fights	179
"Powah!"	187
Blabbermouth	189
Draw the Line	191
Day of Wine and Roses	195
Down on the Farm	197
Duck Soup	201
Experts	203
Follow the Leader	205
Frozen Rain	209
More Ghosts	211
Gifts	215

Gunfight at the OK Corral	219
Hershey Bars	221
Humility	223
Humility, Part II	227
You Are What You Eat	229
Huntin' and Fishin'	231
Dundas Justice	235
IBM 1604 & the Marriage of Tor	243
Interview	247
Jens Speaks	253
Kid Stuff	259
Man's Best Friend	263
Maynard's Duck	267
The Minnesota Dwarf Trout Lilly	271
Mixed Signals	275
Poems for Hobo	277
For Bob Rose	279
Primlefse	281
Caribou Fishing, '84	285
Cannon River Carp	289
Button... Button	295
By the Fire	299
Books & Bookmaking	303
Carleton Lake	307
Cause and Effect	311
Changed by Chance	315
Peace on Earth, Good Will to All People!	317
Bottle Adventures	319
Ytterboe is Dead	321
A Look at the Second Amendment	337
Athletics, Northfield High School, Long Ago	341
The Supreme Court of the United States	343

Northfield Honors WWII Veterans	345
Kernel Dr. Martinson, BA, MA, MBA, PhD	351
Brother Erling's Birthday	355
Cues, Miscues, and Choir Memories	357
The Navy's March of Dimes	373
Chapel	377

Afterword

Remembering Argo	381
Tribute to Lars Kindem	386
Donald McCornack Clark	389
The First Fubar to Fall	390
Hobo Reminiscences	394
Remembering Cricket	397
In Memorium Fubar	399
Mike & Al's in Dundas	400
The Last Rally	401

Preface

Lars Kindem ("Argo") was born in Northfield, Minnesota in 1933 and died in Minneapolis in 2013. Donald Clark ("Hobo")was born in Mitchell, South Dakota in 1935 and died in Carson City, Nevada in 2000. Donald was named "Hobo" by Lars because he was truly a man of the road.

In the 1950s, the self-named Argo emerged as the leader of a band of brothers called "Fubar" and whose bonds of love and loyalty remained constant throughout their lives. The "Dear Donald" letters were written between 1994 and Donald Clark's death in 2000. The letters were addressed to Donald M. Clark ("Hobo"), "late of Northfield, New York City, Portland, Carson City and other environs."

The Argo letters are vintage Lars Kindem as a master storyteller – a collection of mid-20th century Americana with a touch of Mark Twain and Will Rogers. Some of the letters were mailed to Hobo, but most were not. When asked why he didn't mail them, Lars said, "No sense wasting postage – Hobo always shows up sooner or later and we enjoy reading them out loud together, and laughing."

Lars and Donald loved to share memories of their formative years along the Cannon River and Manitou Heights below the "College on the Hill" that Lars lovingly called the "Popstand," St. Olaf College. Since its early founders, few have upheld the inspiration of St. Olaf College as Lars did for so many years with his indelible Norwegian roots.

Lars' parents, Ingvald and Anna Kindem, and three oldest siblings Olaf, Halvor and Andi, came to America from Norway in 1925 and settled in Northfield. Donny's father was a professor at St. Olaf and Lars' father worked as an engineer in the power plant and janitor in Thorson Hall. Anna Kindem was well known for her marvelous homemade lefse and weekly letters to her hometown newspaper in Norway.

The Argo letters provide captivating insights into the formative years Lars and Donny spent growing up together in Northfield in the 1940s and 1950s. Those who knew Lars do not forget his genius, especially words and phrases he coined, his humor, wit, and constant good will. We are fortunate and grateful to have known Lars so well, and for so long.

I wish to thank members of the Kindem family for their assistance in assembling the "Dear Donald" letters. Lars' sons, Tor and Bjørn, preserved handwritten copies of the letters as well as Lars' computer files for safe-keeping and publication – for future "Oles" past, present and future, and for fellow Northfielders.

I would also like to thank Andrew Eggenberger, editor of the Lake City Graphic, for his invaluable assistance in bringing this book to publication with Amazon and helping make it a reality.

B. Wayne Quist ("Hoz") — St. Olaf 1958
Lake City, Minnesota — March 2019

Letters

The Letter

Dear Donald,

I want to discuss with you the most far-reaching, versatile, and important literary form the world has ever known: namely, the letter. You see, the letter lets you publish a portrait of yourself as you choose, a freedom that conversations over the phone cannot grant efficiently because you are dealing with the give and take of the moment; issues you wish to discuss are often lost if you are not working from a prepared script of statements you wish to make or questions you want answered.

My fondness for letter writing is strongest when I get the sense I've entered someone else's mind, someone who opens the door by opening the envelope. I enjoy the intimate pages of people expressing a small part of themselves. Letter writing lets you organize your own repository. There is something good about that.

When I get the monthly phone bill, I am staggered by the amount. Who in the world has called New York? How about Grundy Center, Iowa? This has to stop, I say aloud even though no one is within range of my loud proclamation; and few who would be are inclined to worry about it. Why can't you just sit down and write a letter? It only costs 3 cents. (wait a minute — that's from an old speech. The cost is now 37 cents and heading to a dollar.)

Once, when the world and I were younger, I sat waiting for a friend at a bar, thinking of myself, as those in bars do; occasionally talking to the robot serving up euphemisms of booze, when a politician sidled up to me at the bar. I knew he was a politician because he was wearing a polyester suit. "Whaddaya got ta say?" he opens. I counter with, "You know, you're probably right." "Yer darn right!" says he, "And another thing I wanna tell ya — Can ya keep a secrut?" I assure him I cannot. "Good!" he blurts. "Nobody can nowadays, and any so-and-so who says he can is a liar."

He then goes on to let me in on a secret which he has been holding "close to the vest" as it were: "You vote, right?" "Right." "You probably never voted for me, cuz you're not in my district. Nobody in my district owns a suit. He slaps my knee, laughing. I start to get uneasy. "Here's the deal," he goes on, "You and all of the electorites, ah, electrical, ah fooey, electrolite, I mean, electorate. You guys have the power, you know what I mean? But nobody knows how in the heck to exercise that power, get what I'm saying?" "I don't."

He continues, "What you gotta unnerstand, you know, is this, that if you — you, I'm talkin' about you, the voter, take a pen and paper, and an envelope and put a stamp on it, and write me, an alected official, a letter, from the heart or any other place — I get those letters, you know. Anyway, you take the trouble to write me a letter giving a piece of your mind, that letter represents at least 35 people who feel the same way."

"Really?" I say, following this intense man with my very best listening skills. "That's right. Statistics. That's what they told us on the first day we were in office. Statistics show that most people just complain about the politicians to each other, and never do the real important thing which is to sit right down and write a letter to their public servant."

I thank him profusely for the inside tip, and offer to buy him whatever he is drinking. "That's not a bribe," I state unequivocally, "because I don't live in your district." "No, no, lemme buy you one." Holy smokes! I finally met up with someone who unnerstands. (Understanding comes slowly to me sometimes. But once I catch on, there is no need to repeat the lesson.)

Another type of letter that's misunderstood is the love letter. You never really know what is going on at the receiving end when you write a love letter to a sweetheart. For all you know, she may be reading something entirely different into the text. Or she may, as I suspect, be saying to herself, "How am I going to let him down without a big mess of a scene? The safest way is a letter." Enter the art form, the "Dear John" letter. Now that's the one that hurts. But "It only hurts for a little while," she sang.

But dunning letters are the worst. Most St. Olaf graduates have no idea what to do beside pay up when they receive a dunning letter. Yet, lawyers never pay on time and dentists expect you to delay payment, that's why they charge too much in the first place — they charge interest up front. And the gas and electric guys just turn off your utilities if you do not respond to their letters. I wish I could do that.

It takes time to cultivate a long-lasting friendship, and letters are the way to cement the deal. It takes time to write a letter to keep in touch with friends and classmates. But the time is worth it. How much time does it take to fire off a letter to a friend? Get thee a stop watch. I bet it can be done in less than 20 minutes.

Think of it — 20 minutes to inform, reassure, thank, relate details of your life that you would share with a friend, ask or give advice when needed, express sympathy, or, as I like to do, goof off a little, just for fun, in a letter to a friend like you.

    Lars, aka Argo

Lincoln Street, 1940

Dear Donald,

The year prior to the Japanese attack on Pearl Harbor was memorable for a seven-year-old trying to grow up on Lincoln Street. We still felt the effects of the depression in our family, and there was never enough money to go around, but we didn't seem to miss out on anything.

Living in a large family like mine in those days was an adventure. Did you ever play to a packed house? I did, all the time. We had a much larger family than anyone I knew on the West side of town. I thought I had lots of siblings, and then in 1940, I got one more. Boy, that was a wonderment!

My mother came to me and said she was going to go get a new baby down at the hospital. I was seven years old and it was June 6, 1940. She asked me to help her get into the bathtub, which I did. Not only that, but I washed her back and helped her out of the tub also. I was a good boy.

We went down to the hospital. Along the way, she explained that Dr. Thorson was going to catch the baby. She did not go into detail which was unnecessary. I filled in the details myself in my own mind. I envisioned my mother and Dr. Thorson on the North side lawn of the hospital with outstretched blanket, like Eskimos ready to receive this latest gift from God in heaven.

After leaving mamma at the entrance, I went out to play with Paul Sherwin. On this day we decided to go to Way Park just off St. Olaf Avenue. It was within sight of the hospital, so we could swim while we watched for God to part the clouds and toss down a baby for Mamma and Dr. Thorson to catch.

Nothing resembling the appearance of God or even angels in the sky occurred above the hospital, so we went home for supper. When I got there, the news was out: mamma was in the hospital with a new baby girl. I ate quickly and ran down to the hospital.

There they were. My dad had gone into the nursery and brought the baby to mamma, so she could nurse her. She was a cutie, and mamma said her name was Margit Anne. The nurse was upset with my dad for taking Margit out of the nursery, but mamma said he had seven other children, and it was the natural thing for him to do when he saw the baby crying.

I could hardly wait to hear about the "baby catching" event, how it worked. I remember saying, after seeing the new baby, "Boy, that Dr. Thorson sure is a good catcher!" Right then and there, mamma decided to clue me in. She pulled aside the bed clothes and showed me her abdomen which was all taped up. Then she told me that was where the baby came from.

I asked if I could hold little Baby Margit, and mamma said that would be OK. I asked if I could take her outside and Mamma said that would have to wait until she got older and bigger.

It sure was fun to have a little baby sister! She was so nice! None of my pals had a little baby at home, so I was feeling really special. She was a good baby and seldom cried. I used to sit by her little bed and stare at her, waiting for her to wake up so I could hand her a rattle. I have no recollection of any baby bottles, so in all likelihood, Margit never had a bottle.

At home still, were Andi, Erling, Alf, Roald and me. Olaf and Halvor were gone to the CCC camps by that time. We all took turns baby sitting and trying to get Margit to talk and walk over the next few months.

I think I spent more time than anyone else holding her hands while she learned to take her first steps. Her first words remain a mystery. I bet one of the first was "La" which Andi used on me from time to time when I was very small. So naturally, I tried to get Margit to say my baby name, "La."

The house was crowded in those days. Even so, we took in St. Olaf students who occupied the front bed room upstairs. Mamma and pappa and little Margit had the master bedroom off the kitchen. I was born in that bedroom.

During my younger years, I slept in what we called "the back attic" with Roald, later with pappa. I liked sleeping with pappa because he didn't move much all night, and never hogged the covers. Roald and I used to play cards every night until we fell asleep. There were times when we found frost on the bed posts in the morning.

We still had to make ends meet in this family, so mamma got right back to work with her lefse baking. Her baking was done on a wood-burning stove in the basement, later upstairs in the back porch. The lefse had marks on it from the stove lid or the hour-glass shape in between lids.

Over in the corner were Kennebec potatoes in hundred pound gunny sacks. Mamma said they were the best potatoes for baking lefse. I kept the stove supplied with wood and also stocked the coal bucket when asked. Pappa and I often teamed up to peel the hot potatoes. That was fun. He would give me buttermilk with a spoon of sugar stirred in it for a treat. I love buttermilk to this day.

I delivered lefse to various people around the neighborhood. Now that I think about it, our customers were always "Mrs." something or other. There must have been lots of widows around at that time. I do not remember how much a dozen lefse cost back in 1940, but after the war it was 60 cents a dozen.

One time I carried lefse to Professor Huggenvik. He tipped me a dime, so I bowed and said "Takk skal du ha!" He liked that so much he gave me another dime. Then I said "Mange takk!" I got another dime, so I said "Mange tusen takk!" But he was all out of dimes so he gave me a hug and told me I was a nice boy. I already knew that.

I didn't only deliver lefse for my mother. We also had a large strawberry patch on the spot where the Søvik house now stands. I would pick the berries and sell them, going from door to door. The pints were 15 cents and the quarts, 25 cents. I gave the money to my mother.

We were always looking for a way to make money. One day that same year, 1940, Hans Hansen and I went up to the new house across the corner field on St. Olaf Avenue built by Dr. Marie Malmin Meyer, an English Professor at the college. We picked a wagon full of tulips, taking all she had. She got after me for that one after she caught us at the "Intersection of the World," selling tulips by the Ole Store across from her house. I had to work it off by stacking firewood in her basement.

A few months later, when the heat was off, I asked her if she had any apples on her trees. She said I could help myself. I saw her about two hours later on campus by Ytterboe Hall. I had a big basket full of her apples and was selling them two for a nickel.

Fifty-five years later when I visited Dr. Meyer at the

Northfield Retirement Center she reminded me of the tulips and apples back in 1940. We had a good laugh together.

    Argo — April 13, 1996

Kids hangin' out at 'Olaf

Dear Donald,

I want to take you back to the prewar years for a look at life on Lincoln Street and the St. Olaf campus area. Each day that we were not in Longfellow school or Sunday school or high school, Paul Sherwin would phone me or I would phone him. He was one of my best playmates. He also lived on Lincoln Street, in the house next to the entrance to the athletic field that was later occupied by Ade Christenson and his family.

Paul was an ideal playmate who could heave rocks as well as anyone. He was a brave boy and liked to do the same things as I did for fun. Paul's house was a natural starting point for almost any adventure around the St. Olaf campus. If there was a baseball game, we could walk 30 paces and there we were, shagging foul balls in the grasslands and marsh that later became Lincoln Lane.

Football games were a lot more fun, however, for we patrolled under the bleachers, gathering whatever useful items that dropped down from the fans seated above, and we could look up at the skirts. There were cigarettes already lit that we would find and puff on, but we didn't puff on the ones with lipstick. In those days, women were rather heavy on the red lipstick.

We always found what could be called a gold mine of pop bottles. There were more than you can imagine. Each was worth two cents in cash at the "Ole Store" on St. Olaf Avenue. During football games, we would run like the dickens to get the bottles as they dropped down beneath the bleachers and bring them to Huggenvik's back yard where we stashed them temporarily for safe keeping.

We were real entrepreneurs in the recycling business, but Paul and I weren't the only kids doing this — we had competition. Eddie Tripp and Hans Hansen were there, and Eddie's brother, "Buster," and David Stavig. Each boy had his own pile, and we kept count of our own; there was an honor system back then, not like the business world today; we were all friends, so nobody would "kipe" bottles from another, and we respected each other's stash unless someone started hoarding and got too many bottles.

On a day with no game, we could mosey up Popstand Hill and climb the ski scaffold. Later on, we would usually end up in Tripp's cave. We played hide and seek in those halcyon prewar days without the hassle of dealing with potatoes and onions stored there as they were in later years.

One day when we were playing in the caves we decided to go over on the other side of the hill to raid Lashbrook's watermelon patch. As we crawled through the patch, Helen Lashbrook saw us, opened up the back screen door and hollered, "Who's up there in the watermelon patch?" Eddie cupped his hands and called back, "Nobody but us watermelons!" After she went back into the house we "kiped" two melons and quickly crawled out of there. We took them back to the cave where we ate one, saving the other for the next day's refreshment. But Eddie's older brother "Buster" and his friend kiped it from us; no honor among thieves.

In the winter time, we would go up to the skating rink at St. Olaf located on the front lawn of Agnes Mellby Hall. There wasn't much for us to do there except pile wood on the fire in the stove and warm ourselves. We never had any skates. Sometimes we helped shovel the snow off the ice just for the fun of it. We could also go sledding on Old Main Hill, but that activity required sleds which we had to borrow. My brother Olaf made a sort of toboggan with a frame and three skis that we used sometimes, but it was too heavy to drag back up the steep Old Main hill.

Another adventure was to go up to the dairy barn which stood where the layered parking lot for the Student Center now stands [art department in 2014]. On the way across the athletic fields, we always took a drink from the water fountain located between the track and the baseball diamond. There was a long "bull run" located on the Northeast side of the barn, aimed just about toward where Thorson Hall now stands, but before its completion in 1948. It was a long narrow fenced-in area where the St. Olaf bull was confined in his private exercise area. Would that we had a lion, too, but the bull used to bawl and moo a lot. He had a brass ring in his nose, and I suppose we would bawl too, with a brass ring. We believed that if we ever went near him while wearing any red clothing he would crash out of there and get us.

St. Olaf students had jobs working in the dairy barn, mostly farm boys who knew something about dairy farming. Carleton had the same set up and so did the Odd Fellows' Home. The farmer lived on top of the hill by the south side of where the Student Center now stands. The horse barn stood near there too. George "Peachfuzz" Tripp, Eddie's dad, was the teamster. The team of Belgians was called "Dan" and "Dolly."

We got to play up in the hay mow and liked to jump down from the rafters onto the soft hay below. In winter, "Peachfuzz" Tripp would hitch the team to the snow plow and plow the roads on campus. They also used the team for plowing the field by Thorson and the one below the Old Main, across from our house. Both fields were used to grow corn for silage and alfalfa for hay, on a rotating basis.

Every day a farmer named Schuette with a horse-drawn wagon picked up the leftovers from the kitchens in Ytterboe and Mohn Halls — four barrels full of "slop" in his wagon. In those days, recycled food was used for "slopping the hogs." We didn't do that at our house, for we had no hogs, but we had a five-gallon pail under the sink in the kitchen. The drain was a straight tube which led to the bucket below. The slop bucket contained all the dishwater and food wastes from the kitchen and was carried outside and spread over the garden year around.

We enjoyed going to the basketball games on campus. I remember the 1941 season when the Oles had a good team. Old Pete Pederson furnished us ragamuffins with a ball to play with at half time. We must have put on quite a show on the court in our stocking feet with our running, tackling, scrapping, and occasionally throwing the ball toward the basket which was too high for us to reach with the ball.

After our half time show, we slid under the bleachers at the far end near where the band sat, and watched the game while lying on our stomachs. On one of these occasions, when I was about eight years old, I folded my hands and prayed to God: "Please, God, let Howie Steffans shoot a long shot from the middle of the floor and win the game." I don't remember if he did, but I remember the faith I had that enabled me to talk to God about it.

Once each summer in those prewar years, the St. John's Church congregation had a picnic on the green just south of Ytterboe Hall near the bandstand. Families brought all sorts of "pot luck" dishes to share. We had a grand time.

Especially exciting was when the time came for free ice cream cones. Every kid got two scoops of ice cream and could choose from vanilla, chocolate, strawberry or maple nut flavors. The ice cream came in huge brown rubber insulated containers that resembled somewhat today's large plastic garbage cans, but they were taller and slimmer. Mr. Olberg, partner in the Wolf & Olberg's grocery store by the Northfield National bank, was in charge.

Mr. Olberg was a neighbor and father of my classmate, Alice Jean, who won the 20-yard sprint races on Lincoln Street at my birthday party in 1940. She beat all the boys, including David Stavig, Paul Sherwin, Dick Jacobson and several others. First prize was a ten-cent bag of marbles which was thought to be a very big prize. You could go to the show for a dime. Boy, were the guys ever embarrassed!

Since my birthday was at Easter time, we had an Easter egg hunt in my house. This was a set up. I brought Paul Sherwin, my best friend, into the house before the hunt and revealed the hiding places of the eggs.

There were really only two buildings on campus that I found worth visiting — the gymnasium and the power plant, also referred to as the heating plant. I enjoyed visiting pappa there when he was engineer. It was always very warm and noisy because of the huge coal-burning furnaces which generated steam to produce electricity and heat for the campus buildings. The master switch for turning out all the dormitory lights was there. I think the lights were turned off at about 9:00 pm.

It was lots of fun to take a shower there since we had none at home. The soap was soft, green and not perfumed, but it worked fine. My dad introduced me to the tunnels, but only the entrance. This was a mystery I was able to solve for myself sometime later.

Argo — April 16, 1996

"Sing it to your mother, Lars"

Dear Donald,

Here is a letter I sent to Rolf and Pete Charlston ("Gus"). Their mother was Edith Hjertaas Charlston – Ella Hjertaas Roe was their aunt, and my voice teacher at 'Olaf.

    Argo—

Rolf and Peter, your beloved aunt Ella taught me about song and to be a singer of songs. She taught with great skill out of her rich background of study and performance. How lucky I was that she took me on as a student!

Some months ago, I did an unusual, perhaps strange thing. Going to the Ditmanson wing of the St. Olaf Library, I searched as many old Viking yearbooks as I could to see Ella in her early years. What did she look like and how did she change over the years to become the teacher I loved more than any other at St. Olaf?

She was everywhere. I noted with great interest, though little surprise, reports of her returning from advanced study in Europe. She probably went to considerable expense during the depression to prepare herself to become the most significant and well-known voice teacher in the history of St. Olaf College.

I was a very eager student and prepared diligently for my sessions each week in her beautiful studio. She had pictures and memorabilia everywhere, indicating she had been around and knew many artists.

Ella opened her lovely and cozy home to her students. She had a beautiful method of preparing us for our performances at Steensland. We sang to each other under familiar and not-threatening circumstances. Our friends, her voice students, were supportive. She was in love with each of us and we knew that.

When my turn came to "go on" at Steensland a couple of days hence, we polished up Mozart's "Within This Sacred Dwelling," then a couple others, such as "An Die Musik." I confessed to her that I was somewhat apprehensive about my upcoming performance because a choir buddy, Don Colton, promised to sit up front and laugh at me. I knew he would.

Ella said simply, "Look at me, not at him." He did, and I did, and that was that. Ella won. She knew that I needed to show my Norwegian heritage and skills, so she produced the score of a lovely testimonial, "Du Gamle Mor" (You dear old mother).

I learned the song as well as I could and the day came when we put it all together in her studio. I stood and sang; she sat and played the piano. She encouraged me by turning toward me, raising her hand, palm up, fingers slightly bent, shook it vigorously and said, "Sing it, Lars!" and later in the song, "Sing it from your heart, Lars!" and finally, with all the drama that Ella could muster, she smiled that wonderful smile and wailed, "Sing.....it.....to.....your..... MOTHER, Lars!"

I understood and said, "I'm going to do that right now." I walked out, ran down the Old Main Hill and into my house at 101 Lincoln Street. My mother was in the bakery, dressed in white, baking lefse. "Kom, Mamma, no skal eg synge ein song tip deg!" (C'mon Mom, I'm going to sing you a song!)

We went into the kitchen, she sat down, and I sang that song with those lovely words, "Du Gamle Mor, du sliter arm so sveittan er som blod..." ("You, dear old mother, you work so the sweat is like blood — but it is you who gave me my roots — my heart, my strength and my wild courage, and that is why I will love you dearly wherever on this earth I go.")

As I began the song, I nearly stopped, for in that small kitchen my voice seemed far too large; the volume surprised me not a little. Half way through the first of three verses, I saw the tears streaming down Mamma's floured cheeks. I knew at that moment what Ella knew: this was the song to sing to my mother.

This performance became the most important performance of my entire singing career. After the song, we embraced and Mamma asked me, "Lars, hew titch you to sing like dat?" My response was, "God and Ella."

Every now and then I visit the old music hall where I see and hear ghosts. I touch Ella's studio door and remember. When I visit Oaklawn Cemetery, I always go to the far hill to stand at the grave of Ella Hjertaas Roe. Her grave is between Ole Edvart Rølvaag and F. Melius Christiansen, two other legends of St. Olaf. It occurs to me that those three are well situated in the company of each other.

Ella knows what I am thinking, that standing before her is one who loved her dearly and reveres her memory, one who will forever see that smile and hear her say, "Sing it, Lars! Sing it to your mother, Lars!"

      Lars —

The Bells of Northfield

Dear Donald,

Northfield was probably the best place to grow up in the world! It's my birthright as you will attest, for I was born there, right below the Old Main Hill at 101 Lincoln Street.

You weren't born in Northfield, Hobo, but you achieved the rights of a Northfielder. Your Northfield odyssey led you from Thorson Hall where you lived with your parents, then down to the house on Lincoln Lane, eventually to the Viking stalag Courts across from 101 Lincoln Street – what an odyssey. Fate would decree that at your Viking home one pleasant spring evening you would introduce me to my one and only, the mother of five more Kindems. For that favor, Hobo, I am indebted to you, for you chose well.

There are so many sights and sounds in Northfield that bring back pleasant memories. Imagine waking each morning for a quarter century and looking out the front window at the Old Main on Manitou Heights. What a privilege! And no matter where we stretched our legs or rode bikes in that town, we were constantly advised and informed by the regularity of the daily whistles and bells throughout the town.

The whistle at the Northfield Milk condensery told us when it was seven in the morning and if we were going to be late for school. The same whistle told us when to finish lunch and when to quit work for the day. The bells of St. Dominick's church tolled at noon and six in the evening. No one really needed a timepiece if they were able to see well enough to read, daylight or dark, or hear the correct time of day at important times such as 12:00 o'clock noon and 6:00 in the evening.

There were other bells in town with which we have at least a passing familiarity. We discovered several of them in a collection on the Schilling premises one block south of St. John's Church, a popular hangout for nubile confirmands who had more on the mind than just Luther's Catechism. Remember how we would dash over to Schilling's for a bell or two? Or coming home after the show at the West Theater, filled with the exuberance of youth and stimulated by a session with Abbott & Costello or Loyal and

Hardy (as my cousin, Jake, called them).

It was only natural that we would sneak up on the Schilling bells to give them a ring, not only because they were there, and sounded so good, but also because we knew it passed off old Schilling so much. Imagine, to have an entire front yard full of a variety of bells and objecting to young boys ringing them? Donny, you favored the big locomotive bell and I went for the chimes that played tunes.

My favorite tunes were "Yankee Doodle" and "Mary Had a Little Lamb." Schilling, a collector of note, was not able to collect a fee from us when we visited, and that must have bothered him some. I think he went to bed early, too, so I suppose the ringing of the bells was especially unwelcome. But we sure enjoyed the Schilling bells!

I remember a couple of times when Eddie Tripp and Hans Hansen were along on such a caper. We would talk Hans, who was more foolhardy than we, into going up next to the house and ringing the one on the porch. Lights would go on all over the place and we would run and stand off a short distance and laugh like mad. The formula was always the same: ring as many as possible, run like the blazes, then laugh.

When I got a little older, my experience with the bells got me a very important position as bell ringer at St. John's Church. I was a senior in high school when Old Tendall, the janitor and bell ringer, had to step down because of old age. I applied for the job, explaining to the Reverend Boral Biorn that I knew how to sweep and mop and could ring the bell better than anyone. This was true, of course. Old Tendall taught me.

The bell rope was not quite as thick as the ropes used in the gym for climbing, but it was sturdy. It hung from the belfry, and passed through a hole in the balcony ceiling. Old Quasimodo would have been proud to celebrate his 16th birthday by ringing that bell. Funny thing about the St. John's bell — nobody really knew what note it sounded for sure. For example, I would have someone hold down about six keys on the piano keyboard next to the organ. When I rang the bell as the keys were held down, the strings on the piano, on those notes, would vibrate sympathetically and sing up the scale, like rr--ing--oy--yoy--yoom--ee----.

Tendall instructed me thus: I should take a firm grip on the rope as high as I could reach. Take a deep breath and pull as hard as my weight would allow, all the way down until my hands touched the floor; then grab up as far as I could and pull down hard three more times, all in one continuous motion. Then release, but be sure to grab the end of the rope, so it would not get away from me.

I followed his instruction, but the end of the rope was behind him, out of sight, so I panicked, grabbed the section of rope before me, and it pulled me right off the floor and up in the air. I hung on tightly, of course, so my descent rang the other side of the bell. This went on and I was getting a big kick out of it, singing "Nearer My God To Thee" each time I departed from the floor. I was now a bell ringer par excellence!

My career as a bell ringer involved not only thrashings about in the balcony. During funerals, I set the tone with a light tap each six seconds until the procession of mourners had left. Pastor Bjorn thought it would be a nice touch if I would ring three measured taps at the conclusion of each service. After the third ring had faded away, and after a polite pause, the congregation could leave to go outside and smoke. I practiced diligently ringing the bell for about a week. Imagine how confusing this must have been to those accustomed to the bells of St. Dominick's at noon and at six, but I didn't care.

One day, the organist, G. Winston Cassler, was practicing a piece on the organ. He enjoyed my antics immensely and struck up a tune on the organ, opening all the stops. There we were, Cassler and me, in concert. He was playing a round, "Three Blind Mice" with one hand on each keyboard, and his feet on the pedal keys. I was ringing and riding, confident now in my craft and sure that I would not bolt through the ceiling as I rode the rope up and down. What a concert that was! We sat afterwards and laughed ourselves silly.

The following Sunday, at the conclusion of the service, Mr. Cassler improvised on the organ a beautiful fugue, with statements and subjects and runs flowing all over the place. He winked at me and I caught on. So did Fred Schmidt, our choir director. Cassler's fugue was played in the style of a Bach fugue, but a careful ear would note that it was in reality a very fancied-up version of "Three Blind Mice."

What glorious fun, to hear and ring the Bells of Northfield!
    Argo —

Amerikabrev

Dear Donald,

Here's a short piece from the local news I knew you would like, about Anna's letters to Norway, and a love letter from Ingvald to Anna written in 1918 before they came to America from the old country.

Lars —

Norwegian-American Historical Association (NAHA)
St. Olaf College, Northfield, MN

Anna Sekse Kindem was a correspondent who sent "Americabrev" to a Norwegian newspaper in Odda, Hardanger, called, "Hardanger." Her 141 letters to the Hardanger paper from her home on Lincoln Street were meant to be informative and entertaining. Many topics of the day were addressed to the readers of the paper — family matters, local news of interest, lots of news about St. Olaf College, and other matters. This collection of articles, written in the "hardangermål" dialect used by the newspaper were returned to her by the publisher after publication. Charlotte Jacobson, working for the Norwegian-American Historical Association (NAHA) after her retirement from the Rølvaag Library staff at St. Olaf, translated the articles into English and handed them over to Lars Kindem for review before returning them to the NAHA archives. The dates of Anna Kindem's correspondence were from 1938 until March 1976, three months prior to her death. The following paragraph is from a letter written by Anna in 1953:

"The radio station WCAL is supported by voluntary contributions. Often, people send memorial gifts to the station instead of sending flowers to a funeral for someone they know. Occasionally, some wealthy Norwegians (there are a few) will give hundreds or even thousands of dollars in appreciation of the many services and programs. There are no advertisements. Well, you can say, they advertise God's Word."

Anna Sekse Kindem
Northfield, Minnesota, USA
America

From Ingvald Kindem to Anna Sekse

(Translated by Lars Kindem, son of Ingvald and Anna)
Tyssedal, Norway
August 22, 1918
Dear Anna!

Since we are so far away from each other and as a result have no opportunity to speak with each other, I must avail myself of the only alternative available to me, namely this letter which can bring you my thoughts and feelings.

It is so wonderful to have a friend one can trust and have confidence in. Therefore, as our Lord said, "It is not good that man should remain alone; I will therefore make him one who can be with him." God said that this was absolutely necessary, for he understood that man necessarily must have someone who he could trust and promise himself to, and thus God gave him a partner.

Now I suppose that perhaps you believe that I intend to use this small writing folder to argue such monumental things, but no — a portion of this I prefer to use to tell you once again about my great love for you, my dear Anna.

The first day I saw you remains a living delight for my fantasy. The first time our eyes met, there was a hushed, meaningful, and thought-filled glance. I felt something strange as never before. When I looked into your beautiful eyes, a strange feeling of goodness and well-being came over me which gave me the impression that the look you gave to me was truly from one with a pure soul.

That impression, which is so indelibly impressed upon my heart will never go away. No, each time you enter my thoughts, they become brighter and more clear and I understand more clearly how meaningful the picture of you in that first glance remains. And each time that picture of you comes to mind, it is amplified by purer and more delicately drawn colors and shapes.

With you, Anna, I have found something special that sets you apart and places you above all others whom I have ever known. Your good and faithful heart means everything to me;

for everything, both good and bad lives in the outpourings from the heart.

Your sensitive heart, together with the tenderness of your being which always lingers, and in your actions and your words, has made it such that I cannot contain all of the thoughts of love which have sprung from my young breast. These thoughts have become greater and extend farther and farther.

I wait with longing for that precious, holy moment when we are able to take each other's hand in the faithful promise everlasting to remain with each other. May God help us in our forthcoming union to keep these our promises, and give mutual happiness and blessings to us and to the glory of Him, the Great Master who Himself has established marriage.

I would gladly sit and write page after page when I am writing to you, but time does not permit more right now. A thousand million kisses and hugs and loving greetings from your ever faithful future husband.

Yours,

Ingvald

Fruits of my labors

Dear Donald,

Outside in the yard stand my stalwart children, my beloved trees waiting for the inevitable blasts of winter.

But they won't freeze, no. I will cover their feet with straw and wrap their trunks to protect against critters that gnaw and the intense winter sun that scalds. They will take the long rest until spring when they again will bloom and bring forth fruit — "Fruits of my labors."

They are glad to have me visit them on my daily walk-about, for I treat them with love and respect, and I talk to them. I put food in the eating place and water in the drinking place. Where they need a little grooming, I attend to that also. When they have scrapes and breaks, Argo takes care of that too. I talk to them and they talk with me and each other.

"I planted you first, and you have found favor with me. I am well pleased," I whisper to the large tree in the garden. I tell the tree it is sweet as honey and precious as gold, both worthwhile discoveries for this adventurer. The Honeygold acknowledges it is larger and stronger and has a finer symmetry. But it complains that I have allowed it to carry too heavy a burden at times, resulting in some poorly developed fruit. It reminds me that I only have fallen out of its branches, not those of the other trees. But the Honeygold is pleased to be older and wiser, bigger and better.

Lurking in the back of its mind and mine is the reality that if the tree grows too rapidly, it may become susceptible to fire blight from which there is slight chance of recovery. There is some protection against fire blight, but since I am not licensed, I cannot buy it. So I spray what I can, early in the season during the bloom. This works, but not always.

"You there, Honeycrisp!" I call out. "I have placed you in a favored spot where you will have plenty of sunshine. You are the brightest hope of the university horticulturists. You are designed to have very large fruits with an unusual flavor." The Honeycrisp wonders about its name: "Am I sweet?" it asks. "You are," responds a reassuring Argo. "Not only sweet, but very crisp. Everyone likes a crisp apple. You have the potential to rise above all others in your class; you will be very productive."

As I pass the Honeycrisp, I have to pause to admire the fine specimen with such far-reaching potential. The Honeycrisp grew a remarkable amount this year; it grew so much and so fast that its seven apples were affected by a calcium deficiency. Not to worry, for the remedy is merely to limit the application of nitrogen to slow the growth. It will turn out just fine.

"Over here! Over here!" calls the Prairie Spy to me. It is grateful to live close by the garage to witness all the comings and goings of everyone. Perhaps it enjoys the extra uptake of carbon dioxide from the vehicles in the driveway. The rabbits tried hard to strip the branches long ago, but our favorite Spy made it. The snow plow on a pickup banged it, but the Spy is tough, resilient. Its fruits are very close to the ideal, always tasty, and they keep very well.

More attention is paid to the popular Spy than any other tree by visitors and kids who want a snack. Spy is generous with its gifts, very durable and a heavy producer. The tree when young had an upright habit and Argo waited eight years for it to bear its first fruits. But the long wait was worthwhile. Now the branches are widely spread and very strong. Children will enjoy climbing this one.

The Cortland, by the kennel, traveled farthest to get to where it is, coming from Cornell University's research station in New York. But the Cortland travels well. It is quite different from the others in that it is a "spur" type. This means the apples come from short spurs along its branches. Argo did a good job shaping the branches when it was a young tree and now it is a beautifully formed specimen needing little attention. "Little attention!" exclaims the Cortland, "just leave me be. I know how to produce fine apples. Look at them: they are the deepest red with the white flesh that does not turn brown!"

I assure the Cortland that its apples are beautiful beyond anything I could ever hope. Everyone loves the Cortland, and it is the most versatile of all, good for fresh eating, pies, salads, cooking. And it is true: the Cortland is an independent sort that does not require much pruning or any special attention. Perhaps good breeding has played a part in its success, even though it is quite different from each parent, the old Ben Davis and the tasty McIntosh. It is the only "foreign born" apple we have. All the others are Minnesota apples. But therein lies some of its charm, for the Cortland has blended well into the routine of the garden and will be a steady, if not outstanding producer of beauty and unexcelled taste.

Far off from the others, alone on the western border of the yard grows the Fireside. It is a test plot seedling that barely survived its first season. It is a long keeper, primarily for eating. "Of course!" bawls the Fireside whose name is not a misnomer. "Who wants to be sliced up and cooked?" Well, so be it. Its charm is that it is so very attractive, so solid and with flavor characteristics that are outstanding and not to be found in other varieties. The tree is moderately susceptible to scab and cedar-apple rust, but if treated with protective sprays, it does just fine. The apples on the Fireside hang pendulously, almost like Christmas tree ornaments. The tree carries a heavy burden of fruit which has a tendency to affect the growth patterns of the branches. The apples, indeed, are so beautiful and tasty that one wants to save them for dessert or special occasions. They take kindly to polishing, so a light buffing on one's shirt brings out the best in its radiant colors. The tree is very fertile and has a tendency to overbear.

One day, I stood in the center of the garden, talking to my trees, and listened as I heard them speak to each other about many things. What pleased me most was the comment voiced by one, and echoed by the others: "Argo treats us well and with fairness. Let's face it, we are all different, for we are Fubar trees. We have different designs, shapes, needs and qualities. We have had a few seasons of cold winters and some dry, hot summers. But Argo was always there to warm our feet with straw or give us a soothing cool drink and a good nourishing diet of the right fertilizer, and tell us apple stories."

"That's right!" said another, "And he has studied hard to learn how to prune, spray and groom us all to become the best we can become." "Yes, but the old fart can't stand on a ladder without falling out of my branches sometimes!" "Well," said another, "at least he's trying. Some orchard guys just sit around and do nothing." "Maybe it's God's punishment," puts in another. "Could be, but I doubt it. He never gets hurt badly when he falls from our limbs. Just breaks or loses a pipe now and then."

"Yeah," says another, "Where would we be if he hadn't planted us in Mother Earth?" "Mother who?" "You know very well who I mean!"

I returned to the house, thinking some of the plantings were guess work of a sort, but they all seemed to be doing fine. That's good enough for me. "Fruits of my labors?" I wasn't the one in labor.

Argo —

"Strudel"

Dear Donald,

After receiving a heart-warming greeting card from Suzanne, Class of '90, who writes that I was her favorite teacher, I decided to send you a story she considers her favorite.

It goes like this — my miniature Dachshund, Strudel, affectionately referred to as "Dogus Runtus" while out of his range of hearing, was one of the all-time greats. He never considered himself a runt, and always conducted himself as one who never lacked for self-confidence. He was truly a warrior, I'll have you know.

His self-confidence was very nearly his undoing early on in his short life. It was the month of June in his first half year. We decided to take my boat, the Argo, out to Lake Marion for a little fishing. Present in the boat with me were sons Tor and Bjørn and little Strudel. My big black Argo Lab had not yet arrived in Argoland. I chose names for my sons from the Viking sagas, but "Strudel" came from a cookbook.

The boys and I each had a fishing pole; Strudel came along as an observer. It was his first visit to a lake. In fact, he had no idea whatsoever what a lake was. The lake was calm and smooth as glass. Strudel stood on the seat with his front legs on the gunwale, intently scanning this body of water which to him must have been a great mystery.

Then all of a sudden, with no warning, he jumped overboard, probably expecting to land on the surface of the water, then to walk around on it. Surprise! He not only penetrated the surface but went straight down like a lead weight, totally disappearing from our view. The boys and I were shocked speechless. It looked like he was a goner.

Soon, however, Strudel reappeared on the surface. He was trying to "dog paddle," but the combination of his short, three-inch legs and solid, muscular body with no fat prevented him from staying afloat. Down he went again! "Get the net!" I called to the boys, "Hurry!"

But we were drifting away. Strudel came up for the second

time, eyeballs nearly popping out, gasping for breath, slapping the water frantically with his short front legs. And down he went for the third time! I rarely panic in crisis situations, something I learned as a boy in Northfield as a witness to the demise of several of my young playmates.

This episode was no exception. I knew immediately what to do. I turned on the sonar fish locator, put the Evinrude in reverse, and started to search the depths. There he was, down there about six feet, but coming again toward the surface. One of the boys reached out and netted him. We loved him up a little, not too much, then started fishing again. But Strudel did not fish. He had enough of fishing and remained hidden under the life preservers, finally emerging when we pulled ashore. Strudel never went to that lake again, no, and not to any other.

As long as we are on the topic of Strudel, you may as well follow along on a couple other happenings. Once when I was washing clothes in the kitchen, Strudel was there to observe. I had a stain on my shirt where the principal spit on me that I had to pre-soak with a product called, "Shout It Out!"

The instructions on the container were clear to me so I followed them. I squirted some on the stain and began to shout it out in a loud voice, "Go on, get outta there! Go on, get outta there!" The next thing I noticed was that Strudel had retreated, tail between legs, thinking I was shouting at him. He hid under the sofa and dared look at me only out of the corner of his eye.

Everyone loved Strudel, and we took him everywhere with us, except for fishing. He made the cross-country trip west with Tor, Bjørn and me in about 1982. As things turned out, we nearly lost him, because he fell ill with the dread disease, heart worm. He had to go to hospital and get near-fatal doses of arsenic to eradicate the heart worms which he would then pass in his stool. (Wasn't that a polite way to put it, for a change?)

It didn't matter to us if motels did not allow pets. We took Strudel into our rooms with us, carrying him in his duffle bag. He always slept in this little travel kennel at night, even when he was at home. When he slept during the day, however, he always lay flat on his back. He didn't do tricks much, because we didn't bother with that. We just loved him a lot. The only trick he did with any regularity was to roll over on his back when I said, "Victim!"

Thinking of that trick makes me sad now. Strudel was a replacement for one of our beagles, Argo, who perished when his head became caught in the four-inch grate of a storm sewer, probably while chasing a rabbit. Strudel was present when the remaining beagle, Fubar, was killed by a car on the street in front of our house, also while chasing a rabbit. For many days, Strudel would walk down to the curb and scold the street by barking angrily. That's about all he understood about the episode.

I suspected that Strudel was going into the living room to pee when we were out of the house, so one day I vacuumed carefully in the morning. Then in the afternoon, sure enough, there were his telltale tracks on the carpet. When we finally had to take up the carpet, we found lots of stains on the pad that did not show up on the yellow shag. It sure smelled, though.

Strudel could eat just about anything. He had extremely powerful jaws and sharp teeth which enabled him easily to chew up pork chop and chicken bones. About the only thing we did not feed him was chili. Anyone who feeds a dog chili deserves to be bitten.

I stated earlier that Strudel was a warrior. That was not an idle boast. While away at school, we would usually leave the back door to Donald's smoking room open so that Strudel could go outside to pass. We always left a bowl of water and one of Puppy Chow for his snack times.

One day I came home earlier than usual to find a tremendous uproar in the family room (where Donald smokes). It was bedlam. A critter (that's what we call a ground hog or woodchuck) had entered the room, ostensibly to eat out of Strudel's dish. This was a little too much for our warrior. He was barking furiously at the critter who had by now retreated to the corner under the sofa where Strudel would hide when he got yelled at.

I called out to Tor to get the weapons. He brought a steel garden stake and a garden fork. "We gotta get that guy outta there!" I commanded. "Jab him one!" So Tor took the steel stake, reached behind the sofa and pinned the critter down. Strudel immediately closed with the critter, his attack both furious and devastating. The first thing he did was bite off the critter's scrotum. That quickly got its attention. Then Strudel went to the devil on him to get even with the critter for encroaching on his space. He dragged the critter, who was larger than the dog, outside where he made an end of him. There was blood all over the carpet.

Then, after the critter was dead, Strudel broke all the critter's legs. I heard them crunch under the pressure of Strudel's powerful jaws. The boys and I agree that Strudel was extremely tenacious, and never gave up once he decided to go after critters. That summer, Strudel killed six more critters, all of whom were bigger than he. Our neighbor, Hank, was delighted, for the critters had been raising heck with his garden ever since my beagles, Argo and Fubar, met untimely deaths the year before. Strudel always got two Liva-Snaps from Hank on our daily visits.

The final chapter for our warrior came two years later. He and I had been watching TV about midnight. He sat on the fifth step where he could peer through the stairway bars and see both me and the TV. The time came for him to go out and pass, a signal he gave by going into a spin on the dining room floor.

Out he went. When he wanted to get back in the front door, he always smacked the window once with his paw. When he wanted to get in the back door, he barked twice. That's the way he learned it, and you know dogs — once they learn something, it stays with them.

After a half hour with no signal heard from Strudel, I went out to look. I found him lying on the grass near the Prairie Spy apple tree on the street side of the garage. He could not move, only look at me. What probably had happened was that someone drove in one side of the driveway and out the other, hitting Strudel, and knocking him up on the grass. The car did not stop.

I took a piece of plywood to use as a litter and carried him carefully into the kitchen where he lay by the washing machine. He appeared to have suffered a broken spine. That meant there was really no hope for his recovery.

When I went to check on him at 4:00 a.m., I found Tor sleeping next to him on the floor. Strudel was dead. The next morning I cried all the while I cleaned his blanket. I then washed Strudel for the last time and wrapped his body in a clean pillow case and his clean blanket.

I went outside the kitchen to dig his grave in the flower bed. Tor took the shovel and said, "Here, Pup, let me do it." And he did.

  Argo —

"Dub Dub" Dooley

Dear Donny,

You will remember we had a friend back in our Longfellow School days by the name of Dooley. He had the strange and disconcerting habit of saying everything twice. We called him "Dub Dub" Dooley, because of his doublespeak.

He didn't always talk double. Dub Dub used to stutter badly, but worked his way out of that impediment by singing his sentences. He never stuttered when he sang, so that's what he did most of one summer until he cured himself of stuttering. Once he was cured of stuttering, he enjoyed speaking sentences so much that he repeated them. We figured that was a fair trade-off, but his ma and his teacher in fourth grade, Mrs. Olson, weren't so sure.

One day during recess we located a hole by the school wall about three inches deep and eight inches wide. This was used for playing marbles. Dub Dub didn't have any marbles, but he had ten cents from selling two empty milk bottles. He could have bought a bag of a dozen marbles from Hughes & Heckler Hardware for that kind of dough, but there wasn't enough time, so he asked me if I would sell him some marbles. I told him I only had ten to spare, so I gave him ten marbles for a dime.

John "Soybeans" Sawyer, Dick "Jake" Jacobson, Dub Dub Dooley and I played, shooting in that order. Sawyer was taking his time so Dub Dub said, "Shoot! Shoot! Soybeans, Soybeans!" Sawyer replied, "Shut up! Shut up! Dub Dub!" Sawyer's shot was way off. He blamed Dub Dub and said, "Your turn, Jake." "I heard you. I heard you!" said Jake and shot. "Tough bounce. Tough bounce." said Dub Dub, seeing that Jake was farther off than Soybeans Sawyer. Dub Dub shot and was also off by a foot.

My turn came next. Dub Dub said, "I ain't sayin' nothin'. I ain't sayin' nothin'." "I ain't sayin' nothin' neither," I said. I shot straight into the hole and went to pick up their marbles — my winnings. "Ha, Ha ha, I peed in the hole, peed in the hole, last night, last night," said Dub Dub. I figured he was lying so I said nothing. But one of the girls told Mrs. Olson on him.

Mrs. Olson started the ball rolling as soon as we got back into the classroom. "Delbert Dooley, you may stay after school today." Soybeans Sawyer started to snicker and whispered to me, "Delbert? Is that his real name?" "Yeah, it must be," I whispered back. I felt kinda sorry for him, having a dum dum name like Delbert. We waited outside the door after school for Dub Dub to come out. He never said a word, and we figured it must have been real bad, so we kept quiet and went over to Sawyer's to listen to our afternoon radio programs: Dick Tracy, Superman, and Jack Armstrong, the all-American boy.

Dub Dub didn't return to our school. Mrs. Olson said the family moved to Faribault and he would be going to school there. I heard her talking to Mrs. Olberg, our third grade teacher. She told Mrs. Olberg that Dub Dub was to attend a special school in Faribault.

We never heard any more about Dub Dub until our senior year in high school and our undefeated team played Faribault. Our coach, Ed Byhre, said, "Look out for their quarterback, Dooley. He's magic with the ball." Dooley! I looked at Jake and he looked at me. We both rolled our eyes. So that's where that guy went!

We lost the coin toss and Faribault elected to receive. We nailed the ball carrier. Dub Dub, the quarterback, started the ball rolling, but not the normal way with "Hike!" He said in his count, "Dub-dub, Dub-dub-dub," and the ball was hiked on one of the dubs each time. I was center linebacker, playing just three yards in front of Dooley.

Just before he got down behind the center the first time, he said, "Hi, Lars, how's it goin'?" I didn't know how to react, so I replied, "Fine, fine." He laughed and counted, "Dub-dub-dub" and was gone like a streak of light. But we were really loaded with talent, and stopped Faribault cold all night. I scored twice, and we beat them 21—0 on their homecoming night. The Faribault Daily News reported: Quist 21—Faribault 0!

Dooley had a good year for Faribault and was headed for Notre Dame on a football scholarship. He was cured of his speech problem all right, but he joined up with the National Guard unit in Faribault. They shipped out to Korea during the fall of 1950, our senior year. That was the same time some of our classmates went off to the conflict with the Northfield Guard unit: Russell DeMann, Bernie Rezac, Dale Paulson, Ed

Sorenson, Ray Ozmun and "Sleepy" Wells. Dick Mattson, still a junior, went too.

Dub Dub Dooley made it back from Korea, but not all in one piece. He took two bullets in his legs while on a dangerous mission and got stranded behind enemy lines. He lay there in the freezing cold until they could rescue him, and he lost all five toes on his right foot to frost bite. His football days were over. He came home a hero and was awarded the Silver Star, Unit Citation, Good Conduct Medal, and two Purple Hearts. He went on to Notre Dame on the G. I. Bill, but not a football scholarship. Dooley attended law school there and later signed on with a large Chicago law firm that had over 400 attorneys. He rose to become a full partner in the firm and was General Counsel for Notre Dame for over twenty years — Dub Dub Dooley.

Lars — March 23, 1996

A deed? Indeed
Thoughts on our plots

Dear Donald,

I remember so well when we were kids and the time when I had a nickel to spend at the Ole Store and you were there with me.

I bought some candy that I shared with you, penniless lad that you were. In an attempt not only to be frugal, but also to instill a certain frugality in you, I suggested you only put one piece at a time in your mouth and to go slowly. That way, I figured, I would not have to hand over too much candy.

Now you have a Deed to the property, Donald, indeed. Not just any property, but a choice lot up front in the nicest cemetery in the world. Ah! And in the same vein as my advice on taking it slow with the candy given you, I advise that you postpone taking occupancy too soon.

People who buy new cars usually honk the horn a lot and wave at people they know or don't know so others will see their good fortune at having a new car. That's human nature. Let it be known that you and I are capable of putting a new spin on this trait. We are going to use our bragging rights to show off a cemetery lot worthy of the names Argo and Hobo.

It's all there, Donald: cool shade in summer, shelter from winter blasts, a fine neighborhood and with neighbors who are noteworthy and significant and are remembered just as you and I will be remembered. Oh the peace and tranquility! What we need to decide is the extent to which we might shake things up a bit. Not that we crave notoriety, for you and I have enjoyed a full plate of that. I think we'll leave the neighbors alone in their peace, the peace which will come to us at long last after a rough road and some good times in between journeys.

Your notion to have a tent shape for a tombstone sounds good. It is original. You could consider a point on top, with the face of a clock below so visitors stopping by for a visit can set their watches by the sundial. Perhaps you could have four sides and indicate true north; then on the other sides have E, W, and S respectively. This could be combined with the sundial, or even the tent. If it looks like a tent, be sure to have the flap open with the invitation, "Come on in and join me."

As for my stone, there are many options. The first that comes to mind is going to comfort some: "I forgive you, you scoundrel!" Some may think that statement a trifle insincere, like another insincere comment: "I wish I had worked harder." Or, "Ask yourself: How am I going to get a nice place to rest like this?" There could be some merit in having a pressure-sensitive ash tray between us for the convenience of smokers. As they snuff out a cigarette, the piece activates a solar-powered voice recording or your voice saying, "Thank you!" or "The bar is closed!"

If you like, we could have a menu of buttons numbered one through nine, each to bring forth in our own voices favorite witticisms or loose comments such as, "Lift up your dress!" or, "Button your lip!" or, "I would rather be here than in Monticello." The key to participation, meaningful participation, would be the caveat: "Each message plays only once a month, never at night, or when there is deep snow." How about, "It's a long pull from the Halls of Montezuma."

I tend to favor the incongruous. Perhaps a statement such as "This has been a rude awakening," would be fun. Or perhaps something really original, "The Good are here. The Bad and the Ugly are over there. (Followed by the whistle from the movie. Cracks me up!)

All things considered, Donald, we have a sweet prospect ahead for us to contemplate. A Deed, indeed!

Argo —

Code Name: "Cynthia"

Northfield Connection — brief summary of some of the facts surrounding the life and family ties of one of America's most successful espionage agents in WWII, Amy Elizabeth "Betty" Thorpe, code-named "Cynthia."

Donny,

I got right to work on Cynthia after returning from Boston and Bjørn's MFA Thesis show at Tufts. This afternoon I found details in the Minneapolis Public Library that led to further search in the Northfield News Archives. In a nutshell:

A farmer moved from Hancock, Minnesota to Dennison, later to Washington Street in Northfield. He had a son with the same name who attended Carleton for a while, was a reporter for the Minneapolis Tribune for a while, then received an appointment to the U. S. Naval Academy in 1894. He chose the Marines after graduation and served in the Spanish-American War as a Captain. He was definitely a Fubar type, going over the head of his admiral to Teddy Roosevelt, who personally approved a mission that the Admiral had vetoed — a wild caper. Apparently TR liked the young man's Naval Academy and early service records of wild behavior and brawling and stuff like that. TR definitely liked "cowboy" types.

Later, this Northfield fellow entered NYU Law School and continued on with law and the Marines, serving in Washington, DC and other places abroad, rising to the rank of Colonel. He died in 1934, and is listed in the Washington, DC "Who's Who." He married well, to a graduate of Michigan at Ann Arbor — a Minnesota girl from Morris whose father was in the Minnesota State Legislature. They were married in 1908 at the Fifth Avenue Presbyterian Church in New York City.

On November 22, 1910, a daughter was born at Minneapolis Northwestern Hospital. The family later took up residence in Washington, DC and moved in high society circles. The daughter had two siblings, one of whom changed her name later. This daughter turned out to be America's number one spy during World War II, working under the cover of her marriage of convenience to a British Diplomat. The couple had two children: a son given up for adoption; the daughter remained with her mother for some time.

There may be a connection, not yet established, with the removal of the Enigma Code machine from Warsaw, where they were posted, to Stockholm, thence to the top secret code facility at Bletchley Park in England. In addition, through subterfuge and sleeping around in Washington, DC after returning from Poland in 1938, she got her hands on the Italian Naval Codes and the Vichy French Codes. Her code name was "Cynthia."

Cynthia was stunningly beautiful and loved her work, both in and out of bed. She eventually married her Vichy French liaison after the war and moved with him to his estate castle in France. She died of mouth cancer in 1963; he electrocuted himself with an electric blanket.

I have not found her surviving daughter yet. Cynthia's grandparents never knew their granddaughter was a spy, for they died before all this happened. I do not think she ever visited Northfield, but no one can be sure, of course. At least there is no record of a visit to the grandparents in Northfield that I have found. All in an afternoon's work, plus photo copies of all the news articles and other data.

Here's a summary of some of the facts surrounding the life and family ties of Amy Elizabeth "Betty" Thorpe, code-named "Cynthia." Two brothers from Vermont settled in Northfield Township and Dennison in the middle of the nineteenth century. One, Alvin B. Thorpe, married Louise Jones in 1870. She was 18 years old.

Four years later, in the summer of 1874, she is listed as one of the original guarantors in the fund drive to raise money for St. Olaf's School. Her name is on the list of donors in the Ytterboe Papers. She gave $100, the equivalent today of 25 times that amount, at least. Thorson gave $2,000. Some of the Bunday families in the Northfield area are descendants of A. B. Thorpe, whose daughter, Nora, married W. W. (Willie) Bunday.

The other brother that settled in Northfield Township was George Carleton Thorpe. George C. Thorpe was a successful farmer. The 1870 Census lists his farm and land valuation at $18,000 (well over a million dollars today). In addition to his lands east of Northfield, he held a parcel of land stretching from the Cannon River near the old city dump, across the back road to Dundas, and up to St. Olaf College. In addition, he later had extensive land holdings near Hancock, Minnesota in Stevens County where he became involved in real estate and lucrative loans.

George Carleton Thorpe had a son named George Cyrus Thorpe who was born in Northfield in 1875. The son attended Carleton academy for a year in 1890-91, according to the records in the college archives. George, Jr. went on to the Naval Academy at Annapolis in 1893; was a reporter for a Minneapolis newspaper in 1899; became a Marine officer in the Spanish-American War; later served in Cuba during the insurrection; later the Philippines, and was commandant of marines at Pearl Harbor.

Marine Captain (later Colonel) George C. Thorpe, led the first diplomatic mission to Menelik II in Ethiopia, establishing an American Consulate there. He later attended the Army War College, Naval War College, ran the Marine brig at Portsmouth, wrote several books about military tactics, as well as books on Prohibition and other matters. In the meantime, he managed to earn a master's degree from Brown University and a law degree from NYU. He retired from the Marines as a full colonel in 1922 and made a fortune practicing maritime law in Washington, DC and Boston.

His wife, Cora Wells Thorpe, was the daughter of the prominent H. H. Wells of Morris, Minnesota, who was a former state legislator and senator and successful businessman in Stevens County. Cora became a Washington DC society matron and her picture hangs in the Washington, DC City Hall. She graduated Magna Cum Laude from the University of Michigan, did graduate work at Columbia, Sorbonne, and Munich Universities. The Thorpes had three children: Amy Elizabeth, Jane Wells, and George Wells.

Their oldest child, Amy Elizabeth Thorpe, ("Betty" to friends and family) was born in Minneapolis, November 22, 1910, at Northwestern hospital. She was not raised in Northfield but lived with her parents in Cuba, Santo Domingo, Honolulu (where she wrote a 55-page novel at age eleven: "Fioretta, A Tale of Italy"), and Switzerland where she studied at the Ecole des Essarts at Riant Chateau. She also studied in Paris and Dana Hall in Wellesley, Massachusetts.

Betty never formally attended college but had a "coming out" debutante gala at age 18, fluent in French and Spanish, worldly-wise, having traveled extensively growing up. Betty married a British Diplomat, Arthur Pack at age 19 — the bride was four months pregnant — and left with her husband for various postings from Santiago, Chile to Madrid during the Spanish Civil War, followed by service in Prague just before the Nazi Anschluss in Austria, then Warsaw as war clouds gathered in the summer of 1939.

Betty Thorpe Pack had been on the payroll of British Intelligence department MI 6 since her early days in Warsaw and was paid 20 pounds per week. In Warsaw, she was instrumental in gathering secrets about Polish cryptanalyst work on the German Enigma codes. Earlier, she had shown courage and initiative in burglarizing the office of Otto Henlein, Hitler's stooge in Prague, Czechoslovakia. She stole a map indicating point-by-point the plans of Hitler's invasions in Europe, including Czechoslovakia, Poland, Yugoslavia, Greece, France, and the Ukraine. These items were handed over by Cynthia to the Passport Control in the British Embassy, front for British Secret Intelligence Service (SIS) in countries abroad. Small wonder she was recruited by MI6.

After the Nazi invasion of Poland, Betty and her husband were posted once more to Santiago, Chile where Betty carried on a running battle against Nazi sympathizers in her vehemently anti-Nazi newspaper articles. British Embassy officials feared repercussions even though Betty used the alias Elizabeth Thomas in her articles. Her ailing husband returned to England to convalesce for some months; Betty Pack returned to Washington, DC at the suggestion of British Intelligence, taking a house in Georgetown at 3327 "O" Street and using her maiden name, Elizabeth Thorpe. It was at this time she was given the code name "Cynthia" by her British Intelligence supervisor and handler.

In Washington, DC Cynthia's first assignment involved helping change the minds of some "America First" congressmen, isolationists dedicated to keeping America out of war in Europe. Betty was quite successful with Senator Arthur Vandenberg, whose wife had attended the University of Michigan with Cynthia's mother, Cora, in 1901-1903. Senator Vandenberg liked the girls and Cynthia liked being liked — in line of duty, of course. Her cohorts succeeded in destroying the careers of

Hamilton Fish and others who were blocking Roosevelt's Lend-Lease plans to support England in its war efforts against Nazi Germany.

Cynthia's first important achievement was obtaining the secret Italian Naval Ciphers through the offices of Italian Admiral Lais, Naval Attache, who, years before, frequently lunched with Cynthia when she was teen-ager in school at Dana Hall in Wellesley, and he was on business in Boston. Later in Washington, when Betty was 32 years old and stunningly beautiful in 1942, she was irresistible to the Italian admiral.

David Brinkley covers this episode in four pages of "The War Comes to Washington" and describes how Cynthia stole the critical codes. The Italian Naval Ciphers enabled the British to defeat a much stronger Italian navy at the Battle of Matapan off the coast of Greece. In effect, the Italian navy was neutralized and unable to hinder Allied forces during the landings in North Africa, Sicily, and Italy. Cynthia's work "saved 100,000 lives," according to British Intelligence reports on file at Churchill College, Cambridge.

Cynthia's most dramatic achievement was the "black bag" operation — burglarizing the Vichy French Embassy in DC, just two doors down the street from her mother's residence on Wyoming Street in June of 1942. She and her seduced ally, Charles Brousse, the Vichy French Embassy's Press Attache, cooperated and created a subterfuge with the guard, saying they needed a private place to carry on their affair so Brousse's wife would not find out.

While using the lounge, she let the "Georgia Cracker" in (actually, a Canadian safecracker) through a rear window. He opened the locked door to the code room and deduced the combination to the safe. They passed the large code books out the window to an OSS agent who sped them to the Wardman Park Hotel, Betty's suite, 215 "B," where the pages were immediately photographed and returned to the embassy safe undetected. Several distinguished politicians including Senator Vandenberg, Navy Secretary Frank Knox, and other Washington luminaries also lived at the Wardman Park Hotel at the time.

All this while, Betty was under FBI surveillance because a clerk at her hotel reported her for possibly associating with suspicious persons. The FBI did not know what Elizabeth Thorpe was doing under cover as Cynthia — except that she was spending lots of time with mysterious persons, possibly Nazi sympathizers and other shadowy characters.

Betty Thorpe and her British Diplomat husband, Arthur Pack, were soon divorced and she married her partner in the Vichy French Embassy caper, Capt. Charles Emmanual Brousse. They moved to France to take up residence in Chateau Castellnou, Perpignan, in the Eastern Pyrenees, which Brousse purchased in 1946.

Betty's first husband, Arthur Pack, committed suicide in Santiago, Chile in 1946. Betty died of mouth cancer at her chateau in 1963 and is buried on the grounds. Time magazine printed a full page obituary on December 20, 1963. Her husband, Charles Brousse, accidentally electrocuted himself with an electric blanket ten years later.

Betty and Arthur Pack had two children. Their son, George Pack, like his Northfield-born grandfather, chose a military career. Raised as a foster child in England, he enlisted in the British army and served two tours of duty in the Korean Conflict; on the first tour, he was wounded and decorated for bravery with the Victoria Cross. On his second tour of duty, he was killed in action. His remains are buried in Korea. Their daughter, Denise Avril Beresford Pack, born in Chile, was educated in schools in Chile, France, England, and at Georgetown University. She married, worked for Newsweek, and is said to have committed suicide in the sixties.

The Northfield-born George Cyrus Thorpe, died in 1936 of cancer without knowing that his daughter had become a top allied espionage agent and heroine — one of the most successful espionage agents that Britain and America developed prior to and during World War II. Cora Edna Wells Thorpe, George's wife, born in Morris, Minnesota, died in 1954 at age seventy-three in Washington, DC as a distinguished society matron.

My interests and research are concerned mainly with the forbears of Amy Elizabeth Thorpe, especially the Northfield, Morris, and Hancock, Minnesota connections. It would appear from what has been discovered that Betty Thorpe came from very solid stock. Her grandparents were hard-working farmers and businessmen, elected public servants and entrepreneurs in Rice and Stevens Counties; her father, a career Marine Officer and successful attorney, and her mother, a prominent community activist and socialite in Washington DC. One of her uncles was the US Federal Trade Commissioner.

The pre-World War II and wartime exploits of Amy Elizabeth Thorpe Pack are documented in several good books:

"Room 3604" and "Cynthia" by Harford Montgomery Hyde
"Cast No Shadow" by Mary S. Lovell
"The Man Called Intrepid" by William Stevenson
"Desperate Deception" by Thomas E. Mahl
"Sisterhood of Spies" by Elizabeth P. McIntosh
"Spies" by Ernest Volkman

Lars — September 18, 1999

The Lion, Rampant

Dear Donald,

Enclosed, please find a reward for your diligence, intrepidity and more or less wholesome outlook on life and behavior. This St. Olaf flag, black on gold, pictures the Ole Lion rampant, facing east toward the foe on the river, Carleton. He always faces east, toward the foe.

There are those who would comment that this St. Olaf Lion, rampant, and carrying an ax, represents the symbol of violence. This is true, and no apologies are rendered to the tender. Some may comment that the lion, rampant, stands on one foot, contrary to the instructions of Bernt Julius Muus, our founder, who stated: "The lion should stand firmly on both feet so that it can deliver a telling blow with the ax." Remember, it was Muus who decided what St. Olaf School's emblem should be.

As you see, the Ole Lion does not wear a crown in this version. The Lion of Norway, rampant, however, does. In addition to the symbol of monarchy in Norway, the Norwegian slogan, or battle cry of the sainted Olaf, son of Harald (Olaf Haraldsson, referred after sainthood as "Den Hellige"), was "Fram! Fram! Kristmenn, Krossmenn, Kongsmenn!" It is presumed that the army then followed their leader whom they called, "Olav Digre" (dee-greh — the Stout) into battle.

As you know, they followed him once too often, and that was at Olaf's final battle, the Battle of Stiklestad. Olaf was killed at that time, about 4:00 in the afternoon of Thursday, July 29, 1030. It is not strange that the founder of St. Olaf, B. J. Muus, should memorialize Olaf the Saint, for B. J. was born and raised not far from the battle site and later attended school in Trondheim, where Olaf is buried under the altar, grave number eight. But we note that Muus changed the battle cry somewhat, to "Fram! Fram! Christmenn, Crossmenn!" leaving out "King's men." And the original spelling of "Um! Yah! Yah!" was probably "Um! Ja! Ja!"

I suppose you are wondering what uses you have for this black and gold emblem, this flag. Well now, perhaps you have many. You could pin it up on your bulletin board to cheer you up after leaving your bath. A rhythmic chant of "Um Yah!" while descending your stairs could give you the cadence necessary to keep you from falling down, as I sometimes do; on the way up the stairs, the cry lends encouragement, sometimes needed, to be sure, after a hard day's work. Singing it while waltzing will inspire your partner and enable you to avoid getting your feet stepped on.

A decisive greeting of "Um Yah Yah!" upon answering the telephone will always give you the advantage you need. It will throw tele-solicitors off their pace, leaving them totally confused; you will then easily seize control of the situation. I do this, now and then. The result is rather like what happens when putting a radical spin on the ball while hitting it into your opponent's court.

If you don't mind the suggestion, you could wrap your lunch in this lion, rampant, tie it to the end of your walking stick, place it on your shoulder and go about your daily business looking like a true hobo just arrived in town. Should you decide to do this, it is wise to have a toothpick in your mouth indicating that you have just et, then people will not fear you. But you already knew that.

Although small, one could pin the lion, rampant, under the neck to use as a barber's cloth while giving a ceremonial and punitive haircut to a wise-off Carl. If you were to tuck it under your chin while dining out, a perceptive waitress will conclude that you are a big tipper and extend to you many courtesies, including excellent service and perhaps an extra portion of pride or pudding.

During your next visit to Rice County you may enjoy waiting by the train station in Northfield for the passing of an infrequent train so that you can cheer up the lonely brakeman who is usually downcast because he never gets to steer the locomotive. A brisk wave of the lion, rampant, does wonders in these cases.

You will doubtless recall, from your study of Western lore, that the cowboy had an important item called a "wipes." This was what we today refer to as a kerchief. The wipes had many uses on the range, and you may wish to consider taking into use some uses useful while using snoose. You do use snoose, usen't you? What's the use of using snoose if you ain't used to using it. (Remember when we would shout this at "Squint" Hower? His responses were varied, and always laughable, such as, "Get some snoose yourself and stuff it, damn Scandinavian Cattle!")

Of course you can use the wipes for disguising your identity while rustling cattle, turkeys or sheep, or rustling up certain kinds of grub such as lutefisk. Any bandit worth his salt and pepper would use the wipes to cover his face while carrying out a nefarious scheme like robbing the First National Bank of Northfield, in modern times.

The bank teller would be thoroughly confused, particularly at seeing the "Um Yah Yah!" and lion, rampant. You could add to the confusion by revealing that you are a descendant of Jesse James, and now work for the Northfield Chamber of Commerce. Let me know before you carry off such a caper, for I wish to take photographs for my album, especially of you, but also the lion, rampant. Your wipes can also serve as a sling in the event I should fall out of an apple tree in your presence and break a forearm. It is also useful as a bandage or tourniquet should my faithful dog, Argo, become unduly alarmed and launch a surprise attack. You may, unfortunately shoot yourself in the foot as I have done, on occasion.

You can wipe sweat from your forehead with the lion, rampant, while eating a serving of Argo's red beans and rice. You can hobble your camel, your horse, or your ass — whatever conveyance you choose for your next triumphal entry into Burnsville with your lion, rampant. I can arrange another of those parties we loved so well when we were in college.

Remember "Spin the bottle?" Well, that's out. Think of the big hit you would make playing "Drop the hankie!" Sonja Stepperud would like it a lot.

Give some thought to the possibility of masquerading as a Samurai from Itami or Iwakuni. In which case, you would tie the wipes around your head at the forehead level. That's the part in front, above the eyes. Just in case you forget your money at home and find yourself in a restaurant after dining and cannot pay, you may offer to wipe the dishes with your own wipes.

I wonder if we should inform the conformists that their lion, rampant, is doing a balancing act on one leg and not positioned on two legs as Muus suggested?

I can hear them now: "Go blow your nose, Argo and Hobo. Don't mess with our lion, rampant!"

      Argo —

Writing to Disk

Dear Donald,

This morning, at precisely 2:34 am, I awoke to a revelation of great significance, that of having dreamt a dream hitherto unknown to me. It was so important that I nearly came unhinged and could not return to sleep.

By way of explanation, a little background is in order. First, you must know that I dream just about every night. The dreams are never, it seems, frightful or in any way dreams I would call scary. Often, I have repeat performances, some mildly unpleasant, but not so unpleasant as to keep me awake the rest of the night.

Our brain contains about 100 billion neurons. There are connectors between neurons which, if strung out end to end would measure about 250,000 miles. That's a lot of brain to fill up the skull. Ah, but here's the rub: most of the neurons are affected one way or the other by the time we reach the age of three.

To put it another way, most of what we learn of the world around us is picked up by the time we are three years old. Sure, there is activity in the brain after age three, to be sure. But most of that activity, we call learning, is done by the age of fourteen and it goes downhill from there.

There is a message here: If children sit before a TV, they are bombarded with hundreds of thousands of influential stimuli coming directly from the screen. This means, of course, that thousands of examples of violence are visited upon young viewers; thousands of examples of product sales such as breakfast cereal, and whatever, are also transmitted to, and absorbed by young, impressionable minds.

Does the brain ever get full? Not likely. However, there is another side of the coin: Take, for example, a child reared by parents who cannot speak or hear. If that child does not experience intervention by someone else who will teach the child to speak, by the age of nine that ability will be lost forever. The neurons in the brain that handle such traffic will shut down, and that child will never be able to speak

The obvious course of action for parents and those caring for children must be: Take care that you supervise what your child sees on the TV. Children are great emulators and can easily copy behaviors they observe. If those behaviors are undesirable in the opinions of the parents, then they must take steps to correct the situation.

I stated above that most of our real learning is accomplished by the age of fourteen; further, that the brain does not shut down at that point. We merely apprehend less and less of our total learning, compared with what we learn in early years. Sure, you can teach an old dog new tricks but with some difficulty and lots more effort in the bargain.

What made life so interesting for me early this morning, at 2:34 o'clock, was the nature and substance of my dream. Hitherto, my dreams, as yours, usually revolve around events real or imagined in the distant past. This time I dreamt, vividly (though not in color), that I was moving icons around the screen of my computer, performing very complicated procedures, and most important, writing to disk. I was using my brain in the immediate present to do tasks of the present — not the distant past — or even the recent past. In other words, I was writing to my own brain, thus the metaphor, "Writing to disk."

My wonderful dream, therefore, is testament to my self-assurance that old Kindem has not yet gone to seed. I am continuing to learn new tricks as an old dog, and this is the most pleasant revelation I can possibly imagine.

Just think! The neurons and connectors still work, and I am ready to begin Kindergarten all over again. I now feel confident that I can continue writing to disk.

   Argo, 2/17/1997 at 4:05:42.374 PM (Chief Olympic Timekeeper)

Vacuum Cleaning on Sunday

Dear Donny,

We used a carpet sweeper in the thirties and forties in our home. We did not have the kind of carpet that they have today. We had wooden and linoleum floors with scatter rugs or throw rugs around the house. For most of the cleaning, we would take the rugs out back, drape them over the clothes line and beat them with rug beaters, which are hard to describe, but they resemble more or less, what I would call a rug beater.

I never understood why we had a carpet sweeper since we had no carpet. Maybe it was a matter of keeping up with the neighbors. "Sure, we got a carpet sweeper, use it all the time. Got it from Monkey Wards." Well, we used it rather seldom, because our house was well-appointed for cleaning, having both mops and brooms. In fact, we had a nice broom for upstairs. The old ones ended up in the basement or on the front porch for less fussy work.

Mamma was nifty with the broom, finding out along about the fifth or sixth son that the broom was a very effective tool for restoring order around the place. We didn't have much use for psychologists or interactive communication skills to mediate disputes. Justice was swift, though not very severe — usually a quick swat on the butt to increase speed while being bossed out of the kitchen where there was food to be snitched that wasn't suposta be touched. My father never spanked me. There are other things my father never did: he never laughed out loud; he never bought a drink, and never turned one down. But I digress.

It strikes me as too bad that I have the attitude I do about Saturdays and Sundays. I no longer enjoy them much because now that I am retired I lose my advantage when the weekend rolls around. Other guys, the working stiffs, get to go shopping, running errands and having almost as much fun as I do on a daily basis. But I wonder if they have vacuumed carpets on a Sunday as I did today. I did not wake up at 9:00 this morning thinking, "Ah! I feel wonderful! I guess I'll vacuum the carpets so I can savor this wonderful feeling."

If there is a high to be gotten from vacuuming, I have not yet experienced it. I mean, you can get a wonderful high mopping the kitchen floor if you have a mind to. Or if you put the wrong kind of stuff in the bucket. But if you concentrate really hard, you can make the most of an otherwise onerous task. You have options. Set the height of the roller so you end up with the prettiest patterns as you zigzag the mop across the floor. Make your initials. Look for things lost.

I looked all over for my cigar cutter, lost these past two days, but all I found in the logical spot was the usual collection of Tor's fingernail clippings dating back to last March when I last vacuumed, the day before my birthday. I was looking also under stuff.

Who knows when you are going to find a 1905 buffalo nickel or an Indianhead penny? Got lotsa pine needles from last Christmas. They usually hang around for a while. They can give you nasty punctures if you are barefoot.

Nini told me in June that you have to be careful vacuuming. You can get what is known in family language usage as "a back." She had such a back last year that she couldn't vacuum when I was in Spokane. So I did it for her.

Well, I've been stalling around long enough with the introduction to what I really wanted to tell you. After vacuuming the living room carpet, I go for the stairway. And going up the stairway, I pass the photos that I took of the children I made, (or helped make).

I think to myself as I look at them and smile, "This was surely God's plan, to have me vacuum today." It was time to walk up the stairs and look at this wonderful family which the Lord has given me.

I smile as I put away the vacuum cleaner. It was good to vacuum this Sunday.

    Argo—

Telephone Tricks

Dear Donald,

"Ytterboe Cafeteria!" is a common greeting I use as I pick up the phone, confident of at least a couple of things: the caller may be an Ole and rejoice that somehow I sensed that fact before picking up the receiver. The caller may be a telephone solicitor and be thrown just a little off his script.

I didn't always start with "Ytterboe Cafeteria!" For example, last week while baking a new version of San Francisco Sourdough each day, I was answering with a Chief Inspector Jacques Cleauseau accent, "Boulangerie! Bon jour, mon ami!" Confusion usually reigns, which is precisely why I do this. My kid sister, Margit, for example, started laughing so hard she forgot why she phoned me at nine o'clock in the morning. We had a nice chat anyway, about the weather, cod fish, flatbread and other items of interest.

I have been working on a technique to put a little more spin on the ball when I return it to the caller's court. Take yesterday, for example. I opened with "Um Yah! Yah!" This was followed by a pregnant pause at the other end as the caller marshaled his courage and glanced again at his script. "I'm with the Acme Window and Siding Company and we will have a crew on Williams Drive starting next week. Are you the homeowner?" I could have feigned childishness at that point, saying in a child's voice, "Onga Bonga!" while dropping the phone on the desk and making squeals and all sorts of extraneous noises with rustling paper, wooden spoons on a sauce pot, and rattling a noise maker kept at the ready for such purpose. But I did not do that.

Instead, I launched into my prepared reply: "I'm glad you asked that question. It's kind of a long story, but I took possession of this place in 1971 after first having lived in a ticky tacky new house in a ticky tacky neighborhood in what is referred to by the locals there as "prestigious West Bloomington" where I could on any given day stand on the back stoop at four o'clock in the afternoon and call out: 'Mark! Todd! Scott!' and 42 kids with those names would scramble over to my ticky tacky house to see what the ticky tacky man wanted, but instead I would run inside and hide. So I sold out and bought, or rather took possession of this place which could be called a home by some, by others a hotel, by others a five-star restaurant, by some a refuge in time of trouble and incertitude.

As to home ownership — that may or may not occur, since I owe one heckuva lot of money on this place, the taxes have gone way up and I haven't had work for ten years, nine months, and fourteen days, but I am optimistic about some loans I am taking out with relatives and close friends to tide me over into the next decade. You see my problems are complicated by several issues that perhaps are of my own doing or undoing, as it were. I bought a new car and liked it so much I also bought a new pickup. I also bought not one, but three Remington 11-87 twelve-gauge shotguns, one to have by the front door, one by the back door, and one by the basement door. I also, in my repetitive buying on a credit spree, purchased three vacuum cleaners, top of the Sears line; one for Donald's Smoking Room which I recently remodeled at a cost of $12,000, one for the living room and bedrooms, and one for the basement. Looking forward to the summer season, I bought another canoe and now have three. I also have three fish locators, of course, to go with the water craft. In addition, I bought, also on credit, all new living room furniture and draperies to match my new carpet which I had to take up because of dog "pass" here and there.

My sore back is gone, pretty much, because I bought a new bed and expensive firm mattress and box spring which I got on credit, on sale at Monkey Ward's. I got my kitchen remodeled by Sears to the tune of $9,000, a new furnace, water heater, water softener, new plumbing in the kitchen and laundry. I also bought a new computer and printer for my publishing venture I hope to get off the ground sometime in the future when I am a little more financially stable. I also have three sets of college loans to pay off at a total of $42,000 plus interest. Two years ago I bought a new Sears 8 horsepower snow thrower, a new Sears lawnmower and a $2,000 kennel and run for my faithful dog Argo who enjoys the finer things in life. Last year I bought a $6,000 entertainment center, four years ago I put on new shingles, bought new combination storms and screens to the tune of $5,000 and painted the house with two primer coats and two finish coats of 15-year warranty Sears Best Paint.

Now, what is that you do want?" — "Click."

Lars – (you may use this for your future phone scripts if you wish)

Telephone Tricks, II

Dear Donald

I want you to know you can also throw the telephone solicitors off by reciting a long list of vegetables, such as asparagus, beans, lettuce, cauliflower, okra, and so on — prepare a list of about 40 items to have on hand by the phone.

You may wish to turn the tables on the solicitors by attempting to sell them certain articles at a discount such as: a used sofa, a bike, a cup of coffee, dog leashes, screen door hooks, life insurance. In the latter category, you must of course gather personal data about the caller: age, height, weight, military service, on-going ailments and complaints, recreational drug use, schooling, and whether they have ever been refused insurance for any of the customary reasons. Be sure to inquire whether they are published or if they chew soap or tobacco.

You could also invite them for a personal one-on-one interview conducted on your stairway. Advise them that it will be tape-recorded and they will be charged the usual rate for such appointments, about $30 an hour or portion thereof. They need to be told there are no guarantees.

If they decline the offer of an interview on your stairs, suggest a public place, such as a park bench where you can hold hands without many people noticing. Perhaps they would prefer to watch the CBS Evening News at your place. Ask if they are doing this for a class at school. Ask if they know Jesus. Ask if they ever played semi-pro ball. Ask if they sell naughty pictures. Refer them to Gunder or Argo. Ask if they ever thought of selling plastics or paint.

You could invite them to participate in a word association session with you. If they agree, take notes. Start by saying: "I will give you some nice words, one at a time. Tell me the first thing that comes to mind after you hear the following:" Clark bar; Lewis & Clark; Clark Fork; Clark Gable; Clark Kent; Clark Gee; Clark Throw; Clark Cradle; Clark Take-down; Clark Art; Clark Gun; Clark Boat; Clark Humor.

If they get at least five correct, then tell them they have won first prize.

Argo — March 12, 1996

Flagpole Sitting

Dear Donald

It is said by the wise that one can live by his wits. That is not to state unequivocally that a little elbow grease or greasing the skids doesn't help also. Some would insist the quickest and surest path to success is crossing the palm with silver. That notion, however, lost its appeal in confirmation class when I learned the story of Judas and his evil design in perpetrating a sell-out of Jesus for thirty pieces of silver.

The day after my graduation from Northfield High School, I hit upon a plan to use my wits and a little elbow grease to make a quick buck to send me on my way in the new world. My enthusiasm was prompted by what I thought was to be my final view of the old school. I studied the facade, remembering all the wonderful teachers whose rooms I could enumerate while standing outside Supt. Erling Johnson's office: Miss McCartney, Miss Moynihan, Mrs. Wulfsberg, Miss Overvaag, Miss Labbitt, Paul "Spider" Jorgensen.

The inspiration came to me as though I had been on the road to Damascus. To my right was the flag pole. It had been our flag pole for the past six years and clearly showed signs of wear and neglect. The pole was rusty as all get out. I thought to myself, we can't have a rusty pole flying the colors, no. The smart thing to do was to hurry over to Washington and Longfellow Schools to inspect their flag poles. Sure enough, they were both rusty. Now we were looking as a package deal. These three poles needed painting, and I was the one chosen by God to do the job.

The first thing I did was to find a length of rope. I found some sturdy rope slightly thicker than my thumb and about twenty feet in length. Then I found a board about 1" x 18" x 6" which would make a fine seat for my boatswain's chair. The flag pole by the St. Olaf heating plant on the athletic field side was to become my proving ground for testing the equipment.

"Once a scout, always a scout," I always say. My rank in scouting was Second Class, meaning that I had passed the test on tying knots. I felt I knew rope and could tie just about any kind of knot necessary to accomplish my purpose which was to shinny up and down the flag pole at will, stopping safely and securely at any point.

This strategy involved using my favorite knot, "two half hitches." One double half-hitch could be slid up the pole as far as I could reach. Then, with one foot in the stirrup connected to those half hitches, I could raise the other lower half-hitches, and so on. At any time I could rest on the board which was fastened to the ropes as a seat, just as in a children's swing set. After two enjoyable climbs to the top of the Ole pole which was fifteen feet taller than the school poles, I felt I was ready to make my proposal to the superintendent. I went to his office and knocked at his door. He came out from behind his desk to give me a warm handshake and asked what he could do for me. "The question," I stated confidently, "Is what I can do for you?" He smiled. I liked him, and the fact that he shared the same first name, Erling, as my big brother was another point in his favor. My role as a student was behind me.

I was now a private contractor bidding on a job, and I liked the elevated status this brought to the moment. I politely directed the superintendent's attention to the rusty flag pole outside his window. "I can paint that pole for you, but it will cost you $25.00 — a dollar a foot." He wondered aloud how I knew that the pole was 25 feet tall. I was ready. "See this yardstick? You and I know it is three feet long. Using a lesson I learned in this school, I stood the yard stick on end next to the pole and measured its shadow. Then I measured the shadow cast by the pole and easily arrived at the 25-foot figure."

He beamed at seeing the advantage one of his graduates had gained by learning the lessons well. "Now then, Lars," he went on, "How do you propose to get up and down the pole to scrape and paint?" I assured him that I had invented a device so simple and effective that it would soon surprise him greatly.

I asked if we had a deal, and he said he had to check on the question of insurance. He made a quick call to the school board attorney and then gave his approval. First I had to inform him, reluctantly, that the two other school poles were in worse shape than the high school pole. He took my word that I had inspected them and then agreed to the contract for all three poles at $25.00 each.

I began immediately by moving up the pole at a very brisk pace and wire brushed all the rust off in less than an hour. I could see many people peering at me from windows and enjoying the show — but perhaps not as much as I enjoyed providing the entertainment. The work went as planned, and I finished all three poles in two days. I could have done it in one day were it not for the fact that the first coat of paint needed drying time. Superintendent Johnson was very pleased with my work. He handed me a check in the amount of $75.00 and asked what I was going to do next. I told him my brother, Roald, and I were going to take the train the very next day for the Luther League Convention in Seattle. I did not tell him we were going to ride the freight train and save the fare money, $45.00 provided by St. John's Church. But that's another story.

     Argo — April 4, 1996

Muus Hunt
Gjengangere (Ghosts)

Dear Donald,

Strange things come to light from time to time, like Ibsen's "Ghosts," or Strindberg's "Ghost Sonata" and "The Father" — "sins of the father." Take, for example, the fate of Mrs. Oline Muus and some of the descendants of Pastor Bernt Julius Muus, founder of St. Olaf College.

The Muus descendants in the United States have done well and are leaders in their communities as ministers and solid citizens. Many are graduates of St. Olaf, but no building or edifice on campus is named after B. J. Muus, nor is it likely that more than an obscure bust on the first floor of the Old Main will ever note his name. The reason is scandal — old fashioned family scandal that has resonated in public through generations of the B. J. Muus family:

— infidelity, promiscuity, and a highly publicized Victorian divorce (B. J. Muus v. Oline P. Muus in 1879)

— illegitimacy (their daughter's disgraceful out of wedlock birth, another Victorian scandal in 1881)

— a Nazi collaborator and traitor to the Norwegian fatherland during WW II (the Muus' grandson)

The first scandal started to erupt after Oline Muus broke her leg, claimed Pastor Muus refused to call a doctor, and that she suffered inordinately as a result. But Muus said the local doctor was having an affair with Oline and all of the dirty linen was exposed during subsequent proceedings in the Goodhue County District Court in Red Wing — a whopper of a scandal for the time.

In fact, Muus was exceptionally tight with money and failed to provide basic necessities for his family. He was totally devoted to his mission but neglected his family as a result. This is documented in court records, and the straw that broke the camel's back was Oline's inheritance of $3,700 following her father's death in Norway.

Oline boldly sued Muus and the court records reveal that

Muus had taken control of Oline's inheritance, declaring he was a Norwegian citizen and under Norwegian law the husband controlled all family finances. Oline lost her lawsuit in Goodhue County District Court in December of 1879. She then left Muus and her children, adding more shame to an already highly publicized scandal, moved to Minneapolis among various supporters, and worked at various jobs for sustenance.

Oline took her case to the Minnesota Supreme Court and won, having tested her case for the right of women to keep their inheritance. She was granted a "limited" divorce in 1883 and moved to Columbia, South Dakota. In 1896 Oline joined a Norwegian settlement in Fruithurst, Alabama and purchased several properties with her inheritance. She was a loner and held church services in her home. Oline died in Alabama on September 4, 1922 and is buried there.

Oline's oldest child was Birgitte Magdalena Muus Klüver, (1860-1935) and the next Muus scandal was Birgitte's illegitimate son Sverre, raised by Pastor Muus. Sverre attended St. Olaf several times between 1891 and 1896 and was expelled from Luther College in 1898 after running up a lot of debt. Court records show he worked in Oregon in 1899 after leaving his wife and daughter in Montana. Back in Minneapolis, he worked as a cook and spent 30 days in the Hennepin County workhouse. Sverre had become a hopeless alcoholic and was declared "of unsound mind" by the District Court in Red Wing. He was committed to the Rochester State Hospital for the Insane in 1923 where he spent the rest of his life.

That's the last of the Muus scandals in America. Birgitte Muus moved to Norway sometime in the 1880s or 1890s and married a Norwegian of German ancestry named Klüver. When Pastor B. J. Muus had a stroke in 1899, Birgitte traveled back to Goodhue County and lovingly escorted him to Norway. Muus had been disgraced in America where he had devoted his life as a pioneer Lutheran pastor. He died on May 25, 1900 back home in Trondhjem Norway, having never become an American citizen.

The final Muus scandal developed following World War II when another son of Birgitte, Berndt Julius Muus Klüver (1897-1941), was declared a traitor in Norway. Before the German invasion, Klüver had joined a Nazi-controlled Norwegian police unit called the "Hird."

The Hird was patterned after the Nazi SA (Sturm Abteilung)

headed by Ernst Roehm who was murdered by Hitler in 1934 at a resort near Munich. Hitler's decisive action successfully disbanded the Nazi SA which had become a competitor to Hitler's private army, the SS, but had significantly influenced the Norwegian Hird.

The most infamous Hird gang in Norway operated in and around Trondheim, the area where Pastor B. J. Muus was born and where he died, and where Saint Olaf is buried. The most famous of the Norwegian Nazi gangs was named after its leader, Rinnan Banden (the Rinnan Gang). Rinnan was convicted of 13 murders that he personally committed and was executed after the war. The grandson of Pastor B. J. Muus, Berndt Julius Muus Klüver, was convicted of war crimes and sentenced to five years in prison. His property was confiscated and 25 Norwegians were executed for their war crimes, the last in 1948.

Comes now the son of the convicted Norsk Nazi collaborator, a man named Ole Wilhelm Klüver (great-grandson of Pastor Bernt Julius Muus), who suffers from shame and ostracism still existing in Norway. He wants it to end, for he and others like him carry wounds that will not heal.

Ole has written countless articles in Norwegian newspapers about the children of Nazi collaborators and problems that still exist. He has written a book that no one will publish in Norway. Ole Klüver's wish is that the innocent children of the Nazi collaborators be spared what he considers unjust punishment. Many are ostracized for the actions of their parents or relatives, but maybe the war is not over. (cf. Ibsen's "Ghosts," Strindberg's "Ghost Sonata" and "The Father").

I've now written enough about the Muus family, and I think it is clear why the name "Bernt Julius Muus" does not adorn any building at St. Olaf College, even though he was the founder. To know more, Donald, read Joseph Shaw's book on Muus. It's good, and I gave Joe a lot of information from the Red Wing trials, etc.

Argo —

P.S. St. Olaf's first location in Northfield was across from the high school at the southwest corner of Union and Third streets where the United Church of Christ (Congregational) is located. The Founders bought lots 4, 5, 6, and 7 in Block 24 from the Northfield School District. Harald Thorson, a local businessman, suggested they buy 20 more wooded acres on the hill west of town in 1878 to add to the five acres they already owned; that's how the "Popstand on the Hill" was situated there, and still resides.

Role Models

Dear Donald,

It has been said that role models influence character development. I suppose this to be true, but warn there are two sides to the coin. We who were raised in Northfield had ample opportunity to test the waters, so to speak, in this regard. Up on and around the Hill were many fine examples of do-gooders and psalm singers who were perfectly suited for the task of thumping ideas into our heads with a bible or whatever verbal implement they chose. They were well-meaning, nice folks, for the most part.

But as we come down off the Hill and roam the bottom lands of Northfield, we find equally influential, though contrary influences. That is to say, the role models downtown could provide learning experiences to assist in character development of a different slant. We who were bright learned early on that we could get 35 cents from our moms for a haircut from the barber by Max's "Stop & Shop" named Tell Bud. Further, after having received the haircut money, we could choose instead the barber directly across Third Street near the "Fair Price Market."

That barber, Art Gibbs, would cut your hair with or without a bowl for twenty-five cents, a saving of one thin dime which you could spend at the West Theater or elsewhere. We had a little saying in those days: "You can get your hair cut at Gibbs, but don't Tell Bud."

Art Gibbs was quite a barber. He once gave a guy a haircut while blindfolded. Folks wanted to see if it made any difference. I don't remember the customer's name, but they said he came out about like the rest of the folks who got haircuts from Gibbs. Whenever he slipped and made a bad cut, he would say, "You moved!"

Gibbs lost his ten year old son, Albert, by drowning in the river above the dam. Our only skating rink in those days was the stretch of river between the dam and the Fifth Street bridge upstream. Art's son and a boy named Emil Exner fell through the ice and were swept away by the current under the ice. They didn't find the boys until spring.

The issue of whether Gibbs actually spit in your hair was often rumored but never proved, as far as I know. We know for certain that he chewed tobacco and saw him spit at his potbellied wood stove which had a four inch rim around the bottom. The rim would catch the spittle that didn't sizzle away on the top or belly of the stove. I do not contend that one could float a toy boat in that reservoir, but wooden matches and cigarette butts have drifted around in it.

There was a spittoon, of course, but that apparently was no fun to spit at, for the stove was a larger target and worked better. But if Gibbs did spit in your hair you wouldn't know it, for he used that spicy perfumed raspberry-red Brilliantine in your hair so the dirty comb would slip through while Art slicked down your hair. Besides, the large Chinese boar bristle brush with talcum powder that made you cough as well as smell created a cloud that could camouflage surreptitious spitting activity around your head.

Gibbs never let you sit in the chair so you could face the mirror as he cut your hair, clicking the scissors four times between each actual cut. He was either perfecting his aim or giving you the impression that he was doing sufficient work to justify charging a quarter. So there you sat, wondering what was really going on back there behind your ears. Every kid waited expectantly for some spit to dribble down his neck or be massaged into his scalp. We all knew for a fact he spit in customers' hair because everyone said he did. I never saw him actually do it, but we sure believed he did.

Even though you couldn't see yourself in the mirror, there were plenty of other distractions to hold your attention while in the chair. Directly before you behind the pot-bellied stove along the wall, was a bench where older men pretending to be customers sat. This was usually a collection of Northfield's finest. They occupied the bench during the cold months or on rainy days when sitting in front of the "Fair Price Market" or Martin's Drug (later, Waggoner's Rexall Drug) on the opposite corner was less than inviting.

On any given day you would find the "Barbershop Trio," made up of "Squint" Hower, lead tenor; Lonnie Van Guilder, bass; and Aaron Fredenburg, baritone. From time to time a guest artist from "Hungry Hollow" might join this cacophonous ensemble. The notorious "keeper" of the city dump, Johnny Olson, joined the trio to make it a real barbershop quartet about

1949. Together, they functioned as an orchestra without a conductor—sort of perpetually tuning up.

The "Northfield News" and Northfield "Independent" were the weekly papers, but these guys on the bench provided the daily news. No topic of interest was ever avoided. All the downtown dirt was grist for their mill. They knew a lot about any subject imaginable, including who the original "Kilroy" was.

And interspersed in their nonsensical ramblings were various cuss words punctuated by a great spit of tobacco juice toward the stove. Some spit remained on the chin, to be sure, adding a deeper hue to the already brown, leathery faces that always needed a shave. They wore heavy visor caps, even indoors, and in winter wore those long, wide-lapel greatcoats, usually open at the front, exposing one or two suit coats and vest.

Squint wore a gold ring on the small finger of his left hand. He could wind his left leg clear around his lower right leg, and when he did, took a long time to unwind and stand, so he mostly sat. He was in the Army during World War I and after the war lost an eye in a farming accident with a pitchfork which is why everyone called him "Squint." He may have been in a fight, or drinking, or both. Squint lived on Lincoln Street across from Ade Christenson's, in a house he shared with his brother "Moose" who was a butcher at Armstrong's Ole Store. He may have had another brother too, but I don't remember ever seeing him around.

During the 5 or 10 minutes it took to get clipped, any kid in town could learn a whole glossary of new terms — swear words enough to fill a notebook page. They were usually casually and fluently inserted in the body of a sentence so you had to listen carefully for the new words to memorize. These could be used at play during recess at Longfellow, or muttered under your breath so other kids could hear them but not the teacher. And just think of the terminology that came into play as we stood on the ledge below the dam spearing carp with a sharp stick.

For some reason kids always liked to pick on Squint, most likely because you would always be assured of a response. As we rode our bikes past him, we would call out, "Hey Squint! Get a job!" And he would mutter, "Damn Scandinavian cattle!" Years later, as college students driving by in a car, someone invariably would shout the same advice out the window at Squint and he could always be relied upon to answer, "Get a job yourself, goddamn Scandinavian cattle!"

Across the cement bridge, as we called it, we found other character-building influences around Bridge Square in the persons of the Northfield Police. Chief Barney Wells was an imposing, though slow-moving copper with a very large revolver and plenty of ammo in his belt. Whenever two kids on a bike rode by, he invariably would advise, "One on a wheel!" (the old fashioned term for a bicycle). We invariably would continue on, calling out, "This bike has two wheels!"

There came a time when Barney Wells had to arrest Johnny Olson, one of the barbershop quartette. It happened right on the corner near the "Well." Olson was drunk, and in those days deserved to be arrested. It was the law. When Johnny was placed in the squad car he opened the window, threw out some dollar bills and started screaming, "My money! My money! Barney, get my money!" So Barney got out of the patrol car and chased after the money which was being blown away by the wind. He finally caught up with it in front of the Highway Cafe on Water Street. In the meantime, Olson escaped from the patrol car and ran across the cement bridge by the dam. Barney caught up with him and drove him down to the jail house.

Well, you might know — Olson broke away again. He ran straight down to the river and jumped off the stone wall behind the hotel into the water. It wasn't very deep, but Olson pretended he was about to drown by walking on his knees on the bottom, screaming all the while, "Barney threw me in the river! Barney threw me in the river!" Soon, crowds of people gathered on opposite sides of the river to watch the show. The Northfield Fire Department was called. They rigged up safety ropes and other stuff, plus a long ladder, and four guys went in to rescue Olson. This time Barney got a good hold of Olson's ear and parked him in the jail for the night.

There was another time Barney or some other cop arrested an unfortunate drunk named McCorkell. He had earlier lost one leg up by the Grand Theater when he parked his car, then went down to open the door of his "tuck under" garage. The car rolled down and pinned him against the door and he lost a leg in the accident. Anyway, this poor crippled fellow got locked up in the jail for being drunk in public, and nobody bothered to empty his pockets. So he lit up a cigarette, fell asleep, and the mattress caught fire. He died, helpless, of smoke inhalation in the city jail.

The last time I remember seeing Barney Wells was in 1953 on "Jesse James Day" at the scene of the fire truck rollover behind Hilleboe Hall at St. Olaf. Wendy Miller was first on the scene. When he saw those crushed girls from the St. Paul Drum & Bugle Corps who had been taken for a joy ride up St. Olaf Avenue and through the campus by a drunken fireman, Wendy got sick and threw up. I was the second person to arrive on the scene about halfway down the hill leading to Highway 19. I saw one girl who was apparently dead, another who had her left leg split open like a hot dog.

A tow truck arrived and Barney directed the crew to hoist the fire truck up so we could remove the girls underneath. They got the truck up about two feet, but then the winch let go and dropped the truck onto the girls again. There was much moaning and screaming, and I was nearly crushed too. I crawled under the truck to turn one girl's face because water was coming out of the tank on the truck and she appeared to be drowning. She was gurgling and soon died.

After a time, I saw Barney Wells talking with the confused driver of the fire truck who had been at the wheel when it rolled over. I heard Barney say, "Walt, if you are as drunk now as you were when I saw you about an hour ago, you are in big trouble." No arrest was made, and Walt was not charged at the time, as far as I know, but he did get fired as a result of the accident. The girls' families sued the City of Northfield, but got nothing. That's what I remember about "Jesse James Day" in 1953, except that Barney and Walt were both fired and Northfield changed the name of "Jesse James Day" to "The Defeat of Jesse James Days."

Many people in town were really upset about celebrating a murderer and thief like Jesse James who was probably never even in Northfield during the bank robbery in 1876, which is what local attorney W. W. Pye told me in 1947. He said Jesse James was never indicted or brought to trial because there was no proof "beyond a reasonable doubt" that he was in Northfield during the robbery. If you want more information on this Jesse James business, talk with Hoz. He interviewed W.W. Pye and has a copy of the paper Pye delivered before Aggie Larson and the Rice County Historical Society when she was president.

In between lunches and snacks and coffee and snacks,

Barney's next in command, Lenno Brandt, "Old Five by Five," was most often seen under the big clock on the corner occupied by the Northfield National Bank across from Bridge Square. It was there that some kids on a "scavenger hunt" had to measure him around the middle with a tape measure on Halloween. He measured over fifty inches at the waist and was a good sport about the episode.

Lenno had difficulty driving the patrol car because his big pot belly got in the way of the steering wheel. He would steer by pulling down with his right hand and simultaneously pushing up with his left hand, or the opposite, grunting all the while as he turned a corner, "Woof, woof, woof," or something like that.

Lenno would often stand under the clock observing the pulse of the town. He would wait for the infrequent appearance of a male dog and a boy or boys to arrive at the same corner at the same time. Then he could use the only words we ever heard him speak. He would look at the dog and proclaim, "I don't like that dog, his balls are bigger than mine."

Lenno was a hero in World War I. He was awarded the Distinguished Service Cross (DSC) for extraordinary heroism on October 4, 1918 in armed combat during the Meuse-Argonne offensive. The DCS is the Army's second highest military decoration, ranked just below the Congressional Medal of Honor. The Meuse-Argonne was the deadliest campaign in American history with over 26,000 killed in action and 120,000 casualties. Lenno survived and his official citation states:

"The President of the United States of America, authorized by Act of Congress, July 9, 2018, takes pleasure in presenting the Distinguished Service Cross to Corporal Lenno H. Brandt (ASN: 43704), United States Army, for extraordinary heroism in action while serving with Company I, 16th Infantry Regiment, 1st Division, A.E.F., near Fleville, France, on 4 October 1918. Corporal Brandt, with one companion, advanced ahead of his Company, exposed to heavy fire, and silenced an enemy machine-gun nest which had halted halted his Company."

The third cop on the force, Paul Skauge, was the night cop. He also served as a watchman at St. Olaf. Skauge got off duty at six o'clock each morning. My brother, Erling, worked at the gas station called Campbell's Service Station, the "Tydol-Veedol" in the Malt o'Meal building. The manager was Harold Starks.

Several times when Skauge went off duty, he would go across the cement bridge, pull out his revolver, and shoot carp. He hit quite a few, Erling told me. The police didn't have a target range, so Skauge would just fire off a few rounds at the carp for practice. A stranger passing by at six in the morning might get quite an impression. I suppose Officer Skauge could have done what we all did — go out to the city dump at night, head lights off, load up, turn the headlights on, and blast away at the rats. I never enjoyed it much.

So it was, Donald, that we had all kinds of influences on character development in Northfield. I must say, however, that the good influences far outweighed the bad, and we were lucky to be able to associate with many nice people. Our playmates were lots of fun and really good kids. Our teachers and coaches were excellent examples of good character.

I guess if I were to choose the best, I would have to go with the guys that lived on Lincoln Street and Lincoln Lane. They never let each other down, never shot anyone in the back — they were the real role models.

   Argo — December 16, 1995

Apple Run

Dear Donald,

As you are aware, all my days are interesting; some more than others. In the interest of seeking the interesting, I went on an apple run in Dakota County, and even northern Rice County. Now, an apple run is fun. I load up my trunk with five-gallon pails of apples; I load up the back seat with the faithful Argo, who also enjoys apple runs, and off we go.

Our first stop has multiple purposes. It is to visit my sister, Margit. She needs comforting in her time of trouble. While she and her husband, Wynne, were gone on a four day weekend, the water hose from the sink to the ice maker in the refrigerator broke. The water damage to her lovely house is largely in the basement, but devastating. All the carpet is removed. The piano sits, keys warped as Salvador Dali's, like undulating rubber, forever silent.

The gift of apples starts us off on the right foot. She takes enough for her neighbor, too. We then discuss the upcoming visit of the king of Norway. This should be fun. I've never met a king I didn't like. Margit will wear a Norwegian costume. Maybe I should too, and some medals, Donald. Remember when we dressed in tuxedos for the symphony and wore track medals? That was a kick, Mr. Ambassador.

I helped Margit choose carpet, a privilege that comes rarely. My technique is to observe carefully which sample she prefers or seems to prefer and say, "You're right! That's the one. Definitely. I see what you mean — it has those brown flecks that match the woodwork. Uh-uh, you don't really need a high pile anyway — just shows vacuum cleaner trails. You know, this one will not show dirt, not hardly, no. Yes, definitely, you can't go wrong. Take it. Ya, that's the one."

Carpet samples are put away. That's what big brothers are for, to help out in major decisions. Margit notices I am well-groomed and dressed in a mode she likes. We discuss her new job as a tourist guide to the Twin Cities. She is well prepared for this exciting new chapter in her life. I sure like her enthusiasm — she will be a great guide. Margit suggests I could use a new car and that it probably should be a recreational vehicle, a Blazer. I suppose, some day. But it will be tough to step down from a big black limo. We say so long, and I head on down the road towards Farmington and my favorite nephew, Charlie. He and I do things together that my sons and I don't seem to be able to do, that is, except for Bjørn, before he got a girlfriend.

Charlie lives in a new house with a lot landscaped by Mulligan of Northfield. (No, not the townies, these guys live out on Highway 19). He comes out of the house in jeans and a pajama top, so I know it is not yet 11:00 a.m. Charlie likes my apples, and his wife, "Peterson," as he calls her, does too. I suggest apple crisp. They concur. Charlie and I discuss the November deer hunt. I tell him I have applied for the doe permit lottery. He hints I may want to visit him at the Log House for the grouse hunt, at which time we can also zero-in the rifles. This I enjoy. I like to shoot, and am not bad at it, even with my bad eye. Once I took Nini and kids and our dog Viking out trap shooting. It was a blast. Nini enjoyed it so much. We never did it again, a fact which now makes me ashamed of myself.

Anyway, I ask Charlie if I need to buy a deer rifle. No, you can use the Ruger M-30, which shoots a Russian 7.62 x 39 mm. 123 gr. soft point. Charlie is going to have a scope installed and the rifle bore-sighted. We can then fine-tune it on the gravel pit range where everybody else in the area does. My former skier, Doug Erickson, is the Conversation Officer there at Tower, Minnesota. He will show me good hunting spots.

You remember how we camped out at Caribou Lake and did target shooting and trap shooting. That sure was fun. Bjørn and I have done the same. Here's what is a blast: I take a stack of yellow clay targets, walk around the woods among the yellow-leafed trees, and place the targets on stumps, in crotches (of trees). Then Bjørn and I, armed with .22 rifles, scan the area for the hard-to-spot targets. We discovered something interesting. When you hit those clay targets dead center like Alvin York would do, they break not. So you have to walk up on one for a look-see to verify, then go back and pull a little to the left or right of center to break the target and know you are shooting well. Charcoal briquettes really go "Puff!" But I digress.

After leaving Charlie's place which is two miles north of Farmington, I find brother Erling, planting a shrub in the front yard. I give him and his nice wife, Joyce, a report on Bjørn in

Norway. We talk about their coming visit to El Paso for the annual reunion of the 442nd Bomber Group. Former senator George McGovern is one of the guys in the Group. I give them a pail of apples. Apple crisp is on the menu. Joyce gives me fattigmann and sandbakkels (Norsk cupcake). Then I am off to Northfield.

As you know, the road to Northfield takes you past the Castle Gardens Club, still there, where we used to buy set-ups or a bottle of beer for a quarter, a T-bone steak for a dollar. As I drive past the old truck garden onion flats, I notice the ground level appears to be about two feet lower than it was fifty years ago. Must be the sod farming they do now. When I was twelve years old, we were picked up by a truck at 5:00 a.m. and taken out to the "Monk" Festler truck garden. He is the man who stored his onions and potatoes in Tripp's cave.

I disturb myself to remember, for ten or fifteen cents an hour, straddling on my knees a very long row of onions; taking also a row to the left and one to the right, and pushing the weeds away from the onions by thumb. It was a formidable task for a boy of twelve to look down his three rows, a quarter of a mile long, knowing when he finally had crawled to the end, he would have to turn around and take another three rows back to the starting place. It was shivering cold for an hour or so, then too hot. We were thirsty and hungry, but had to finish a row before taking a drink or a leak. No one ever said, "Nice going." No one knew how we felt inside or out, no one cared and there was always someone looking down at you.

More pleasant things come to mind as I enter Northfield. There's the picture of a cow and those words again. Can you imagine a small town with two great colleges? It surely is an interesting place to live. Driving up St. Olaf Avenue brings memories. There we see former homes of Glasoe, Haakon Carlson, Melius Christiansen, Donhowe, Homer Mason, finally the Ole Store and then the intersection of the world, Lincoln Street and St. Olaf Avenue. Up the avenue: Bjork, Mellby, Malmin Meyer, Lee, Holland, Schmidt, Hegland, A.O. Lee, Armstrong, Huggenvik, Norstad, Biorn, Granskou, Jørgen Thompson and then finally, 'Olaf.

It's all changed now, but we don't care. We just want to remember the way it was, because that's what counts. At St. Olaf, I visit WCAL. Paul Peterson, the station manager says it is OK to put a basket of apples in the employee "break" room. I have a large basket with the very best apples for fresh eating. I place a note by the apples: "These Honeygold apples are chemical-free, and they are washed," anticipating questions in the minds of those who will help themselves.

Paul gets a bagful. I gave one to his wife last week. I tell Paul that one of the apples is the "Main Apple." He is pleased when I tell him the main apple is the very best one on a tree, reserved for a friend. I go around the station clasping hands, enthusiastically telling them they are the greatest, and that WCAL really scored a "coup" with its series "The Lives of the Children." It is good to see people respond to compliments sincerely given. They know me from before, so they know I speak truth.

I always seem to have an errand at the bookstore. I need a couple refill roller balls and a St. Olaf Choir CD which has a song that brings tears, it is so beautiful. The name of the song is "Set Me As A Seal" ("...upon your heart, for love is strong as death.") from Song of Solomon. There are absolutely no pen refills in the bookstore. They are using up pens faster than the bookstore can supply them. The woman sends me downtown to the stationer's. "Nice town you have here," I offer. The saleswoman, about twenty years old, responds, "Ya, I'd rather raise kids here than in the Cities." "You got that right," says I, taking off my cap as a gesture of respect that earlier impressed the young lady in the bakery. "Nobody ever did that for me before. I think it's very nice," said she. I am glad to have changed my ways. Being an older gentleman is fun. People enjoy being treated with respect and good humor.

We return to the campus. Dog Argo likes to take a pass around the trees in back of Agnes Mellby Hall, so after that we leave for home. We stop at the Fireside Orchard half way to I-35W to see Bob, the owner. He and I are on this apple kick. Bob is glad to see me again and says, "C'mon, I'll show you around." He shows the cavernous warehouse, kept at 34 degrees, which holds over 10,000 bushels. Then we drive up and down certain rows to see a variety of cultivars. He enjoys hearing my compliments for he knows they come from the heart and from one who knows something about it. He proudly shows examples of expert grafting. We sample a new apple, "Sweet Sixteen," and it is good.

We discuss harvest, timing, ante climacteric, senescence, and after a while he asks if I studied biology. No, but it was my most valuable subject. Without any fancy talk, he says, "Boy, I wish you would come work with me." I tell him right out that my goal is to live out my life as a gentleman farmer without ever holding down a job. He remarks that I seem to know and care a lot more about apples than many in the business. He enjoys hearing me tell of my trees, how I do a walk around each night to check on them, knowing every branch. I tell him my mother was from a fruit farm in Norway, just up the road from Hovland, Hardanger. We have a certain kinship here. I tell him of the death of my Superior Plum tree last week. His diagnosis is immediate and correct: birch borers got at the base of the trunk, girdling the cambium layer under the bark. He was right. I look around the attractive sales room where they have all sorts of goodies, and select a half pound of Penuche. I haven't had that for a few decades.

Faithful Argo and I return home, drive past some places where we will hunt pheasants next month. When we get home, I notice immediately that there is an apple missing. Yes, of all those hundreds of apples, I miss one. My new Honeycrisp, at the edge of the garden on the street side had seven big ones when I left in the morning. One hung pendulously from the bottom branch, too visibly, and someone could not resist the temptation. I bet it was my neighbor, Mrs. B. who rides her bike, carrying a knapsack, looking for targets of opportunity. She will enjoy it, and that's one less apple to take along on my next apple run.

   Argo — October 14, 1997

Boys Will Be Boys

Dear Donald,

We had a guy in the tenth grade by the name of Billy who had a special talent. He could bend his left arm backward at the elbow. Billy had what they called "slippery joints" — double-double-jointed.

One time he was acting up in Emma Overvaag's English class and she made him stay after school. He faked a fall by the pencil sharpener and came up with his arm bent backwards. "I broke my arm!" he said, "I need to go down to the nurse." She let him do that and he walked out of school to freedom. He wore a fake sling to class for a couple days afterward so she wouldn't get wise.

Paul Sherwin was another guy who had to stay after school — in Miss McCartney's 8th grade arithmetic class. One time he said his grandmother died so she let him go. Then she died again, but Miss McCartney said, "I thought she already died?" Paul said, "She really did, this time."

So he escaped again. The third time she died it didn't work, so Paul stayed after, but he was cunning. He went to sharpen his pencil, and there by the sharpener was a 10-pound lead sash weight that anchored the rope which went up through two pulleys and lowered the 24" globe above her desk.

He untied the rope and the globe crashed down on Miss McCartney's desktop right in front of her face. It made a heckuva racket and scared her out of her wits. Paul ran away, unnoticed. The principal, William F. Carlson, found out that Paul was being a nuisance in class, so he told Miss McCartney she should detain him after school. "I don't dare," she said, "He lets the globe down on my head." The principal just shook his head and walked away.

There was another guy by the name of "Poof" Norgren who always had one up his sleeve. We called him "Poof" because he would pass gas silently and could stink up a classroom like you wouldn't believe! He also bought some smelly poop stuff at Tiny's Smoke Shop downtown to have on hand in a little vial for emergencies. Any time he had to stay after school, he would go up to the teacher with the smell coming out of his pocket and say, "I had a accident, did it in my pants, needa go home." It worked once with every teacher.

We also had a guy we called "Onion Skin" Hanson. His skin would molt like a snake about once every three months. He would sit there in class and peel it off. Once in a while when a girl would stare at him, he would peel off a strip, put it in his mouth, chew it and say, "Umm, good!" One girl threw up all over her desk when she saw that. The study hall teacher, Ken Heacock, made Hanson clean up the mess and then stay after school. His brother, "Smiley" Hanson, had false teeth and would take out his upper plate and wipe the teeth off on his sleeve. The same girl saw that and barfed again. Mr. Heacock made Smiley clean up that mess, too, and stay after.

We once made a deal with our basketball manager at the B-squad game against Faribault. He took the needle and deflated the ball — not so you could see it, just enough so it wouldn't bounce. When we started the second half with a jump ball one of our guys said, "Whatever you do, don't dribble the ball."

We passed the ball until Dick Jacobson got an easy layup, then Faribault got the ball out of bounds. The guy who got the ball tried to dribble but the ball wouldn't bounce and stayed down on the floor. I quickly grabbed it and passed it to Tommy Thomas for another easy bucket. The referee stopped the game and called for another ball but did not take away the points. During the time out, our coach, Ed Byhre, who was not in on the stunt, nevertheless figured that something was wrong. He went over to the scoring table and made them take away the questionable four points. He was an honest man and a good coach.

We never did any more of that kind of stuff until we played Faribault again. They had a guy named Tom who used to walk across my path during the track season to throw me off stride when I was pole vaulting. He was guarding me really close and liked to put his hand in front of my face and say stuff to irritate me. I fixed him good with a quick fake to the right and without looking gave him a shot in the face with the ball as hard as I could. The referee called a technical foul, but Tom was so affected he missed the bucket by three feet. The poor chump sat on the bench for the rest of the game. A few years later we became classmates at St. Olaf.

Dear Donald

I remember when Luke Johnson moved to Northfield. His parents were missionaries to Madagascar and were to spend a year in Northfield on furlough. We called him "Lefty" because he was born with two left hands, but one was on the right arm, so when he had mittens on, nobody could tell the difference. I befriended Lefty right away because I never had a friend before who had two left hands, and I thought it was quite the deal. Lefty was a big kid, about six foot two and 190 lbs.

We were in the tenth grade and had Fred Simonich for woodworking shop. Lefty asked Simonich if it was all right to be in class since he had two left hands. Simonich told him that was OK, because "A lot of kids in this shop are all thumbs so having two left hands is no big deal," he said. Simonich asked him if he played basketball. Lefty said he had played some in Madagascar when he and his brother stood a couple of guys in a game of horse. Simonich wanted to know which hand he dribbled with and Lefty said, "My left." Then Simonich asked him if he was a left-handed shooter. Lefty said he was sort of ambidextrous, but really preferred baseball.

So Simonich took him up to the baseball coach, Loyal Burmeister. He told "Burma" that he had a hot prospect for him. Simonich told Burma that Lefty was a double lefty and could pitch left-handed with either arm. Burma asked Lefty if he batted left-handed. He said he did. They went down to the old gym where John Westerlund, our gym teacher, had the kids playing catch with baseballs. Wes asked Burma what he wanted. He told Wes he wanted to find out what kind of stuff the kid had, and could he pitch a few to the catcher, Dale Quist?

Well, everybody stopped what they were doing to see what kind of stuff the new kid had. They could already see he was biggern heck. He would catch the ball with his left hand, then wind up kinda weird and throw a curve ball with the other. He only threw curves. One hand curved the ball sharply down and in like a sharp cutter. The other curved the ball down and out. They put up some real good hitters like Bernie, Bing and Corky against him and they all ducked; the ball curved so much it scared the heck out of them.

Then they took him up to Ed Byhre, our football coach. Ed said he never had a lefty passer so after school they tried him out over in Central Park behind the school. He would run to the left and throw with the left. Then he ran to the right and passed with the other left. But the receivers couldn't handle Lefty's passes. He threw the ball like a bullet. "We got a live one here," I heard Byhre say to Simonich.

The next Monday I looked for Lefty in school. He was not there, not even in woodworking shop. Simonich announced, "I guess we lost Lefty. He moved to Watertown, South Dakota to live with his grandparents because his folks went back to Madagascar."

Lars — March 2, 1996

Grandparents

Dear Donald,

I never knew my grandparents. This fact has come more into focus now that I am in the grandparent stage of this life and it makes me feel a bit sad. But at the same time, it makes me feel privileged, because I am now able to do things they never had the pleasure of doing, namely, to enjoy the issue of my issue.

Now that we have placed the issue of the issue of my issue on a positive mode, we can go forward with more enthusiasm for the topic. You must first have a little background if you are to understand fully how this issue came to be an issue for one who in his dotage wants to dote on his grandchild at Christmas time or any other time.

Three of my grandparents lived and died in Norway. The fourth, my father's father, moved to Portland in the nineteenth century, and in his remaining sixty years, never came (or went) back east or back to Norway. You are doing better than he, although there remains a distinction between coming east or going south. Some folks went south by going west, but that's another story.

Back to my grandparents. My mom's mom and dad were farmers who came originally from the province of Telemark, Norway. Their name was Romtveit, which became, according to Norwegian usage, Sekse, when they chose a farm called Sekse as their homestead. My mom was born there, hence her surname, Sekse. Her father died in 1930; her mother, in 1943.

I couldn't visit grandpa because I was not yet born and I couldn't visit either of my grandmas because of the depression and the war. They probably would have liked me, because the role of grandparents toward their grandchildren is not to judge them, but to accept them. They cannot choose their grandchildren; grandchildren cannot choose their ancestors.

You know something about my father's father, for you were present when I picked up his death certificate while I was in Portland last June. I often wondered what had become of him. You know that his 93-year old body was donated to the

University of Oregon Medical School. He abandoned his wife and small children in Norway when my father, a twin, was one year old. But he did not abandon me, so I hold no grudge though I think it would have been most enjoyable to sit on the knee of an honest-to-goodness Norwegian storyteller to learn how it's done to perfection.

My father's mother did the best she could do in Norway under her difficult circumstances. She had a hard life, and that became my father's inheritance. As a matter of fact, I never saw my father laugh out loud. It's tough to do that while you are going from the frying pan into the fire, as it were.

But in his later years, he became the quintessential grandpa to 29 grandchildren that we know of. He was never a "poseur." His grandchildren knew that, of course, because it is very difficult to fool kids. Although he was a bit of a hard guy early on, he mellowed to become what a grandpa should be — a kindly old gentleman who is always welcome and who always welcomes the grandchildren.

They say that children are the best philosophers because they always ask, "Why?" It can be fairly said of grandpas that they become philosophers too, having learned not only to ask questions, but to question the answers. You are familiar with the old saw which was my father's credo: "The more I learn, the more I realize how little I know."

I know you know that too, for I know you have been reading Kierkegaard who claimed, "If I think, I am not." My father never agreed with that conclusion, being a strict Hegelian logician. However, he was always willing to listen to another version of the truth. He used to sit forward on the edge of his chair as I spoke, cupping his hand by one ear. He finally got a hearing aid — in fact the smallest I had ever seen. I asked him, "What kind is it?" and he replied, "Oh, about five o'clock."

Where was I? Oh yes. We were discussing grandparents. "Beware Greeks bearing gifts," was the admonition for centuries. Does that apply to Greek grandpas? I hope not, I think not (Don't agree with that last sentence!). I wonder what the guys who own the Greek restaurants in America and who are grandfathers think of that slogan?

Grandpas enjoy bearing gifts for their beloved grandchildren, at least until the kids are old enough to ask to borrow the car. I am currently preparing myself for negotiating proposals I will need to offer Northwest Airlines in the event there is a dispute over excess carry-on gifts. I hope they have the Christmas spirit so I won't have to play hard ball, no.

But I am prepared as a final offer to state, "All right. You win. I'm a Greek bearing gifts, I give up, the presents stay on the plane, I leave. Now are you happy?" But what could happen is that some masochistic flight attendant might be burned off for having to work on Christmas Day and just might say, "OK, have it your way."

My little princess, Arianna, will be glad to see her grandpa, and bearing Christmas presents will have nothing to do with it. I know how to be a grandpa, having studied my father in his role for forty-five years. There is a bond that develops between grandparents and grandchildren that is unexplainable. We know how to manage things and be patient, for the most part.

At present, the stories I tell Arianna are the same old fairy tales and rhymes that are so familiar. But just wait until she gets to be about ten years old and says, "Grandpa, tell me about when you were a little boy in Northfield." I'll have to make up something, for my childhood was so uneventful. (What did you say about that? Oh.)

Speaking of events — I'll always remember the day last June when Arianna, who got up before I did one morning, and was in the living room when I entered. She let out a squeal of pure delight at seeing her grandpa. I let out a whoop in response, and we were off to another great start of another wonderful day together.

Sonja has taught Arianna well. My grandparents should have been so fortunate. Each time I phone, Arianna gets on the phone and says, "I love you, Grandpa!"

     Argo —

Angel Arianna

From Spokane, WA - April 29, 1996

Dear Donald,

One particularly useful art I learned at my mother's knee was that of reading coffee grounds in a cup. This carries with it an elevated status, for coffee grounds are infinitely more difficult to read than tea leaves.

This particular morning, I recall that I had to pull the coffee filter and tilt it somewhat in order to get some good grounds for the day's predictions. Normally, Nini (former wife, elevated in status because she is the mother of my children), would send me on my way with some astrological counseling gleaned from the daily paper which had little else to offer. However, I missed the morning's counseling session because I overslept. I should like to share with you what I learned, together with the background.

First and foremost, it is very likely that my principal position in the hereafter will be supervisory in nature and somewhat broad in scope. After the customary negotiations with St. Peter — sentry at the Pearly Gates — sessions to which I look forward eagerly because of the attendant haggling process, I intend to remain steadfast in my position that I am best suited for looking after angels, especially good-looking ones.

I know this to be true because of my current position, looking after the angel Arianna, a responsibility I take seriously. This morning, Sonja, Arianna's mother, had her set up in basic black, pony tail and dangling earrings which she just now removed. I asked her if she had ever heard of Miss Hilleboe. She had. The only connection I can imagine is that Grandma Nini had related a few of her less onerous escapades while at 'Olaf, but nevertheless had at the time at least a nodding acquaintanceship with your former neighbor on Lincoln Lane, Gertrude Hilleboe.

Lest you feel too puffed up about having had a neighbor named Gertrude, may I remind you that for some years I had Gertrude Sovik as a next door neighbor. A fine name, to be sure, one which shall be the basis for a song I intend to write — in Norwegian, of course. But I digress again.

My mention of Miss Hilleboe very likely prompted my four-year old granddaughter, Arianna, to remove her earrings. My preliminary conclusion is that Arianna is grooming for eventual acceptance at St. Olaf, and wants to present an innocent image not unlike that of her grandma, Nini.

It follows, therefore, that she needs to be careful to avoid wearing red dresses, patent leather shoes, and so on. I know Nini avoided wearing these; furthermore, I don't recall her sitting on my lap without a Minneapolis phone book between us. She may have tried, of course, before she came to know better. I know you discovered her while you both were students at St. Olaf, and learned that she wanted to date a hero and that is why you called on me to take her out. I digress.

Another reason I am convinced Arianna is a St. Olaf gal is that when I just put a St. Olaf Choir CD on the stereo she asked me to dance, which I did. As we danced, I hummed the low notes which I could feel rumbling in my chest and which Arianna enjoyed. "It isn't everyone," I explained to her, "who has a St. Olaf Choir bass for a grandfather." We danced on, blissfully, for in my heart I now knew her theme — "I love the boys who dance slowly," for it runs in her maternal ancestry. Then comes the tender pat on the cheek as I am touched by an angel who says lovingly, "You are a nice boy, Grandpa."

In nearly two weeks of angel watching, I have received only a single rebuke. It was brought on by me after becoming tired of holding my hands full of rocks from the flower bed which she entrusted to me for safekeeping. I threw them back on the rock pile. She was on me in an instant, shaking her index finger as one disciplining a child, saying, "Don't throw rocks! Never! Never! Be nice!"

Satan never had a tail like mine, which I metaphorically put quickly between my legs and bounded up the stairs to the relative safety of the deck. I'm telling you, Donald, you have to watch it around here. At the top of the stairs, I began to laugh. She called out to me, "That's not funny!"

I knew I was in some deep doo-doo that I couldn't wiggle out of with a simple offer of jelly beans and M&Ms from my stash on the top cupboard shelf. My peace offering would also require a generous draft of Hires root beer. This, your supplicant did. Coupled with more St. Olaf Choir tunes, these items made everything "all better" as they say in pre-juvenile circles to indicate the absence of pain, that healing is complete.

As my little angel was dining on her lunch of rice pilaf, I explained to her the day's itinerary. After lunch, a nap. After the nap — which is required — we embark on our next adventure, a long stroll in the stroller. As they say, angels need to learn to stroll before they can fly.

After the stroll, it's rehearsal time. I have selected for today's drill, Alan Hovhaness' Symphony No. 50, "Mt. St. Helens," movement III, Volcano. This dramatic eruption scene with kettle drums and huge cymbals is useful for teaching marching band skills. After the initial blasts of the big drums which will knock us off our feet and send us tumbling as if shot by cannons, we arise and march to the marcato beat of the score.

I lead, marching as I was taught while playing a policeman in the 'Olaf production of "Pirates of Penzance." It is for Arianna to follow, toy saxophone in hand. We will march around the house like the St. Olaf lion, rampant, until the repose of the aftermath with soothing violins, horn and trumpet cause us to sit, listen and enjoy. Words of appreciation are respectfully spoken at this point: "I love this music." Then as the climax approaches with its stately grandeur, we gesture wildly as we follow the grand march heavenward, like Christian Soldiers marching, as Baring-Gould so memorably put it, "...as to war."

Our command performance will be this evening before an admiring and appreciative audience — Nini, mother of my children, who will doubtless remark, "It's too loud!"

    Lars — Friday, April 10, 1998, 3:22 PM

Many Glacier Hotel

Dear Donny,

I thought I would share some memories of Glacier Park and Many Glacier Hotel from the Fubar summers of 1956-1959. Several Fubars were there — Marty, Gunder, Stud, Hoz, Scuba, scoundrel Tyrant. Rawhide was head bellman for a couple of years and we were reminiscing recently. Here is an email I sent to Rawhide in response to some questions.

    Argo —

Rawhide — it was 1957 right after the Ytterboe incident. I arrived in Whitefish, Montana on a freight train with Marty and hitchhiked over Going to the Sun highway. I knew that Mrs. Seilseth, wife of the general manager of the Many Glacier hotel, was a singer, perhaps in the St. Olaf Choir, and that her husband Lloyd grew up in Northfield.

I went up to the office where Mrs. Seilseth was running the elevator music system, and said: "How do you do, Mrs. Seilseth, my name is Lars Kindem. I was born and raised in Northfield on Lincoln Street below Old Main. I stood in the St. Olaf Choir (an archaic term that means something to the older cognoscenti) for three years; I cared for F. Melius Christiansen as my patient before he died. I want a job in the Grill."

Thunder clapped as her hands came together — "Lloyd! Lloyd! I have found a replacement for that young man who did not show up for his job in the Grill, and he is a marvelous Northfield boy!" I was hired on the spot, for $45.00 a month plus room, board and tips.

Night clerk Ray Kinley was definitely a legend at Many Glacier. I recall Rawhide slipping down to the kitchen and bringing back to the front desk two bowls of ice cream and other goodies for Ray in the wee hours of the morning. Ray had a room next to the liquor store in 1959. Mine was down the hall.

Ray was elevated from night desk to assistant manager in the summer of '59 under Ashby Stiff, a hotel management guy and all-around "prack" from Florida State. He had been assistant manager in 1958 under Mr. Lundberg, a hulking, bald, Swede with a Ph.D. in hotel management.

All of us were fired at the end of the season when Rawhide was there. The reason I got rehired was the result of some small talk during a party near the U of M campus in Minneapolis with a guy who had a contract to be a garbage truck driver at Many Glacier Hotel but did not intend to go. I got the contract from him, crossed out his name and inserted mine.

Mr. Lundberg, the manager in 1958, liked me a lot. I first drove a stake-bed truck which held all 26 of the garbage cans from the kitchen. Mrs. Roady was still there. I would take the cans halfway to Sherburne to the dump and feed the grizzly bears who kept a respectful distance while I off-loaded the garbage. I then would drive over to the log supply and load up an entire truckload each day of 4-foot logs for the fireplaces. I loved the work and it kept me in good shape.

One day I went in to Dr. Lundberg and said, "Doc, you aren't making any money off the bar by the dining room. I can fix that." He asked how, and I said, "I want to have a wine cart loaded with crushed ice, wines, pre-mixed martinis and the like, and hawk the wares in the fashion of those London street merchants, singing." He said he had heard of such a thing and ordered the carpenters to build a wine cart after my design. Then, of course, I became Sommelier or wine steward, from 4:00 pm on each day.

As luck would have it, a convention of about 550 bankers from the Northwestern and 1st Bank groups held a convention at the hotel. I set up a bar right in the lobby by the front door and made a fortune. Then I asked the front desk who the big shots were. I had champagne buckets with ice sent up to their rooms, compliments of management. I think I sent four buckets. That evening, Dr. Lundberg said to me: "Lars, that was a stroke of marketing genius. You created an atmosphere of good will such as I never could have dreamt."

The next evening, at the big banquet, someone ordered champagne. He had two choices: Taylor's New York at $3.50, which I said was not good enough for him and his party, and Mumm's Cordon Bleu, at $16.00 the bottle. He ordered two of the best. I ran back to the bar and had the four waiters in red coats, towel over left arm, march in step with me to the table.

"I'll take the cork," said the man. Oh boy. I popped open the cork and handed it to him. "No, what that expression means is that I will take the first sip to see if it is all right." I did as he instructed, and my assistants poured. We had a hard time getting back to the bar for everyone wanted champagne and we quickly sold all the expensive stuff in stock.

I ran downstairs to the liquor store and said to Sandy Sanderson, the store manager, "Get every bottle of sparkling and white wines you have in the store and rush them up to the walk-in freezer in the kitchen. We're gonna sell them all." He did as I asked.

We sold every bottle he had and we made $5,500 that night. Later, in the Grill, the bankers, who by now had their snoots full, asked if we could stay open another hour. I said we would for $20.00 tip for each of the thirteen people on duty. They said OK. We did it and everyone was happy.

The next day Dr. Lundberg called me in for an accounting to be sure that all the rumors he had heard could be verified. After my account, he said: "Lars, I am prepared to offer you the job next summer as Beverage Manager for the hotel. You will be paid handsomely. Only the chef and I will be paid more. In addition, I want you to serve as House Officer because I don't want that St. Paul dick around with his sidearm and you will have to straighten out the Saturday night brawls between the cowboys and the Indians."

I said, "OK, provided that I may name my assistant manager (Gunder); further, that I have a room in the hotel and full dining privileges, my automobile, and full privileges at McDonald, Prince of Wales and Entrance." He said, "You know how to bargain. The answer was "Yes" to everything, and "Welcome aboard the management team." Did I celebrate that night at the Hydro, with champagne, while the others drank Great Falls Select (of course, I was fired at the end of my third year too)!

I liked the Hydro a lot. One night, my second year, I think, I returned to my room in the dorm and found a huge buffalo head under the covers in my bed. Someone had lifted it off the wall in the main lounge where we used to slide under the partition to kipe stuff from the store, such as Pendleton shirts.

The next year, they sealed it off pretty good. I ruined my Voigtlander Vitessa camera at the dock from Swiftcurrent to Grinnell Lake. Standing with one foot on the dock, the other on the gunwale, I did the expected — the splits — and went straight down. Heck of a deal. Ruined the shutter mechanism. I remember Rawhide tossed a hunting knife at a meandering deer across the lake from Many Glacier Hotel. I think he regretted that act of thoughtlessness, but for sure no real harm was intended.

Stud was a kick as a houseboy. Dan Ketter ("Tyrant") was a con man. Some of the Oles were silly, the girls, especially. Marty had a silly girlfriend there. Rawhide's was sensible, pure, smart. She was gorgeous and a very good singer in the group of Madrigals we formed. The gardener at the time claimed he was fooling around with Mrs. Seilseth in the greenhouse, never confirmed this for sure, but the word got around.

Gunder and I had a racket going. I never worked the Grill; walked around wearing a tie and sport coat, glad-handing the guests, as instructed by the manager, for working the cash register detracts from managerial capacity! Gunder took all the tabs I signed, put them under the cash drawer, and at the end of the night, tore 'em up.

We still had a bar cost much lower than former years — 24% as opposed to 27%. The Dining Room cost was around 35%. So the owners, Knutson Construction Co. from Minneapolis, liked us a lot. In addition to the Madrigal singers we formed a troupe that did musicals, such as "My Fair Lady" and "South Pacific," among others. One year a professional troupe traveled from hotel to hotel doing shows. Nobody liked them.

One day during my second year there when I was starting out as wine steward and manning the upstairs service bar alone (The Interlaken Room), a big, handsome dude in a red and black checkered lumberjack shirt came up and said, "Hello, Sonny, give me a light Scotch, neat." I did not know what the heck a light Scotch was, so I went for the Haig & Haig Pinch bottle.

He said, "No, Sonny, that's not a light Scotch — try Cutty Sark there..." I served him. It was 75 cents and he tipped me a quarter. The next day, he was in a party that climbed Chief Mountain. He was a man who formerly was a "high rent" boy in the homosexual community in Hollywood in the early thirties — the guy that got George Cukor fired as Director of "Gone With the Wind," ostensibly because Cukor knew of his past activities and he did not want to be exposed. His name, Clark Gable.

Then there was the lady who always took the same lakeside room and lakeside table for a week each year. She had honeymooned there as a newlywed and her husband had passed away. She wanted the memories and she got them. She was about sixty years old and was treated with a deference not shown to everyone. People liked the story a lot. Would I die next week if I had that kind of devotion and loyalty from a wife. The heck I would.

You remember in 1957 during the cleanup before the arrival of the guests when a houseboy hiked up to the shrinking glacier we called "South America." He got between a grizzly sow and her cubs. The bear chewed off one buttocks, half of his shoulder, and buried them in a shallow grave. The kid spent two years in plastic surgery routines at the University of Pennsylvania hospitals. And I witnessed the grizzly first hand who wrestled the garbage cans by the kitchen and behind the Grill. One night the watchman prevented me from blundering into a bear by the kitchen on my way from the Grill to the dorm. The watchman, a young man from Texas, stood on the walk bridge, shining a flashlight on the bear, and said, "Y'all betta git back into the hotel. They's a bear over yonder by the kitchen. Ah'm gitten the heck outta heah mahself!"

We have not, of course, forgotten the times I furnished Rawhide with orders of drinks that he finished off in the bellman's room. Or that marvelous married couple who were bellhops? I remember vividly when she was at the travel desk in the lobby and the wind blew her papers onto the floor. Her response was plain and direct when she called out in a loud voice, "Close the god-damn door!"

Or Roald Tweet, later professor of English in Illinois, who had a game leg and a pronounced limp. He would drip water from the sink onto his nose so it looked like he was sweating a lot. Good for tips, I suppose. One of our buddies later set up a dental practice five blocks from Roosevelt High where I taught. I never went to see him because I never really knew him.

The gearjammers told tourists, "See them glaciers up yonder under that there ridge called the Garden Wall? Well, that white stuff, that's not snow; we had a warm spell and the snow all melted and filled up the lake, so they shipped in a couple hundred bales of cotton from Georgia just to make it look white and good."

And don't forget, Mebust ("Scuba") came to visit us from Kalispell. And Hoz was there, Gunder, Stud, Marty too, a "Meeting at the Summit" of FUBARS in 1957 when I hired a couple of them in the bar.

I returned to Many Glacier in 1980 and Ray Kinley was the gardener. He remembered everyone, and very well. The summer before, the entire ground floor was flooded when melting snow elevated Swiftcurrent about six feet. What a mess. I stopped at the Grill. The guy who waited on me was an Ole but he did not really fit in. He did not know how to enjoy the place as we obviously did. The "Honeymoon" cabin on the peak of the garden wall to the left is still there, but I do not know if it is used for fire-watching. Maybe. Hope so.

    Lars —

"La Biche" – The Doe

Dear Donald,

After a while, say a couple years, one settles in to his retirement, or as Gus calls it, "free agency" and adjusts patterns of living for the long haul. That's what retirement should be, and I know you have studied this too.

With a list of cautions drawn up in preparation for various onslaughts upon the innards such as the prostate, the liver, the heart and the gut, one plays with the cards he is dealt or deals to himself. A timetable, that's what we need, so we can anticipate the next curve ball.

Well, I said years ago that I would retire and read my father's books. I do not refer here to the printed page — rather a look back at what he learned, then taught me, especially as he got older. We cannot, of course, return to ninth grade, a time when we knew all the answers, no. But we certainly can draw upon a panoply of experiences to take us, more or less erect, into the next millennium.

As retirement approached, I devised a scheme which is yet unfulfilled. I wanted to write Latin to my friends, talk French to the ladies, call my dog in German, discuss truth in Norwegian with my children, and only use Swedish to swear at my servants and neighbors and help Hoz with his translations.

But my neighbors are insufficiently prepared in Latin. The kind of French I would use to address the ladies would only get me a slap in the face. My dog would be offended by Teutonic commands, would not respond and I don't like German shepherds. Discussing anything with my children in Norwegian would run up a large long distance phone bill. The only servant I ever had ran off years ago with a Burnsville cop, and my neighbors deserve the kind of lashing that cannot be done with the tongue.

So the old woodsman has had to make the kind of adjustments that are easiest to accomplish — get the gun, shoot the pheasant, get another firearm, hunt the deer. In between outings, talk to my faithful dog and cook supper, then write to my friend,

Donald. It is so simple, so straight-forward, so important that the other matters fade into insignificance.

It is about the latter form of hunting mentioned above that I wish to report to you at this juncture. You know about my rather studious approach when embarking upon a new adventure. I bought and read five books on the deer and the art of deer hunting. I sat for days in my living room practicing behaviors one uses at a deer stand in the woods, sitting nearly motionless in my easy chair while staring into the woods to attempt to discern the slightest movement of anything.

While doing this, I enjoyed many cups of coffee, listened to the St. Olaf Choir and several symphonies and stoked the pipe now and then. I mulled over all the details I had learned and needed to know for the hunt which began on November 4, 1995. I turned sixty-two in March and was ready. It's about time, says I.

My nephew, Charlie, lent me a shootin' iron, a Ruger "mini 30." We sighted in the rifles in a gravel pit, but I ran out of ammo and time before I could reach the near-perfection I like to attain. I was satisfied I could shoot anything within fifty yards; beyond that, there would be the possibility of a miss. The obvious solution, then, would be to get into a woods situation where only short range shots would be available and necessary.

Off to the hunt. We saw nothing to shoot during our early morning and twilight efforts the first weekend. However, I encountered a gray timber wolf at close quarters, about twenty feet, and that sight pleased me, making the visit to the woods enjoyable.

The second weekend was going to be different. After having become somewhat familiar with the venue, I felt confident we would achieve success. Then the best thing happened. We got 4-5 inches of new snow during the night — the so-called "tracking snow." Now we had a quiet woods and white snow to silhouette the target.

I had also prepared myself better this time with mittens, hand warmers, pacs with felt insoles, and a new blaze-orange hooded hunting coat. The hood was very practical, not only for containing my body warmth and keeping the snow out of my neck.

And I discovered something new. On the stand, I could rotate my head inside the hood while the hood remained motionless. Secondly, moving my head ever so slightly made a noise as my cap rubbed the inside of the hood which could be heard by no one except me. But that was enough to warn me not to make sudden movements with my head and it made me cautious.

I carried with me into the depths of a cedar swamp a small folding stool, parking it next to a cedar tree, with six other cedars in an array before me, all upwind. This gave me a field of view — cross and upwind of a fairly wide area — lots of trees, but some open spots. Thus ensconced, I sat nearly motionless for ten minutes.

My approach to the deer stand had been accomplished with stealth, and no twigs were broken by my measured footsteps. My rifle stood at the ready, butt on my thigh and barrel up against the tree. I breathed slowly, calmly, quietly, like meditation.

It is difficult to summon here the feelings I had the instant la biche (the doe) walked silently into my field of view. "So this is the way it is," I thought, "here we go." The doe looked directly at me. Nothing can explain the profound unawareness of her brow. I thought, "Do not blink, Argo, do not move, hold your breath."

Then began the extremely slow movements to bring the rifle to bear. Each time the doe lowered her head, I moved slightly a little more. The doe signaled by swishing her tail before each time she raised her head. She looked directly at me at least four times.

This all took about two minutes, it seemed, but finally I sighted her through the scope, the crosshairs and post on her right shoulder. This was a little higher than I would have liked, but necessary because a horizontal log covered the preferred spot.

Now I was on target and ready, but it then occurred to me that the "positive" safety would click, alarming the doe when I made ready to shoot. So I rapidly clicked off the safety and quickly pulled the trigger just as the doe responded to the "click" sound.

The instant the doe heard the click, she jumped and I fired almost at the same instant. I confess to blinking when firing, but I knew the shot had struck, perhaps a vital spot. As the doe bounded off, I decided to wait, motionless, in case a buck was following.

As I waited, I noticed that the doe, who had bolted off to my right, had circled back some distance to the left from which she had come. I saw her only because she swished her white tail as an alarm signal. I would not have seen this had I not remained at my post.

After twenty-five minutes, I decided to track the doe. I went to the spot where she stood when shot, tied a blaze orange tape to a twig to mark the starting spot of the trail. At that place I found two tufts of hair. Then about twenty feet along her path of flight I found the first blood spatter on the snow. There was a spatter to the right of each track left by her bounding leaps.

My assumption that the doe would lie down to rest and not be able to rise proved true. I found her lying on her left side and saw the gaping wound in her rib cage. Her nose and mouth had a bloody foam; the lungs had been hit. It was over. I tagged the doe with the only doe permit in our party.

I marked with blaze orange tape my exit path from the woods as I went to secure a rope and the plastic sled but we had forgotten the sled. I tied the forelegs to the neck, fastened the tow rope and started to drag the doe. This was heavy work. I needed to get the doe out to the road by the truck, for it was now nearly dark and I could not see to dress out the doe properly.

Nephew Charlie came to assist in the drag which was moderately strenuous because of fallen logs and thick underbrush in our path. Our third partner, Tom, offered to dress out the doe while I held the flashlight. Charlie went back to the cabin for the trailer, and we brought the doe back to the boat house where Charlie had rigged up a pulley from a log. We cleaned out the cavity with water and hoisted the doe by a hanger inserted in the hind legs.

Charlie and Tom were excited and pleased at our good fortune after many outings in extremely cold conditions. I remember being rather quiet about the whole episode. I did not cheer or whoop, only waved my arms as I left the woods to signal Charlie at his stand up the hill that I had scored. I did what I knew and the doe did what she knew. I respect her, for she had me outclassed in the woods in every way except this — I had the ability to reason, and I could plan ahead what I was going to do; plus, I was armed.

Tom estimated the dressed-out weight at about 120 pounds. I guessed 140 pounds. At any rate, we are dividing the steaks, chops and sausages three ways, and we all will have some nice venison dinners with our families, thanks to the doe. The doe would not have died of old age, I am told. Neither will I — yet.

Here I am, Donald, sixty-two years old. The first deer I ever saw in the woods while deer hunting went down at 30 yards with a 123 grain bullet, the only shot I have ever taken at a deer. Argo sits now at 1.000 "per cent" with nowhere to go now but down.

Oh well. My satisfaction is that I did everything right the first time. I think my father would have been pleased that I read some new books and got my first doe, "La Biche."

    Argo —

TZXCCVBNM6969
(Security)

Dear Donald,

I think you will agree that this topic gives leave for all sorts of mischief, idle banter, mother of pearl and yo-yo. It became clear to me when I awoke this morning that it might be risky to venture out onto the streets. Not that I am superstitious or overly paranoid, but they may be waiting for me around the corner. Besides, just because you're not paranoid, doesn't mean they aren't out to get you. What is important is that you convince them that you are out to get them. Ah, yes! That feels much better!

So my research for a friend took me to unusual places today, including one of the Minneapolis high schools, Southwest, as you can plainly see by the crummy envelope wrapping this letter. Security is tight at the public schools nowadays and visitors have to sign in at the front desk. I should state at the outset that my mission had a somewhat frivolous purpose in addition to the serious.

I know the principal because he used to be assistant principal at Roosevelt, where I hearkened to the voices of the children who would cry out, "Kindem rules!" And so I behaved accordingly, using the "powah" granted by the masses to harass the administration who are inevitably and always in the wrong. This guy, the principal, I picked on mercilessly — he would either run away in retreat or lock his door when he saw me approach.

This visit was no different. All I really wanted to do, since I had not seen him for about six years, was to sit in his office with my feet up on his desk, light my pipe, and call out to the secretary to fetch us a cup of coffee, would you please. We would engage in preliminary small talk, sparring a little, as the paranoid little turnip with a mail order Ph.D. would try to gauge my purpose and try to fend off the inevitable assault on his psyche, morale, qualifications, motives, grammar, and of course the imperfections of his college.

He was always a shifty little cunnilingarian. As I was signing in as "George Mikan" on the form attached to a clipboard for that purpose, he spied me through the door of his office, walked over and closed and locked the steel door to his office. A steel door, no less — ultimate in modern principal protection. Does he also wear body armor and carry a weapon?

A young bumkin, Eloise the receptionist, was on the phone. The principal's secretary, who calls herself, "Administrative Assistant," in the sign on the door, picked up her phone. I knew who was calling — it was that little guy I just saw go hiding in the principal's office and he was now telling his administrative assistant to "Bar the door, Jennie, I'm in conference the rest of the day." Barred from seeing the principal, and having nothing better to do and with no weapons or dynamite in my possession, I walked over to the library which is now euphemistically called the "Media Center." I would think it more appropriate if it was called the "Center for Mediums." They need a crystal ball to try to figure out what is going to happen next in the zoo they permit themselves to call a school.

Just to test the waters, I walked over to a rowdy bunch of library loafers. How could they ever know that I once, as a teacher, had an Easter egg hunt in our library which demolished the place. Books on the floor, kids going through the librarian's desk, files, closet — The Great Easter Hunt of '71. But I digress.

I asked the standard, "What's heppnin' bro?" A rather fat ninth grader in bib overalls responds, "It's cool, Man." I walk behind the counter, which is square with a desk in the center, and start dialing a number on the phone. The library lady, as I call them, just looks and stares, wondering what's up. Bear in mind, I haven't shaved for three days and am clad in dirty Tee shirt, cargo pants, and wearing my Ole baseball cap. Then I ask her, the library lady, "Do you have a secretary?" She says, "Yes, over there behind those glass windows, but I think she's on break." "That's OK," says I, and walk into the secretary's office.

By now you know what I am after: a crummy school envelope for Hobo's letter and one for Gus. I crave envelopes with logos and much as those guys over there in the Middle East crave other things. She left a key in the desk drawer. I turn it, and "Voila," the mother lode of envelopes with logos appears. I filch two, for I need only to prove the elements to Hobo and Gus, for they are Fubars and understand.

The very fat black kid in bib overalls stands in the doorway. "You lookin' for candy, man? She don' keep it there no mo, it go missin'. She keep it in huh pøs." I move on past him, mumbling, "Thanks, man," and leave the library which sounds more like a third grade recess period than a library. I walk down the corridor past a uniformed policeman and teacher's aide guarding a door. They nod, "Good morning," and I return the compliment and go out the door.

I am thinking of the elements of a crime — Actus Reus, Mens Rea, intent, and it dawns on me that we may have just had a burglary here. Aw, no way — I was just testing the building security. I get the heck out of there.

        Argo — Alternative title: "Security"

Predictions

Dear Donald,

As you have so often proved, it's easy to predict the future, but sometimes hard to get it right. To assist in our attempts to predict the future, should we choose to do so, perhaps we ought to have a shelf of books on the topic — "Things that make us smart."

But then maybe the smart people are in fact more reluctant to predict the future than the less smart. The latter don't know what is going on, perhaps don't care, and thus possess the reckless abandon necessary to go out on a limb, just like some apple pickers I know.

Sure, the apple pickers have a tendency to extend their reach to the point of over-reach in order to gather the finest fruits which hang way up there, or far out there. That's why some guys tumble off ladders while harvesting fruit. It is useless to claim that falling off ladders of a different sort while in the quest for fruit of a different sort does not occur. But of course it does for you and I are witnesses to that truth, and we have the scars to prove it.

Perhaps we should arrange a round table discussion on the topic of showing scars. I can provide the table. It is where I now sit to write these lines. We could introduce the topic by eliciting admissions of a less probatory nature about falling, for example: I have indeed fallen from an apple tree more than once but never, so far as I can recall, have I fallen off a bar stool. I only fell off a toilet stool once, and that wasn't my fault. I have never fallen out of a barber's chair, but I have taken a tumble or two from a desk at our favorite college.

Again, it was not entirely my fault. Someone, a Fubar, cried out, "Exostentialism!" (Sic!) and I had to go down, immediately and with fervor, because that's the way we did things when we were fit and in college. We always did things fervently because we didn't know any better. We had not yet read the books on the smart shelf, you see.

How does one strike a balance between fervor, passion and

intelligence? But, does one? It seems to me that of the three, fervor gets the nod in some areas of endeavor. We pray fervently to God. We exhort our athletes fervently before and during the competition. But we have a tendency to hold back somewhat on the fervor when it comes to pulling the trigger on a dollar to buy something we really don't need. While driving, we do not approach a stop sign with fervor, but instead kick in the intelligence quotient so that we don't bash into the car ahead or worse, a pedestrian, and we may still retain some passion.

Yes indeed, intelligence is a wonderful thing. It can lead us to one of life's great joys, appreciation. We can appreciate art in so many ways if we have the intelligence to understand its deeper meaning. We can enjoy a simple event such as a dinner with a friend if we understand the concept of appreciation. We may awaken in the morning, appreciative of the fact that we survived the night with its terrors and can face a new day refreshed, always asking the right question: "Ah! What new adventure is in store for us today?" I call that sort of attitude "enthusiasm."

It isn't hard for old friends to get fired up or enthusiastic about lots of things. The conversation is always good. You cannot have conversation without enthusiasm for the subject. Otherwise, it would be dead. I like people who can eagerly pursue just about any sort of project, provided there is no negative effect on me or on mine. Some people can get enthusiastic over a bowl of oatmeal. Now that is a blessing!

So now, back to the topic at hand — predicting the future. I suppose I can go out on a limb, at least insofar as the short term is concerned. I will state unequivocally that come May we will be whistling the tune, "Now is the month of May-ing, when merry lads are playing, fa-la-la-la-la."

You and I will travel some and see the sights of your choosing. We will camp out, should you desire, and we will shoot the gun. Interspersed in all these grand activities will be a few mealtimes at Argo's "5-star bistro," lots of relaxing time for naps and calm reflection and reading.

There will be evidence of fervor, passion, intelligence, appreciation, enthusiasm and good old fashioned friendship, with lots of laughs — how's that for a prediction!.

Argo — April 8, 1996

The Past Is Prologue

The Penguin said to another penguin, "You look like you're wearing a tuxedo." The second penguin said, "Maybe I am."

Dear Donald,

I usually consider myself innocent, even if I'm not. In this regard, I take the scientific approach which cannot measure moral responsibility. That way, I can avoid painful, perhaps false conclusions by others when it is convenient, which is usually the case.

Perhaps some conflict in our lives arose because we were not fully accepted into the local society represented by the "Jesus in the Manger" group and dominated by old-line professor families. Besides, small town mentality and provincialism were always evident, causing people to act strangely to outsiders but yet understand each other so well. They did not understand, however, that some of their old values had expired and were totally dead.

Over the years, we had experienced a sort of industrial revolution in Northfield. Lincoln Street got paved. The teamster at St. Olaf, George "Peachfuzz" Tripp, no longer handled teams and the horses went out to permanent pasture. The football was pumped up with air, not stuffed with sawdust. The marching band no longer marched, but sat down to play concerts that were far too long, with far too many clarinet and oboe solos.

The wading pool in Wade Park was filled in with black dirt and sod so the children could not splash, and there would be more grass to mow with gas-powered mowers. Women started going to the hospital to give birth instead of toughing it out at home with bloody rags. The telephones were outfitted with dials and the party lines gave way to more expensive private lines with no more "rubbernecking."

City gas service pipes snaked underground everywhere, ready to blow up the entire West side if they were scratched. People no longer used coal bins for coal, nor iceboxes for Cannon River ice, nor chopping blocks for chopping wood, or chopping off heads of chickens they now bought plucked and dressed at the

Ole Store.

Women were driving automobiles, the price of gas a quarter, oil 15 cents a quart. Skating on the ice pond above the dam was prohibited, and nobody rented canoes on the Cannon River, which lacked a poet then and still yet now.

Some smart guys on the Hill held out the premise that our personalities were so complex that we very often tried to make ourselves believe that we knew ourselves and could determine what we should or should not do — and in doing so, we actually were self-deceivers. We were affected by so many different factors of heredity, environment and chance, and were conditioned to act and react in certain ways that some felt we could not fully understand ourselves.

Others tried to cover up their basic drives with intellectual calm and reason, but that was not enough. They still sent someone to Dundas or The Cities to buy their "wine" for them. They experienced great anxiety because they were false to themselves and others and tried to cover up their own weaknesses. They were the self-deceivers.

Enter Donaldo — Scourge of the Dakota Prairie — who was prepared to do battle, either on his own terms or theirs. It didn't matter, no. For he had as his companion, one they called Lars, who was similarly guided by the Per Gyntian watchwords, "Unto thine own self be sufficient."

Hobo and Argo traveled far and wide throughout Rice County and elsewhere, using conveyances that were at hand — catching automobile bumpers to slide the icy streets in army surplus boots; the gondola car of a Great Northern freight train; or the ultimate in speed and comfort, a 1956 red and white Buick Special.

In their vast travels, they saw many astounding things and created humorous situations — "sights mortal eyes should not have seen." They may have been spelunking or discovering the best of Heath Creak, or liberating a muskmelon for a midnight dessert. Their activities were mostly out of doors, and always fun. Oftentimes their outings could be described as "a laugh a minute."

They jumped through many of society's hoops, but freely chose which ones. Others, of course, were ignored. They heard Miguel de Unamuno say, "The crowd may cheer or they may boo — it matters not, for I alone am in the ring facing the bull."

It would be gratuitous to state that Donald and Lars could have added chapters to the Quixotic state of which Unamuno spoke. Yes, they tilted at windmills, but only because they were there, and it was fun.

"Grow old with me, the best is yet to be," someone said. Perhaps that expression should be our mutual advisory to guide us, laughingly, into the next millennium and beyond, for "the past is prologue."

   Argo —

Options

Dear Donald,

It is somewhat distressing to read in the newspaper or hear from the presidential candidates the expression, "...decent, hard-working, patriotic Americans..." I suppose they are referring to those people who are the electorate.

Now I consider you to be decent and patriotic, Hobo, an assessment you perhaps agree applies also to Argo. However, in your case as well as mine, I draw the line at the label, "hard-working." My guess is that a significant number of voters whose votes really count on election day are, as we, not "hard-working," but simply retired, i.e., because they became tired of working.

We gratefully accept the designation, "decent" as well as "patriotic." I have never met a retired person (free agent) who did not consider himself both. But let us face the facts: we do not have to tolerate among us those who would malign us by referring to us generically as hard-working, no. Those days are over, gone, done. We do not seek work; we do not accept it; we are retired. Many of us, to be sure, balk at cleaning the bathroom or straightening out the bedroom. There are others who can do those things.

My father often used the slogan, "Vork kom først!" But that was then, this is now. The very thought of going to work makes me whimper and go into paroxysms of anxiety. My pension is not scheduled to run out until I die. If it does not prove to be sufficient over the long haul, so be it. I have been poor, as have you, and it doesn't take a genius to figure out that we are able to function fairly well and get along fine without most of the frills.

Honesty compels me to admit that at one time I had the reputation of being a hard worker who associated with hard-working people. Make no mistake, however, I do not want to have written on my stone, "I wish I had worked harder." No, Donald, rather than being labeled hard-working, I would aspire to somewhat loftier labels, such as: thinker, or poet, or even philosopher, which includes both the foregoing.

Others may choose labels with a specificity more directly related to their understanding of me and to their association with me, such as: loyal friend, passable cook, baker of daily bread, orchardist who tried his best, singer of songs, lover of children and dogs, or just a lover. We can also get into values-oriented schemes here, although I do not, as the politicians do, confuse values with virtues, no.

I have always valued the privilege of going out with rod or gun to harvest food for me and my family. In this regard, I have proceeded with resolute determination to succeed in the endeavor and enjoy to the fullest the pleasure of the attempt. Am I thus to be labeled a hard-working hunter or fisherman? No, of course not. Rather, I am a fun-loving or pleasure seeking hunter or fisherman. You catch the difference here — these are sporting activities, and outdoor sports are supposed to be fun, not work.

As I sit and write these words, I am not thinking of writing as hard work. I cannot assess the merits of the thinking or of the poetry or the philosophy. All I know is, this is not work. You recall that when we were young, we always found the humorous side of people and events. We laughed a lot. We still do and that makes all the difference in our outlook on life.

Many of the so-called "hard-working, decent, patriotic Americans" cannot laugh. A cursory glance at the current crop of presidential aspirants shows clearly that they are hard-working. To conclude that they are decent and patriotic Americans stretches the bounds of credulity to the breaking point. Their decency originated in the outhouse and their brand of patriotism should remain in the outhouse.

So now, fellow "professional loafer," I salute you and me for the decency we both have to admit we never again want to report for work, or to a supervisor, whatever that misconstruction means.

We, Donald, want more than anything else to be left alone — the most precious right in America, even though it is not specified in the constitution. We must always have our options.

      Argo — March 4, 1996

Oddfellows' Home

Dear Donald,

I never tried to figure out the meaning of the name, "Odd Fellows' Home" or "IOOF." It's just as well, for no matter what the words stand for, the "Home" as we called it was at once an old folks' home and an orphanage.

The Home was a very significant institution in Northfield along with St. Olaf, Carleton, and the Baker School. I'm not sure, but I think it has sometimes been the last pause for some on their way to Oaklawn Cemetery. You and I have seen the neat rows of stones identifying former residents of "Three Rings" in the Southeast corner of Oaklawn, just beyond the graves of Aggie Larson, Josephine Notvedt, and Eddie Tripp.

I delivered newspapers at the Odd Fellows' Home while in the employ of the owner of the Pantorium, Morrie Jennes, commonly referred to by some as the "paper boss." However, we referred to him as "More-ass Jen-ass" and the paper we delivered as the "Star Junkel."

Making the rounds to collect was quite a kick. Knock at the door, call out loudly, "Collect!" Enter to greet someone always seated, sometimes awake, usually with a blanket over the lap. The payment came from a small coin purse fastened with a snap — the old kind everyone used in those days. The change was always correct and was traded for a small stamp from the collection book.

"Old Man Moses" always tipped a dime; the others frequently offered Christmas candy left over from the previous decade that stuck together after many years in the jar, and which gave off a strange smell. I always thanked them very kindly but never ate the candy which I figured could make an end of me.

The orphanage section was located at the far easterly section of the building shaded by huge black walnut trees. Across the street was the home of Bill Otterstad, who astounded his high school observers by allegedly being able to type 100 errorless words a minute with a glass of water balanced on his left wrist.

On the corner was the house where classmate David Dybvig spent his first year in Northfield. But they weren't locked in at night as the kids in the Home were. Those kids, probably without exception, could hardly wait to move out when they got old enough.

The orphans had to work on the farm to earn their keep. The boss of the place, a man called Mr. Owens, was a hard taskmaster, except with the older girls. His office was usually locked with the shades drawn and people wondered what went on in there.

I made friends easily in the forties and enjoyed going to the "Home" to play basketball in a gym converted from a swimming pool — it had a low ceiling and you had to shoot line drives with no arch to avoid hitting the ceiling. It was the dustiest place in the world, and dust would fly up out of the loose floor boards when you dribbled the ball on them. Consequently, we learned to shoot and pass, primarily — tactics later demanded by our high school coach, Ozzie Simonich.

The Odd Fellows' farm had lots of dairy cows, large vegetable garden, and an apple orchard bordering Forest Avenue across from Gangsei's house, next to Sawyer's. A large grape arbor with Concord grapes stood behind the kitchen. Inside the huge barn was a pump room, milk cooling room, several stanchions for the milk cows, a pen for newborn calves and two side rooms, whitewashed, with no lights except for two small windows. There was about eight inches of black dirt on the floors. In one room they grew mushrooms; in the other, celery. In addition, they had a large chicken coop, a horse shed, and a coop for geese which was situated by a pond kept filled with pumped-in artesian well water.

I recall vividly two visits to the dairy barn when I was in the seventh grade. First, I was in the company of one of my good friends and a classmate, George (Denton) Toombs, who lived at the Home. We were fellow campers with the scouts of Troop 313, specifically at Camp Pa-Hu-Ca on Fish Lake about three miles east of St. Patrick. Denton left his mark in white paint inside the outhouse in camp where it remains today: "Denton Toombs, IOOF 1946." But I digress.

We went into the barn where Omar "Guts" Anderson, second in brute strength only to his brother, Whitey, was engaged in some foolishness. I asked him to show how strong he was. He crawled under a large cow with his back under the cow's belly and raised the cow off the floor. She did not like that much. She mooed and pedaled her hind legs in the air, then "Guts" let her down. His brother Whitey, then a junior at NHS, was star fullback and defensive tackle on the football team. I remember some of his quotes: "Any man who has the audacity to pass gas in my face, I can lick." — "If I don't get 25 tackles, I figure I played a lousy game."

Whitey was very tough, sometimes even brutish. I recall once when I was in the eighth grade, showering in the locker room, he entered and demanded, "Make way for a real man!" I did not move, so he delivered two quick chops with the edge of his hand — the first to my Adam's apple, the second to my solar plexus. I went down and struggled to breathe for quite some time. No one came to my assistance, so I crawled out of the shower to my locker where I suffered my hurt and humiliation in private.

There was another brother, Al, who beat the stuffing out of Mr. Owens and got kicked out of the Home. My family took him in, and he roomed at our house while he went to St. Olaf. He was a good ski jumper. Al graduated from St. Olaf and became a probation officer in Faribault, I think. I have not seen him these forty-five years. He died last year.

A second memorable visit to the dairy barn occurred when I was in the seventh grade. We brought large grocery sacks along on Halloween. One guy would hold open the sack while the other would yank the cow's tail until she dropped a cow pie. We took offerings from four cows and left to do our mischief, which was to set a bag on a front doorstep, light it on fire, then ring the doorbell and run and laugh. It was up to the home owner to come out and stamp out the fire in the dung-filled sack. Nobody did, so then we then went downtown to soap and wax store windows and sneak into the "Frankenstein Meets the Wolf Man" show at the West.

The last time I ever visited the Home was in 1971. I harvested from the ground two bushel baskets of choice black walnuts. These I took to my present residence where I had moved my family the week before. I put the walnuts in a pile in the back yard next to the woods. The squirrels came and planted them for me in two days.

Now I have dozens of beautiful black walnut trees in the woods behind my house — not odd fellows, these — choice black walnut trees from Northfield's "Home."

       Argo — December, 1995

Not All the Vikings Are Dead

Dear Donald,

Today, Bjørn, recently of Europe, finished cleaning his room after four days of effort. I don't dare look for fear I'll embarrass him by fainting. He found old books, records, pictures and any number and variety of things that one would find after ten years of neglect. He did not reveal, nor did he list all the items that might make a parent curious or lead to a more formal inquiry.

However, he did place a couple of sheets of paper on the kitchen table before me — one, the back of a grocery sack, the other, an old sheet of notebook paper. Both seemed related in subject matter but were impossible to read or decipher, so I ignored them, since I was busy baking bread.

The bread is a special edition I created for my granddaughter, Arianna. She named it "Grandpa Bread." The bread is made with "Golden Buffalo" flour and cracked wheat. I made two thick long loaves and one hearth loaf. Bjørn, tasting it, pronounced it "Serious major league..." and a few other adjectives used by those under the age of thirty. The fact that he ate fourteen slices tells all. So now I have two loaves remaining to feed the multitudes, but that's another story, not so hard to do.

Whenever I encounter the word "story," I think of St. Olaf where so many stories originate. There were giants in the earth in those days, and there were Vikings. The original Vikings had a singular goal in life which was to die in battle, for then they would ascend to Valhalla, where they would spend an eternity fighting and eating and making more Vikings.

I had a visionary dream about a noble Viking that you need to know about. Things were somewhat turned around, but nevertheless became clear to me — an impartial but interested observer in my earlier existence. In this vision I was horse, a majestic horse, a fine horse, a strong, brave and swift horse that excelled in crowded battle, shoving, prancing, stomping, always moving forward, always in the fore. My rider was Olaf Haraldsson, also known as Olaf Digre, later sainted — the soon-to-be sainted "St. Olaf."

Olaf led me throughout the land as he forcibly made Christians of the people. It was immensely interesting for me, a common fjord horse, to see the panorama which is Norway. We circled huge mountains, floated across vast fjords and spent a good deal of our time meeting new people and new horses, Christianizing them.

About once a week we enjoyed a skirmish which pleased me greatly, for afterward I got to eat my fill and choose my next lovely filly. They all liked me a lot and seemed to enjoy the fleeting relationships with no reins attached, for I was bold and good in the manger, and very strong but tender.

It was after one such skirmish that I first saw the "Main Viking." He, among others, had been captured by Olaf Digre, "The Stout," as his friends called him. Olaf was certainly husky, as I can attest, having borne him and his heavy armor throughout the land, and he drank a lot of barleyed mead and ale.

On this occasion, as before, the captive Vikings were bound together by the ankles with rope and sat on a log. Each, in turn, was asked by Olaf if he wished to become baptized and become a Christian. Those who said "Ja!" were immediately released and took their place behind the king. Those who refused — and there were many — were beheaded on the spot.

Olaf had two henchmen who took turns lopping off heads. They turned to the next Viking who sat with arms folded across his chest in a gesture of defiance. His hair and beard were long, the hair reaching beyond his shoulders. He spat at the two executioners and blurted out, "Don't spill blood on my hair!"

I twitched my ears in disbelief, for I knew there was going to be a little problem here. Olaf Digre dismounted, much to my relief. He placed both fists on his waist and glared at this young upstart who was challenging his executioners. The assistant gathered the Viking's abundant flowing hair and pulled it toward him, exposing the Viking's neck to a clean downward swing with the big ax.

The ax man swung the ax with all his might, and just at that instant, the Viking jerked his head backward. The assistant's hands, clutching the hair, were in the path of the ax which severed both his arms at the wrists. The ax went into the ground; the Viking quickly grabbed it and split the executioner's head in two like a melon. I stomped my hooves and neighed in applause at seeing this wonderment.

Olaf stepped forward and asked, "Who is this fair man with the courage of ten?" The Viking replied, "They call me Donald-the-Fair, and they say Francis is my fadduh. Not all the real Vikings are dead."

Olaf asked, "Will you come and serve me?" The Viking responded, "Who asks?" Olaf said, "He asks who has the power to ask — your King!" "Yes, of course I will!" said Donald, and embraced the king.

Olaf pointed to me, the nation's prize horse, and said, "This, brave Viking, shall be your faithful steed. Together you will cut down the enemy as a farmer cuts down wheat."

Donald asked, "What is the name of the horse?" The king said, "Argo," and so it was that Olaf and Donald and Argo fought many battles together, according to the Norse Saga that records achievements of men strong and bold of old.

That, dear friend, was my dream-vision, but now I am in the kitchen, at the round table with big bread before me and the prospect of a glorious weekend ahead. I call Bjørn to me, and I ask, "Bjørn, are all the original Vikings dead?" He pauses, momentarily, deep in thought. "No," says he, "Two remain: you and Donald." I thank him and we embrace each other.

It is then that I remember those two pieces of paper, the brown paper and the notebook paper with the strange lines, markings and notations and I ask, "What the heck are these all about?" Bjorn's response comes to me like the calm report of one who has just brought home his semester grades and all of them are "A"s.

"These," he explains, "are diagrams of all the St. Olaf tunnels. I have verified every detail, such as entrances, and all matters of interest. I have described every tunnel."

I study the diagrams and see that what he claims is true. He states he will use the computer to make professional-quality maps.

Now I know: Not all the Vikings are dead.

    Argo —

Pop Hill and the Popstand

Dear Donald,

I can't think of a hill that has been the site of so much fun for so many people as Pop Hill at St.'Olaf. Crowning the hill in the old days were the two ski jumps built there; the first dating from some time in the thirties, the reconstruction about 1946. At the base of the North slope was the network of limestone caves to explore.

Defining the exact location of the hill and the dimensions of the land that should be included as part of Pop Hill is somewhat problematic. Howard Hong might argue about this point for I say the hill should be defined by the boundaries from about fifty yards south of the old ski jump site to about fifty yards north and east of the cave property; thence over the top of the hill from the caves and about fifty yards to the level section where Howard and Edna Hong built their stone house next to Thorson hall.

The reason for this rather specific delineation is the fact that Pop Hill derives its name from the business carried on there in the early 1900s — a brewery turned into a soda pop factory after the onset of Prohibition, with cold storage in the Platteville limestone caves below. The College became well known as "The Popstand" during Prohibition because of the flurry of activity in the caves under Pop Hill. Bootleggers knew it as a good place to do business because of the location of the sainted school and the innocence of distributing "soda pop" and drinks like "Orange Crush" that provided additional cover for much needed business activities. When people said, "Let's go to the Popstand," everyone knew it was not for "soda pop," and a lot of people made a lot of money in the process. Oh well.

But Pop Hill is just a part of the greater geological area called Manitou Heights; in fact it is an extension of the Pop Hill sandstone deposit that the entire Popstand is built upon. In 1945 St. Olaf Professor of Biology Edward W. Schmidt, emeritus, one of Mohn's early hires, published "The Geology of Manitou Heights" that describes the formation of Manitou Heights (elevation 1,085.96 feet) and surrounding geography, as well as a description of Pop Hill.

The entire promontory upon which Thorson Hall stands, and virtually all of Manitou Heights, is one large deposit of Platteville limestone and St. Peter sandstone. The formations of sandstone and limestone on Manitou Heights are the oldest geological feature around Northfield. Both types of rock are the result of sedimentation when the Midwest was submerged under a continental ocean over 500 million years ago. Sandstone was formed by erosion and limestone by decaying biological matter.

I quote from Professor Schmidt's study:

"Platteville limestone underlies the top soil from the northwest rim of the hill to a line drawn from a little distance east of Mohn hall to Ytterboe hall. When a tunnel was dug from the heating plant to Mohn hall, it revealed some limestone near the hall. The trench dug from the Old Main to the heating plant exposed only stratified St. Peter sandstone. Some streaks in this showed beautiful colors."

And for the naming of Manitou Heights, I quote from the 1913, '14, '15 Viking, page 118:

"According to an article written in the Manitou Messenger by Mrs. Anna Mohn, the wife of St. Olaf's first president, the faculty of the newly established St. Olaf's school gave the name of Manitou Heights to the wood covered hills which formed a part of the school grounds, and the valley just mentioned [Norway Valley] they named 'The Vale of Tawasentha' from its supposed likeness to the valley described in Longfellow's Hiawatha."

But enough of that; let's talk about the ski slide. During the forties and early fifties, the jump was the site of many collegiate ski jumping tournaments. My brother, Erling, together with Paul Stavig and Rolf Huggenvik, trained on that hill in preparation for the state high school meet in which those three as a team finished second in 1943. Other youngsters came along in the mid-forties, including several who did not continue jumping beyond the age of twelve or so. Included in that group were my brothers, Roald and Alf, and their buddies. They became interested in basketball.

I took my first five jumps at age nine in 1942. The only boy I ever saw who was about that young a ski jumper went off a couple times at about age ten under duress and on crooked skis. I made him do it, for I wanted to teach the boy, now a Fourth

District Judge, something about the excitement of the sport. His name is Peder Hong and Howard was his fadduh. Peder learned in one short lesson that when you stand at the top of the slide summoning courage to launch yourself down the ramp, you have to make a decision. There is no walking back down with skis in tow. You go into it with eyes wide open — very wide open. You make a commitment to go, and you then have to live with that commitment. That's a valuable lesson for a youngster to learn. It is a rite of passage.

I continued jumping throughout my college years. We had a good team which included some Norwegian "ringers" and we easily trounced Carleton and all the other colleges except UMD (Duluth). They killed us. They had a guy named Arvid Slotness, a victim of polio with a badly crippled leg who beat most of our guys. We had lots of snow the winter of 1951-52, and we were always going after the legendary hill distance record which everyone believed to be ninety-four feet. A jump that far is extremely hazardous, for at one point you depart from the curvature of the landing slope and do not return until the dip, or transitional curve to the outrun. In other words, you land nearly on the flat from a great height, and can really get busted up. I usually jumped about seventy-five feet.

At the St. Olaf Winter Sports Day Tournament my freshman year, hundreds of irreverent Ole students were present to witness the anticipated carnage. They armed themselves with snowballs to fling at the airborne targets, a few chosen Ole jumpers. When they announced my name, Wendy Miller, my longtime friend, became unhinged. I had never told him that I was a ski jumper. Wendy jumped up on the knoll of the landing hill directly in front of the takeoff, shook his fist at me and hollered for all to hear, "Kindem, I'm not going to let you do it! Come down off there, you're an idiot!" I waved him off and sped down the ramp.

As soon as I jumped, they fired snowballs, but only one of them hit me — in the right hip. I had one ski that was 7 feet 9 inches in length, the other, 8 feet, so never really could balance them properly. I don't know who won, but I didn't. To this day I find it convenient to blame Wendy for my rather mediocre effort. My consolation is that at least I dared go off the jump. I intend to remind him of that detail annually until we're both doddering old timers who won't care much one way or the other. Perhaps.

Down the hill northward was the home of the Tripp family headed by the St. Olaf teamster, George "Peach fuzz" Tripp. I sang at his funeral in 1956. His youngest son, Eddie, who died of cancer about 1950, was one of the best playmates I or anyone ever had. Eddie had access to the fantastic network of limestone caves on the property they rented from St. Olaf.

To get a picture in your mind of the floor plan of the caves, you have to think about a view from above. Imagine a three leaf clover. The entryway was about twenty feet wide, and ten feet high. Where the tunnels branched off, they were twelve feet wide, and the passageways with domed ceilings, about ten feet high. You entered at yard level through a large shed which at one time housed the brewery and "soda pop" bottling equipment. The actual floor of the cave was at the foot of a forty foot downward ramp, about six feet below the level of the yard.

Hundreds of names and initials were carved into the sandstone walls of the cave. During the mid-forties, Marvin "Monk" Festler, a Northfield truck gardener, used the main chamber for storing sacks of potatoes and onions grown at Castle Gardens. There was a slatted floor in the main chamber and the pallets of bags were lifted onto piles that reached to the ceiling. The three side tunnels had no flooring, just sandstone. It was great sport to play tag or "hide and seek" in the cave. It was also a fine storage place for a couple watermelons and some muskmelons removed from Lashbrook's plot to the northwest, just beyond the woods.

No one ever used a flashlight, but I remember trying to use a candle. There was always a draft of cool fifty-seven-degree air that rushed to get out through the entrance. There was at least one air vent through the ceiling which terminated above ground behind the Hong house near Thorson.

We played hard in those days. I remember when some guy or guys would hide out way back in the pitch black darkness. Someone would go back there armed with a half dozen hard "Kennebec" potatoes that were the best ones for lefse, and heave them like baseballs into the dark until someone either got hit or otherwise surrendered. I don't remember what we called that game, maybe "hit or miss." One time, poor Hans Hansen, ran smack into the sandstone wall and got a thump on the noggin on the upper right side above his temple. He was out of touch for a few minutes and then went home. He later developed a brain tumor which may have caused his blindness a couple of years later.

Of greatest interest to all the kids was the narrow tunnel which led straight north from the northerly cloverleaf of the big cave. At the end of this forty-foot long tunnel in which one had to crawl on all fours was a set of vertical bars, similar to jail house bars. No one ever got past those bars as far as I know, but everyone wanted to try. On the other side, according to legend, was a large quantity of gold in the form of coins in gunny sacks. Some say the gold was hidden there by Jesse James, or by the former owner when the US went off the gold standard; others opined the guy liked to collect a lot of gold so hoarders couldn't get it. All we knew for certain was that the gold was there, just beyond the bars, and there had been a cave-in on top of it, burying it forever.

We searched diligently above ground at the spot in question, and indeed found a sunken area about as large as a two car garage in area. So many had gone at it with shovels that the site looked like a common sand dig or start of a gravel pit. This proved, of course, that the gold was still there. Any enterprising adventurer with proper drilling equipment using metal detectors could find it. How do I know for certain? Because "Peachfuzz" Tripp told me with a straight face, and I believed him. He was an honest, hard-working teamster who harnessed his Belgians, Dan and Dolly, and took care of business for the St. Olaf farm. He even plowed and graded the campus roads.

We used to slide down the east slope of Pop Hill, aiming toward the intersection of Lincoln and Greenvale. At the bottom of the woods was a barbed wire fence. We would twist a stick between the lower two strands of wire, thus raising the height of the lower barbed wire and enabling us to go under the fence on our sleds in full careen. One boy missed the center of the opening and got one heckuva gash from above his forehead all the way back the top of his head. Boy, did he bleed! I lent him my cap to put on top of his own so he would not get blood all over the new jacket he got for Christmas. After a couple more slides, he decided to get on home for supper. I bet he caught it from his ma — she brought my cap back to our house. I told her she could keep it, but she wouldn't. I didn't want to tell her that I got all the caps I needed in the warming house at the St. Olaf skating rink in front of Agnes Mellby Hall. Ole students often left caps there.

It was fun to climb up to the top of the ski jump scaffold in the summertime. Some people got scared just looking down the back side of the tower. I also remember that on Pop Hill there were plots of honeysuckle, those pretty four-pronged flowers with a drop of sweet nectar at the end of each prong. John Sawyer, "Skookie" Norem and I sipped nectar from at least 500 of them one day in 1942 and became ill and Huggenvik came to our rescue.

I have often thought since our days at St. Olaf that someone should build another ski jump on Pop Hill, or maybe start selling "soda pop" and other beverages in the caves again, or give tours. The students need diversions while at college. I bet the women nowadays would take up ski jumping there too. Why not? They now have an ice hockey team.

Next time you come here to visit, Donald, we can take a walk around to see the ghosts at Pop Hill — Eddie, Hans and the others. It will be fun to be together again, exploring Pop Hill at the Popstand.

Argo —

Pride

"Pride goeth before the fall," — or does it?

Dear Donald,

During a recent interview I was asked, "Are you proud to be a St. Olaf man?" Of course I replied, "Of course I am."

She inquired further, "Proud of anything else, Argo?" The response: "Why, yes, there is something. I have, for example a fine fiberglass pole-vaulting pole out in back. Very few people can duplicate that."

What does that mean — that any possession you have that someone else does not have makes you proud? Oh, no, no, no. That was just one example of something I just sort of feel good about. That doesn't mean I intend to use my pole every day. Why, I can get hurt all I want just by falling out of apple trees.

The point is merely: I think it is neat, that a "has been" pole vaulter still clings to a vestige of his past. Anything wrong with that? No, it's kinda like saving photos in an album or old yearbooks — exactly. But right now I feel really good about something I would like to share with you.

You see, I have a toilet that flushes blue. No one in the neighborhood knows about this, and no guests have seen it; my children don't even know about it. Hobo, think of it now. Of all the toilets in Dakota County, I probably have the onliest one that flushes blue.

My dad was kinda like that when he was a newcomer to America. Ma asked him to build what Norwegians call an "ute do" (outhouse). Ingvald said "Ja" and went to work. When he was finished, mamma complained, "We have the only square-holer in all of Dakota County!" Ingvald did not have a coping saw, so he could not cope a round one. But he had a cross-cut saw and he coped square with that. If we had owned a regular round-holer, or even a two-holer, there would really be no bragging rights.

I went to Knox Lumber, Menard's, all the places to examine the various agents to place in the toilet tank. It had to be blue. Just think how dumb it would look if I had a toilet that flushes yellow? No improvement there. Nor brown — that would look even worse, and red was out of mind.

I have kept my blue-flush toilet a secret in the basement. Even faithful dog Argo doesn't drink out of it, no. And he's never been upstairs, so he doesn't even know about the other two toilets that flush clear, chlorine-smelling water. Nothing. Now if I were to install the other color you are thinking about, red, there would be problems with guests who would summon assistance and holler, "CALL 911! — 911!"

No, there are little secrets I will keep. Only a very select few will be invited to use the basement toilet. FUBAR guys still prefer to "pass" outside, so they may miss out on the fun, but that doesn't matter, no. I have to admit going in the woods outside is still the best, but I can take pride in my special toilet that flushes blue.

I won't even try to deal with issues such as what happens if something falls out of a shirt pocket into the toilet, or you drop your watch in. The point is, I take pride in having my very own toilet that flushes blue.

If you have one too, then you know what I mean about pride. If you don't — too bad.

Argo — Aug. 25, 1995

Relativity

Dear Donald,

In keeping with my pledge to retire and read my father's books I sat down yesterday with a volume he left for me. It was Einstein's Theory of Relativity.

I read first the Special Theory, then the General Theory. I am pleased to report that I understood both, a source of joy to an aging scholar. But the question arises — what good will it do me? Let us examine the question more closely.

For starters, I worked on the Fourth Dimensional Continuum, with absolute space relative to time. Imagining my flag pole wanting to reach the clouds, I established the requisite fixed reference points in order to calculate the length of pole required. In order to verify my work, I searched for the two fixed length rods in order to replicate the experiment, but alas, they were not to be found. It can wait until tomorrow.

Now, regarding time, Einstein and I concur. If you stand by the side of the road with a timepiece and I have one which is identical, but am in my vehicle traveling past you, my clock will be slower. Similarly, if we each have a pole vaulting pole, identical lengths, and I travel while you stand, my pole, if held so that it is aimed forward, will be shorter than yours as I pass by you. Nifty!

If you stand on the embankment to observe a train pass by and I am walking forward on the train, you would assume my walking speed to be train speed plus walking speed. Answer: NO. Just like a fighter plane traveling at 500 feet per second shoots a machine gun with bullets that have a velocity of 3200 feet per second, the total speed of the bullets would seem to be 500 plus 3200, or 3700 feet per second. Again, NO. Good guess, though.

Now visualize the same experiment in the train using a flashlight beam in a vacuum, and you will get the point. I like Einstein, for he was correct when he stated $E=mc^2$. His formula is useful on nights when I am afraid of the dark. My task becomes simply to turn off the light switch on the wall and attempt to "beat the light to bed." This exercise usually results in breakage and bedlam, and in general a more frightening experience than simply turning off the reading lamp on my bedstead. But you will understand, Donald — I had to try out E=mc2 and see if it works.

Laying aside the special and general theories of relativity, envision, if you will, Argo sitting attentively next to his short wave radio receiver. It is tuned to 2.5, 5.0, 10.0, 15.0, or 20.0 megacycles, (depending upon time of day and other factors), chronograph in hand, listening to the tick-tock of the Ft. Collins, Colorado, timepiece and waiting for the precise time to be called out at the exact second, the exact minute, the exact hour of Greenwich Mean Time.

It is the night we change over to daylight savings time. I set three stop watches, each in turn, run them for two hours, stop them simultaneously, and check for the inevitable deviation. I then choose the middle one, if three times are given, or one of two if those two match.

This watch is then used to set all the clocks in the house forward one hour to the correct daylight savings time. I then sleep peacefully with the knowledge that the time is right.

      Argo — April 6, 1996 (Chief Olympian Timekeeper)

Reputation

Dear Donald,

I can name a few people who did not attend St. Olaf College but nevertheless did quite well, considering — Emiliano Zapata, Marlon Brando, T. Allen Fisher and Torstein Veblen, to name a few.

In spite of the fact that some notables cannot credit a St. Olaf education as the principal ingredient in their successful climb to fame and fortune, we nonetheless may with some confidence conclude that the St. Olaf reputation is quite legendary. For example, Wendy Miller was hitch-hiking in the far west when a Catholic priest picked him up. Making small talk, the priest asked Wendy what he was doing in life. Wendy told the priest that he was currently a student at St. Olaf College. "Oh," said the priest, "That's one of our finest saints and very best colleges!"

Then there was a colleague of mine, Lynn Smith, a biology teacher at North High School who told of an experience he heard of during his first year teaching in Dick Werdahl's home town, Kenyon. It seems an elementary teacher asked the third graders to make a map of the United States, including the main cities. One child turned in a beautiful outline map of the US. A small dot and small print indicated New York, a larger dot, "The Cities;" a still larger dot and larger print, "Kenyon." And the largest mark, a large circle, was labeled, "ST. OLAF."

It was a custom for students in my classes at Roosevelt High School in the old days to rise and stand respectfully as I entered the classroom as they do in Norway. The students would remain standing until I greeted them with a warm, "Umm Yah Yah" and asked them to take their seats. On one particular day after they sat down, I noticed something was amiss. The students, usually talkative, remained silent, staring at me. Naturally, I first checked my seat to see if it had been booby-trapped with a fart pillow or perhaps thumb tacks. Nothing of the sort. Still they stared intently, but I noticed smirks on the faces of some of the boys.

Then I saw the blackboard at the rear of the room. Someone

had taken a piece of chalk about an inch long, held it sideways and written across the entire blackboard, "CARLETON—THE ENEMY!" in two-foot high letters. Their reaction was uproarious the instant they knew that I saw the message. After they quieted down in order to hear my reaction, I instructed them: "Tell me who did it! Rat on the SOB.! Squeal on the one who wrote that on the board!" They unanimously pointed to my top student, a 4.0 guy named Mattson.

I said, "Mattson, for that stunt you earned an A for the trimester!" I then invited him to come forward and sit at my right hand at the extra desk, a place of honor for people of superior perception and status — and sense of history. His application to attend St. Olaf was later turned down, so he attended a lighter weight state school in western Minnesota called U of M - Morris.

I told him that with his attitude and good sense, he would do all right. Just to make sure, I suggested he look up an old Ole buddy, Athletic Director, Noel Olson, '54, and use my name.

I never heard from him again after that school year. Do you suppose he actually did a little name-dropping with Noel? Could it have backfired? Could Mattson and I have overestimated the value of my reputation?

   Argo — February 15, 1996

San Francisco Beckons

Dear Donny,

I suppose you have already seen your recent interview with Isabella BT Goliath), or maybe not, so here it is.

Argo —

Headline: Hobo on Road Again, "San Francisco Beckons, Triumphant Return Hailed"

(Exclusive by Isabella BT Goliath, special Northfield corespondent)

Returning to San Francisco for a two-week visit, eh, Donald?, our ace Northfield interviewer asks politely.

"Yes, I suppose you could say that," replies our friend known in Fubar circles as "Hobo."

By the way, Hobo, if I may be so bold...

"You may. Many are," says a friendly Hobo.

Tell us then, how did you get the name, Hobo?

"It was given to me by my best friend, my friend of longest standing, Argo."

Go on...

"I will, thank you. You see, Argo had a scholarship to the University of Oslo Summer School in 1953, the year I graduated from the famous Northfield High School back in Minnesota. He and a fellow named Peterson had contracted to drive a rental car to be delivered to someone in New York City. Argo drove over to my residence at 31 Lincoln Lane and invited me to ride along just for the fun of it."

Were you surprised?

"Yes, certainly, and pleased. I asked my fadduh, and he said it would be OK because Lars was so trustworthy and good and nice, so we left within the hour."

Any incidents?

"Yes, there was one. I recall seeing a sign at a place in Ohio which read, 'President slept here' or some such nonsense."

What did you do?

"As I was about to say, the driver, I have forgotten which it was, certainly not I, swerved into a parking place rather hurriedly, and delivered a resounding smack to the stump of a tree which was obviously too close to the curb."

Any damage or injuries?

"No injuries, but one heck of a lot of damage to the left front quarter panel. It was not our vehicle, so it did not bother us much, no."

Which president are we talking about?

"I don't know, one of 'em. We left, right quick. Argo did not have a driver's license either, so maybe he was at the wheel. We had, in those halcyon days a certain aversion to police authorities, and so we decided to continue toward New York, heading east without further delay."

Anything else to report?

"Yes, my right arm got quite sunburned from leaning it out the window of the car."

Were the others also sunburned in the same fashion?

"I think one of them was. Whoever was not driving, I guess."

How long did the journey to the "Big Apple" take?

"We drove straight through so as not to hit any more stumps along the way, so we made it in less than eighteen hours."

You guys must have been traveling at a high rate of speed.

"I would imagine so because Argo usually does. I never looked at the speedometer, however."

Was this your first visit to New York City?

"Yes, none of us had been there before."

How then did you find your way around the city?

"We stopped at the entrance to the Holland Tunnel and asked a policeman where he thought we were. Then he asked where we were going. After we told him the address, he jumped on the running board and said he would take us there, and sure enough, we got a sort of police escort, as it were, right into the bowels of Manhattan. He got off where he lived, and explained further where we should drive. Nothing to it."

I suppose you delivered the auto with a smashed front fender without incident?

"Yes, of course. Argo parked the vehicle where the dent would be hidden from view. We signed off on the car, and left."

Where did you go then?

"My companions had to catch a ship, so to speak, so we took a bus over to Pier 91 at the foot of Morton Street, on the East River."

My, you have a good memory for details.

"Yes."

What then?

"Argo told me I was on my own, and asked how much in American dollars I had in my pocket. I told him something well under $5.00. He suggested I hike over to either the 34th or 50th Street Greyhound bus depot, buy a ticket to the first destination outside of New York City, perhaps some place in Pennsylvania, then hop off the bus and hitchhike back to Northfield — City of Cows, Colleges and Contentment."

And you followed his instructions?

"Up to a point, yes. You see, I fell asleep on the bus. I was sitting in the window seat at the rear, and no one thought to waken me. So my ride took me all the way to St. Louis where I disembarked, as they say."

I think you mean, "Got off," don't you?

"I don't see where you get off telling me where I got off or if I got off!" steamed an irate Hobo.

Nevertheless, you made it safely back to Northfield, City of Cows, Colleges and Contentment?

"Yes, I did. From what I understand, Argo did in fact get on that ship, the 13,500 ton Norwegian-America Line ship, the 'Stavangerfjord' and sailed off to Norway for the summer."

Sailed?

"You know what I mean. Interestingly enough, that was the same ship that brought Argo's parents and three siblings from Norway to the United States back in 1923."

Siblings?

"Yes, brothers and sisters."

So now, Hobo, when was your rather interesting nickname first used?

"Argo returned, unscathed, from the summer in Norway and we met at the Ole Store. He said to me, 'well, I see you made it back all right with a detour through St. Louis; you would make a good Hobo.'"

And that's how it was?

"That's the way I remember it."

By the way, Hobo, as long as we're on the subject, are you really going to visit San Francisco?

"Yes, soon, it beckons"

    Argo — Interview by Isabella "Big Tits" Goliath

The First Pick: Pluck & Pack

Dear Donald,

The apple pick is on, sort of. It has to be this way — I start with Prairie Spy, because they have begun to drop. I picked three five-gallon pails of premium apples yesterday and left about another 4-5 bushels to hang. They were not ripe enough to pick. I immediately chilled the washed apples in ice water, then refrigerated them. I will give Bjorn's friend Mara all she wants, for she seems to prefer the Spy. Tor is getting two bags of the best today, plus a sampler of Honey Crisp. Some will go to Northfield, to friends, and to my WCAL buddies at St. Olaf.

They say the apple does not fall far from the tree. So when I was walking toward the west on the boulevard by the garden, I was surprised to find a Haralson from the dwarf on the corner, 20 feet from the tree. "Magic," says I. Or else someone was chased by Argo during the time I was at Mara's show, and the perp dropped one. I noticed that some branches on the Dwarf as well as on the Cortland by the kennel are picked clean.

This must be because they are hidden from view behind the garage — time for some sleuthing. So I set up the alarm system, with fine monofilament line strung from the power pole, around the flag stake, and into the kitchen to a loud buzzer. No one came last night. Maybe the thefts occur during daylight hours by passersby? So now I do what I do, just as the St. Albans Goat. I will start today on processing the fallen fruits into juice and also start dehydrating slices for the winter storehouse.

The record of 14 bushels from the Honeygold in the garden will surely be surpassed this year. They hang pendulously in thick clusters. With about 120 of that size per bushel, there will be lots of fine apples to give away and process. I can do both very well. When I am making juice, canning, drying apples and baking bread at the same time the kitchen is really buzzing. It is, as they say, a production kitchen. Old Larsemann II moves fast and smartly, and a lot gets done.

But that is the way it is supposed to be, if one is also to be able to take time out for pheasants, which starts next weekend. Think of faithful dog Argo and me, carrying far too many shotgun shells and a few apples in the pockets, going farther and farther afield than the others in search of better chance.

After a noon hour break, the opportunity improves as the pickup trucks with kennels in the back line up at the various country spots for their long-awaited beer and lunch.

The guys are all out of shape; their dogs bushed; a couple of beers and they say, "They ain't birds around like they used to be. Heck with it."

They continue to drink their beer, getting more and more tired and unavailable for the afternoon hunt, rationalizing: "Them birds'll still be there next week, give 'em a rest. My ol lady wants me to do the storms and screens anyway."

"Yeah," says another, "I got a heckuva blister from these new huntin' boots. Rex is all tuckered out anyways. We always have better luck after the corn and beans are picked anyway, cuz then they're all concentrated in the sloughs."

A third chimes in, supporting the other two buddies, "I'm hung over from last night anyway, thought I'd have to hang it up by ten. When it comes right down to it, I like pheasant hunting with the guys, but I would just a soon eat Kentucky fried chicken anyways."

Anyways. Yes, any way to get out of a tough "sitjiation" while saving face with the boys. But a man has to have a few stock phrases to use when he is in a tough spot. Or to protect himself (some of the boys say "pertect") when he knows he has gone a little over the edge of the comfort zone.

The legs are stiff and sore, the back aches from carrying the shotgun; he's hot and sweaty and intelligent enough to see "there ain't much chance for birds anyway, what with all them guys from the cities trompin' around the good places to hunt. Why, a man could even get kilt!"

Ah, faithful black Lab Argo — we don't give up that easily. The only thing that makes us hang it up is when it is obvious that Argo won't hunt any more. Maybe he knows that after we get home he is going to get the biggest supper in the world and the rare pat on the back reserved for special occasions like this.

I will be thinking about Bjorn and remembering the good old days when we, father and son and dog, did the thing that a trio such as we are supposed to do every autumn until something beyond the control of anyone stops the routine. Bjorn will hunt again.

So will I and the day will come when we will remember Argo, and how he could find birds so well. I suppose it will be fair game to remember also that he was fond of trotting back to the car sometimes, perhaps too fond for my liking.

But maybe we should remember him, when the time comes, in a manner that each of us wants to be remembered — without the serious flaws.

It is true Hobo — the Dead should get by with everything; the apple pick, too.

      Argo — Oct. 5, 1997

The Fortune Cookie

Dear Donald,

Affixed by hand at the top of this page you will find the message from a fortune cookie.

Initially, I thought it would delight you as well as provide a good snack if I were to enclose the cookie and its fortune in this letter. However, discretion got the better of valor again, and I ate the cookie with good conscience, but I saved the message for you.

Which is not to say I did not make some attempt to enclose the whole cookie, but the envelope just got too thick. I envisioned, as I crouched down so that my eye level would be on a plane with the envelope while sitting at my round table where we have gathered and talked many hours, that the envelope certainly would not remain fat after the post office got through with it.

Some of those post office thrips have been known to step on an envelope to flatten it, thus enabling it to go through the canceling machine. Think of the Timex watches and Easter eggs from grandpas that have suffered this maltreatment. I suppose I could have flattened your cookie myself, but you don't want to get an envelope full of crumbs. So I ate it, but you have the benefit of the fortune.

Which brings me back to the topic at hand, the so-called fortune cookie and its ubiquitous message. The Chinese had a purpose in inventing this medium that transcends the motives of other print media. I cannot remember anyone winning a fortune from what I have ever read in a fortune cookie in my entire life. They are always a passing fancy, not a fortune. They are a nice frill after eating egg foo yung in a Chinese restaurant and are best shared with dinner partners. "Who got the best one? Which one is best?" Ah! There's the genius of the inscrutable descendants of Kung Fu Tse. The messages are always equal in cheeriness, always wishing you well, like winning a dollar in a lottery. Not much, but still a dollar.

You may rightly ask, "What is a dollar?" Well, let me tell you. It's like when you are a little kid with a single penny who goes into the Armstrong Ole Store to stand before the grandest collection and display of good things ever seen in this world. You see it all, your eyes roving over the display case of penny candies that you long since memorized. You accept the challenge of getting the most possible for your money, a penny's worth.

Hobo, it always would come down to the caramel, that excruciatingly delectable caramel, that same delightful caramel you have had many times before. You look at everything in the Ole Store, select that one, that caramel in the very front, the biggest one, and Mr. Armstrong hands it over to you with a friendly smile. You give him your penny and go outside the Ole Store, sit down on the ledge alone, unwrap your precious caramel that always has a little bit of stubborn paper stuck on it that won't peel off. But that doesn't matter, no way, never.

The hard caramel quickly goes into your mouth, scrap of paper included, and you know exactly what it will taste like as you slowly work your caramel through your mouth with your tongue until the warmth of your dripping saliva works all the way through your delightful experience with your one-cent caramel, constantly testing the sweetness and the juiciness in your mouth.

Your carmel soon becomes so soft and chewy it's almost ready to swallow, but you can't let that happen. Your jaw aches from chewing such a tasty morsel and you want to postpone the inevitable swallowing, but there it goes, you can't stop it, straight down it goes, lost forever.

And right at that moment of ultimate delight, you realize you have received the greatest treat in the world for a lot of money and you think, "What if I had a whole dollar, a hundred times that many.

Wow, that much would buy 100 caramels; I'm sure glad I learned math at Longfellow."

Argo — Sept. 8, 1995

The Pour

Dear Donald,

If you want to have a really good time at the same time you're learning something new, go to Flaten Hall in the basement of the old Art Barn at St. Olaf and watch them pour. This is not coffee I'm talking about, or whatever they may be pouring over at Thorson. We're talking bronze here — hot bronze — over 2,000 degrees F.

A kind invitation from Mara takes me down I-35W and east on Highway 19, up the back entrance to St. Olaf, along the edge of Norway Valley we know so well, and over to the old Art Barn. I thought you might enjoy a report on one facet of the Art Department inasmuch as you have changed your life major to art and naturally might be interested.

I walk down to the lower level which is at ground level on the south side. Groping my way down the stairs, I am somewhat apprehensive. It sounds like a jet airplane getting ready for takeoff. I slow down, but then see Mara, and everything is "copacetic" as Jimmy Durante used to say.

Mara is partly garbed in what is de rigeur for the day — leather jacket and chaps, foot guards, extra leggings similar to what mountain men such as "Liver Eating" Johnson wore, and a blue hood for neck and head protection that looks rather like those worn by the gunnery crew in the movie, "The Guns of Navaronne." Protective eye wear is required, and near at hand are face masks similar to what the welders wear — flip up, flip down.

Melissa and Jane are there to assist in the pour. A very muscular senior named Andrew appears to be the main man. He is carefully feeding chunks of bronze into the crucible which sits over a very hot fire that roars upward past the crucible and lid about a foot. Overhead is a large round vent that exhausts the gases, but not the noise.

I look around the room and wonder if it is all right to stay. I have a visit with Melissa as she straps on her gear. She graduated in art a couple years ago just like Mara; Jane is a senior. They are privileged to be allowed to use the facilities there.

I have known Melissa for a couple years, having viewed her work at two art shows in which Mara also participated — Steensland and also the downtown gallery that you and I visited. Melissa's paintings show lots of bucolic scenes, very calm, ordered, sweet and peaceful. She must be from the farm. She is very talented.

I look around the room and see a well-equipped metals shop with several items of equipment for bending and cutting. Warning signs are everywhere, and it is clear that this is no hangout for a ninth grader, too many ways to get injured.

Samples of bronze in various stages of development or rejection are seen. I look closely at two bronze hammers, one has a bronze handle with knobs on it, The craftsmanship looks good to me. Over in the corner stands the furnace, roaring and emitting a high pitched noise.

I wonder why they don't wear ear plugs, but they are young and therefore indestructible. I begin to wish I had bought mine, but there's nothing to be done about that.

I ask Mara about the molds. She informs that they are outside in the kiln, remaining very hot. "You don't pour hot bronze into cold molds," she states to her guest. In the center of the floor are nine 5-gallon pails of sand where the molds will be placed just prior to the pour.

I recognize some of the equipment like the straight edge skimmer Mara will use to skim off impurities before and during the pour. There is a six foot-long temperature probe to gauge the progress of the molten bronze cooking in the crucible. Mara takes the probe in hand, adjusts her face guard and rests the tip near the top of the hole spewing out flames.

It looks as though she is warming the probe before putting it into the melting pot. She then inserts the tip in the pot and takes a reading from the face of the gauge which is electronic — digital, about 4" x 6"— in a housing at the end of the probe.

I do not get to see it, no, I'm not going anywhere near that "fire from hell." The probe glows red almost immediately, but comes out, indicating the metal is about 100 degrees below the desired temperature, just over 2,000 degrees F.

All they can do is wait, and let the furnace do its work. In the meantime, Andrew probes the molten bronze with a rod to determine if there are any clumps of unmelted bronze in the pot.

After another half hour, the reading shows 2,057, which is adequate. Out the door to the outside kiln they go. Each member of the crew dons elbow-length asbestos-lined gloves. They take with them a wheelbarrow which has a layer of chicken wire in the box.

As the kiln is opened, we see a beautiful, bright orange inside, and also the standing molds which glow hot orange. Andrew extracts the molds with long tongs and places them carefully into the wheelbarrow. Andrew then wheels it inside, not seeing the fresh doggie-do in his path. He steps in it. I wonder what I would have said. He does not say that.

A man and woman enter the room. He begins to assist in packing the molds in the pails of sand. They pour sand into each pail to steady the molds whose openings are covered with the gloved hands. Some gloves begin to smoke. There is a slight spilling of sand into a mold or two.

These have to be taken up and re-seated in another pail after being emptied of the unwanted grains of sand in the molds. I wonder why there isn't some sort of reverse bellows, or sand sucker with a metal tip to suck out grains of sand. A possible invention for someone?

Andrew takes another temperature reading. It is ready. The vent is moved aside; the brick cover with a hole at the top is also swung aside. I ask, "How much does the crucible or pot weigh?" The answer, about 120 pounds of bronze and a 15-pound crucible. The glowing crucible is about nine inches across at the top, about 15 inches in height.

The lifting tool is clamped securely onto the crucible which is then lifted out of the furnace and gingerly placed onto two bricks in the pouring harness. The pouring harness is of steel, weighs perhaps 20 pounds, and has two T-bar handles about five feet on either side of the glowing crucible. Mara skims and whacks the skimming tool on the cement floor. Molten matter spatters.

Someone immediately shovels sand on the chunks. On the floor surrounding the pails containing the molds is a layer of sand to prevent the metal from getting on the cement floor.

Here we go, the pour is on! Big Andrew takes one side of the apparatus, two gals the other side. I can see the technique: they have to crouch down low enough to get the crucible reasonably close to the apertures into which the bronze will be poured.

Each time they tilt the crucible to pour, the liquid runs out, looking like a small river of molten lava. It does not always pour directly into the mold openings which appear to be slightly smaller than a Dixie Cup. The hot metal rolls onto the sand, sometimes spreading beyond the pails. These blobs are immediately covered with sand. What we have here is a smoothly functioning team of people who know exactly what they are doing. As the molten metal is poured into each mold, Mara regulates the top surface of the liquid with her skimming tool. As each mold is filled, she calls out, "Up!" and the crew moves the glowing crucible to the next of nine molds.

The entire pour takes only about five minutes. After that, ingot molds are placed on the floor. The remainder of the bronze in the crucible is poured into the ingot molds, making several bars of bronze. The crucible is then returned to the lifter harness and placed back into the furnace to cool. Masks come off, revealing beads of perspiration on every forehead.

It has been hot work, and the entire room is rather warm. Mara and the other members of the team go around and spit on the red hot surface of molten orange glowing bronze in each mold. This appears to be a "good luck" gesture or else some sort of pagan 'Olaf ritual inherited from the original Vikings.

The tension is over for me. I have no idea if the artists were tense. Perhaps they were, since they certainly took great pains to do the job right. It was a professional operation that was a most interesting spectacle to witness.

Once again I was impressed by what 'Olaf offers students. That place has something for everyone, and I am so glad to see these talented young people in action. They have found a place where they can really do good work. I know you would have enjoyed it very much.

Mara said the items cast, handles for fireplace tools, need to cool overnight. Then the mold material will be chiseled off. That's as far as we got on the topic. I was glad to have been there, not only because I wanted to see Mara in action doing something she does well.

It is more than that. We support by our attendance the music concerts and athletic contests involving students. To my way of thinking, we should support and show appreciation for the art students by attending their shows and seeing them in action.

They seem to enjoy the company, and it certainly is worth the time and effort when you are in town to see the pour.

Argo — December, 1995

The Price of Tea

As someone we know said, "there's a sucker born every day."

Dear Donald,

Just a few minutes ago, the electrical power company came and installed a new meter at no cost to me, or so it would seem I received a free meter. It took only the time required to yank the old one out and shove the new one onto its four prongs.

I thanked the representative for the new meter which should make a lot of difference in my quality of life. However, I have not yet figured out how. I get a new water meter tomorrow. I didn't order that item either, and there is no apparent cost for it.

The only thing I can think of is the meters must be old and slipping somewhat in my favor. It's like the gasoline pump. You have no way of knowing if it is correct, except for the inspection certificate, but is that right? There is a meter that shows gallons and another, dollars and cents. Are they adjusted correctly? Is it possible there could be a million gas pumps that cheat people 200 times each, every day, including Sundays?

You may answer that one for yourself, on faith. The point is: we are at the mercy of those who supply power and water and gas to our homes. We don't have the foggiest notion of how much they are fudging on the bills because of rigged meters. How does one check on them? "What you see is what you get?"

If you go out and buy fifty feet of rope off a coil at the hardware store, you can see the measurement done. This fact is reassuring, naturally. The guys at the meat market in Brooklyn and elsewhere who had their fingers on the scale have now been replaced by the guys who weigh your "hambigger" unseen in the back room. They wrap it in plastic and price stamp it. Were the tray and two sheets of absorbent paper weighed too and are they part of the cost when the meat was weighed, or are they a calculated tare?

These guys are like the people responsible for filling cans of beer or soda pop. How do you know the cans are full, as claimed? The Heinz people recently got caught cheating an ounce on the catsup — which could have been going on since you were ten years old. That's a lot of ketchup. Their excuse: the moisture content shrank because of porous plastic bottles. Oh come now!

In the old days, you could tell by looking at the milk bottle how much cream there was in a quart. Now the milk is homogenized and you can never know for sure the difference between 1%, 2% or so-called "whole" milk. Does a pound of coffee in the can really weigh a pound? Have you ever weighed it? Now they are down-sizing, putting 14 ounces of coffee into a can that looks to the casual observer like a pound can.

Remember when smart guys would look down at 3.2 beer because it was considered too weak? Actually, in Minnesota, strong beer is only 0.8 of one per cent stronger. The confusion occurs when you consider that the alcohol content in 3.2 beer is measured by weight. The alcohol in strong beer is measured by volume. One would assume that strong beer is 25% stronger than 3.2 beer (0.8% compared to 3.2%, right?). Now how in the world do you figure that one out? I care more about the price of milk because I drink milk and not beer.

We purchase oranges designated by the industry as 24s or 36s or 48s or some other count, meaning that there are so many oranges per crate, depending on size. The crates weigh the same, but when the oranges are bigger, they cost a lot more. Is bigger better? The fruits come from the same trees, as a rule.

Who decides the price of fish heads and scraps that you objected to so vociferously at the market here? Is the price negotiable, as a sport coat from Nate's? Ever bother to count the pills in a bottle of 500? Scares you, doesn't it? Sell a million bottles and there are 2,000 free bottles for the company if there are only 499 pills in each bottle of 500. Pretty good deal for Wall Street.

How much would a daily paper or a Sunday edition cost if you requested only the news and sports or certain other sections and told them they could keep the want ads and other junk? Same for the post office — reduce the cost of first class stamps and charge advertisers more for junk mail.

Here's my lab experiment. Take a pound of coffee and keep track of how many cups you brew out of that pound. You will thus arrive at a price per cup. Then go out and order a cup of java at big-bucks Starbucks and figure out the per cent of mark-up on that cup. Aside from the ambiance considerations, it seems that the profit margin is more akin to that found in a jewelry store, eh?

Then go home, look in the mirror and ask yourself, "What in heck is going on here, Old Buddy?" We call this rigmarole the "Law of Supply and Demand," straight from Adam Smith. All the rest is bull. It's true. They keep figuring out how much they can get by with before the bough breaks. That is one reason why a St. Paul money lender made $65 million last year, up from $29 million the year before.

Another example — I got $36.00 when I retired (one dollar for each year of service). I had paid $7.00 annually into the social fund from which the "Golden Parachute" was withdrawn. I should have paid myself more, or at least walked off with some school supplies such as some chalk and blackboard erasers. I suppose I could have stomped a hole in the floor with my foot as did the Viking, Donaldo, who was brought before the King of Norway and asked to flex his muscles and show his strength.

Sometimes I go to the discount stores to buy huntin' and fishin' stuff. Seeing the price stickers, often two or three on top of the other, makes me wish I could change the numbers on my pay check too. No can do.

A couple of decades ago, while shopping at Monkey Wards, I saw a new model vacuum cleaner displayed on the first day it was offered for sale. It had a sale tag which read, "Was $192.00 - Now $172.00." I determined to keep an eye on that bit of fiction which I monitored over the next two years. Over the course of the two-year period, the same prices were posted on the same model. At no time, including the first day the model was introduced, was the machine priced at $192. After two years, the model was discontinued, and a new model came out. I never shopped there again.

People who shop in the produce department of a food market have an advantage, or so it seems. Seeing a bin full of cucumbers or green bell peppers at 59 cents each is your license to pick out the best you can find. This works fine for other items, too, until you get to the strawberries, which suffer from over-handling.

Actually, the best strawberries are eaten summarily by the little old ladies of either sex, ostensibly to taste but probably to get revenge on the store owners. The remainder may perhaps be sneezed upon or handled by customers' hands. You have no idea where those hands have been before they fondled strawberries, moving some out of the way to get at the good ones underneath.

What gets me, Donald, is that we get pushed around, ignored, cheated and otherwise mishandled in more ways than I can recount here. Our nation's early leaders took matters into their own hands — they dressed up in some wild Indian garb, put on the war paint and tossed the tea into the Boston Fjord. All things considered, the price of tea in England was higher, but they never threw it into their fjord. Of course not. Why would people in a "nation of shopkeepers" do such a thing?

Now you know why America had a revolution and became independent. They got fed up with the shopkeepers, and the price of tea.

Argo — April 1, 1996

The Rookie

Dear Donald,

Every now and then we hearken back to the voices of the past and confront memories of events, stunts, tricks, ploys and, of course, mischief.

I am reminded of a cocky English teacher at Roosevelt High School who moved into the classroom across the corridor from my classroom, 311. He was definitely a smarty and reminded me of Malvolio with his cross-dressing and let it be known he was an Augsburg man. That's nothing to tell people. They will immediately wonder if the guy's head is screwed on right.

He had all the right stuff — tweed sport coats, preppy ties, pastel shirts, and baggy trousers. His hair was, after the fashion of the day, swept back, and, I suspect, slightly greased with Brylcreem, just a little dab. He had a Clark Gable mustache, and what I have always disliked in a man, the habit of arching the eyebrows toward the center of his wrinkled brow as if to solicit sympathy. He could well use some of that, to be sure.

The only reason I did not immediately manhandle him to hinder his rather affected demeanor was that he had joined the choral group in which I was singing. He was a good bass by Augsburg standards, just utility by St. Olaf standards, although he could find happiness in the chapel choir, perhaps. So I did not want unduly to injure him.

That is not to say I did not find it necessary to teach him a lesson or two. I got a girl to phone his room saying she was calling from the office. Would he please report to the assistant principal's office in five minutes? He agreed.

As soon as I saw him pass my room, I ran over to his classroom and announced, "Now class, we're going to have a little fun with your teacher aren't we?" They immediately lit up. "Take all your books and things and follow me!" We walked out of his classroom and into a vacant room in the corner. I pulled the door shade down and instructed the kids to remain in the room and under no circumstances were they to leave.

After a time came a knock at my door. "What is it?" I said,

pretending to be irritated by the interruption. He rather meekly said, "My class is gone. I don't know where they are. What shall I do?"

"Well," said the sage old Argo, stroking his beard, "I think you had better go look for them. Check the lunchroom. They probably assumed you wouldn't mind if they took an extra lunch period."

He went, presumably to the lunchroom, then returned, empty handed. I told him he had better not report this to the administration or he would get into trouble for losing a class.

"Is the whole class gone?" I asked incredulously.

"Yes," he moaned. "Oh Boy. You're in big trouble!" I said to him. The bell soon rang, and that was that.

The next day, a beautiful, warm spring day, I decided to set him straight on the matter of the "disappearing" class. I entered his room at the beginning of the period and he had not yet returned from his coffee break in the lounge. I couldn't resist the temptation. "Kids! Kids! C'mon, we're going out to the football field and 'catch some rays' on the bleachers!"

Boy, they hustled out of that room in a hurry! We went to the bleachers, I sat them down and said, "Today is your holiday from English class. I want you to sit here and enjoy the nice warm sunshine. At the end of the period, just go back into school and continue with your classes. You play your cards right and we might do this again sometime."

I had been gone from my classroom about ten minutes. When I entered, I could scarcely believe my eyes! My class was there, the furniture was all backward, including steel wardrobe, book cases, my desk; all the pupils were facing the rear of the room. It dawned on me that the tables had been turned on me by the rookie across the hall.

Neither of us ever spoke about this again. There was only one explanation — he must have spent his freshman year in college at St. Olaf, then transferred to Augsburg — the rookie!

    Argo —

The Screen

Dear Donny,

One of our heroes, Edvard Munch, painted the most valuable painting in the world. It is called "The Scream." Munch could doubtless have learned from your eclectic, rampant expressionism and use of color, but we are talking here not about "The Scream" ("Skriket," pronounced "skree keh" in Norsk). We're talking the screen, as in screen door, or screen window.

About three years ago, I installed new combination windows and screens in this old house. The rear entry door I did myself. Whenever one gets something new, be it an automobile, bicycle, television, computer, vaulting pole, or such, one wonders from time to time when the thing will be wrecked, and by whom.

Whenever I damage something, I am my worst whip, castigating myself for carelessness or stupidity. Anyone overhearing such conversations would probably request that I use a little more restraint, showing mercy to the dummy at whom I am railing and hurling verbal slaps. Naturally, I have not too much difficulty in indulging myself, so I then walk away, vowing to be more careful.

I had a bad night last night and awoke at 4:00 am. Following my usual procedure in such instances, I felt around to determine if I was still alive or dreaming. I had been sleeping in the basement where it usually is cooler, as a rule, 75.6 degrees F., with lower humidity than upstairs.

In addition, the basement is always dark unless one switches on a light or leaves a cigarette burning in the ash tray. I don't do that, no. Avoiding the flashlight at hand, I blundered toward the light switch, but became turned around, finding myself instead in the store room. Being too sick to laugh out loud, I merely groped my way out of there.

I fixed a pot of coffee, waved at faithful dog Argo in your smoking room, the back porch, and waited for the morning paper to arrive. I ate breakfast cereal made in Northfield, toasted oats. We buy Northfield cereals here. Eating a bowl of cereal made me tired, so I decided to set the trap for squirrels and retire again.

I left the doors in the porch family room closed so that Argo would not do what he does when the trap springs — run out, circle, and worry the critters. I needed faithful Argo to stay inside and not bark and carry on so I could get a couple hours of sleep.

Well, he barked anyway, my plans and wishes notwithstanding. I went upstairs, saw a critter in the trap and a curious squirrel teasing it. So I got my piece and shot the squirrel from the window. Dog Argo went nuts. He had already clawed and pawed the back door screen, the new one, into shreds while trying to get out while I was trying to sleep.

I could have prevented the damage to the screen. Faithful Argo could have been instructed to stay away; the storm window could have been lowered; the door left ajar. The sensible thing is to blame myself for the screen damage. Dog Argo, he don't know, no how. So now I gotta go get some screening material and fix it. When it is fixed, I will be proud, but wonder who will wreck it the next time. Next time I will fill the space with a counterfeit rendition of "The Scream," a Hobo oil.

When I feel better, I will sojourn to St. Olaf for a visit, ostensibly to the library, but you and I know there is more to St. Olaf than the library, like the heating tunnels. Yesterday I visited with Sidney Rand, on campus as an advance man for the October visit of the King of Norway. The King has been here before, but I can't remember when. Argo will likely be invited to the dinner party in Minneapolis and will attend. I took my mother when King Olav was here, sometime in the sixties. She thought that was pretty nice. I did too. They fed us well, and my momma said at the end, "If I am going to get any more, I'd prefer to have it in cash."

Strange how the collegians seem younger each year. I wonder if they know it is the fate of the young to become the old? I used to tease students who would ask, "Hey, Kindem, how'd you get bald?" My answers were often unsettling:

I wore a baseball cap backwards. I used to shower daily, at least once, and each time you shower, hair is lost. I recommend washing hair only once every ten days or so, or else you will get bald too. Men who get bald have more testosterone in their system, and are more manly, and less likely to be gay. When I was young, they all had long hair. Too much sex will cause a loss of hair, they say. Drinking beer has the same effect, that of destroying the amino acids of the fufufnik in the scradgamootin. Hamburgers, french fries and pizza have ingredients that also cause hair loss.

I just received a call from daughter, Nina, whose fever has subsided, and the doc says she does not have mono. So I don't have to go to Florida and bring her back here, no. What a relief! It's tough to have sick children, even when they get older.

Sorry about the "lenth" of this letter, as they say on Staten Island and environs. As Ole used to say: I'm not up to "power"; the map's in the "glove apartment"; no more chance than a snow ball in a "bombfire"; you got a "levolver"?

Thank you for the talisman, Hobo. I did not have one. Now I have the powah. I am counting on it to cure my cold. And thanks for the constellation Argo. I knew it not.

In signing off, here's one for you — I was doing newspaper research yesterday in the Carleton library, covering births in Minneapolis of boys born in 1933. I found a boy born to Mrs. Gay Argo, 2936 Stevens Avenue South. I got out of there. A very sweet coed helped me install the film in the microfilm machine. Had I been a student, I quickly would have forgotten all about my studies.

Well, got to go to lunch now. See you when you come — through the screen.

      Argo —

The Shade

Dear Donald,

The summer before our tenth grade we had a guy who transferred to Northfield from California because his father got a job at Carleton. I think his father was in the astronomy department.

Anyway, the kid's name was Royce and we called him "Royster Doyster" because he had the habit of wearing sun glasses all the time. Royster Doyster claimed that he had damaged his eyes while watching a solar eclipse. He even wore his shades when he went to the show. And he even wore his shades while swimming in Carleton Lake, which made our lifeguard, John Westerlund, laugh himself silly.

When school started, Royster Doyster was put in the fourth-hour tenth grade history class taught by Clarence Sandberg. Also in that class were "Sleepy" Wells, "Bojinks" Boe, "Pills Pals" Paulson, "Feed the Hogs" Rezac, "Big Cheese" Paulson, "Soybeans" Sawyer, "Lardbutt...," "Sabang Sabong...," "Fudd...," "Toady" DeMann, "Lambo" Lamberty, "Snip" Snesrud, "Harley Bush Leagues" Wagner, "Corky" Fossum, "Jawannagetbeadup" and "Howdyawannapayitoutayerpocketorcayshcaysh" Raadt. They called me "Lefse" because that's what I always had for lunch.

Trouble started right away when Royster Doyster came a half day late the first day of school. He walked into Mr. Sandberg's classroom dressed in his wild California style. He had a necklace, earring, hair style with a crew cut on top, slicked back long hair on the sides and a duck's tail in back. He wore pointed brown and white shoes, zoot-suit pants with key chain, a baggy lavender shirt, and those constant sun glasses — the kind pilots wore, aviator glasses with gold rims.

"Holy smokes!" I said to Sleepy, waking him up, "Would you look at that!" Mr. Sandberg tilted his head down so he could see over the tops of his glasses. He looked at this apparition, wiped his mouth as he always did before saying something he thought clever, and bawled, "What are ya doin' with those Hollywood glasses on?"

Royster Doyster responded, "Because I'm from Hollywood, man." We all laughed at that. "Take 'em off anyway, and sit down over there by the windows!" barked Sandberg, embarrassed and miffed because the kid sneaked in a one-liner on him.

Royster Doyster took off the glasses, extended his arms in front of him like Frankenstein, and blundered into Donna Mae Reynolds first, then Alice Jean Olberg, then Leon Nicolai, and finally banged into the radiator, spilling onto the floor the gallon cans of water Sandberg had placed there to provide humidity for the room.

While this charade was going on, Royster Doyster was calling out loudly, "I can't see! I can't see! My eyes! My eyes! Help me!" The water splashed on Nicolai and on Sleepy, who jumped up and started hollering, "I'm all wet! I'm all wet!"

Everybody on that side of the room jumped up, desks tumbled, girls screamed, some guys swore, pandemonium ensued. Sleepy jumped up on his desk as I had done on mine. Mr. Sandberg walked out and came back into the room with William F. Carlson, our steel-eyed Principal. Somebody was going to get it, for sure.

Mr. Carlson looked calm as always, cold sober and unsmiling in his wire-rimmed glasses. It was hard to rattle Old Stone Face. He stood with his arms folded, staring, and motioned to Royster Doyster. We turned him toward Carlson and gave him a shove. "Where am I? Where am I? I'm injured, can't see! I'm injured! Help!"

Mr. Carlson then addressed him calmly, "What seems to be the matter with the gears in your head? Do you want all of us to feel sorry for you?" Royster Doyster turned to the class, arms outstretched, palms up, pleading, "Is he talking to me? Who's he talking to? Who is this guy?"

Mr. Carlson asked slowly, "What are you going to do for an encore?" Royster Doyster pointed at Mr. Sandberg, "He made me take off my glasses. I can't see a thing without them!"

"Well," said Mr. Carlson, slowly, "Put them on. You'll need them to find your way home. Get your hat and coat."

They walked away. As they walked down the hall, we could plainly hear Mr. Carlson say, "Don't you know that when you fool with me you might just as well go outside and ram your head into a tree. That's as far as you are going to get here."

Clarence Sandberg resumed teaching, asking our class the same question he asked his classes every year: "What do you call those armored vehicles used during the war that have a big dome with a cannon and caterpillar treads?"

"Tanks!" I hollered. "You're welcome," said Sandberg, and we settled down to normal classroom routine. We never saw Royster Doyster again. They said he transferred to Shattuck Military Academy in Faribault, an adventure for all — shades at night.

Lars — March 2, 1996 — brother Erling's Birthday

The Minnesota State Fair

It has often been said by the Burnsville master gardener that the Minnesota State Fair is the greatest show on earth. He ought to know, having gone off and on to the Fair since 1950. Your favorite Northfield reporter recently asked Argo about the Fair. His valued comments follow in a letter to his long-time friend Donald Clark who resides humbly in San Francisco.

Dear Donny,

The State Fair is unpretentious. No promises are made. It is just there. And it has always been about the same, year in and year out. That is what people expect, and that is what they want, by and large.

But that is not to say that there are no changes. Obviously, an entirely new set of birds and animals are there each year. Not to mention the fruits, vegetables, crafts, grandstand shows, and even this year, a brand spanking new Midway to attract people who can't stand to be away from the loud noises and neon of downtown or Lake Street.

Or the country bumpies who have never seen a freak show or the latest version of the tilt-a-whirl; who do not yet have personal knowledge that you can't really beat the odds throwing baseballs at bowling pins or milk bottles. Besides, the Midway is a place where people go. And people are attracted to crowds, and auto accidents.

For me, the most fun thing at the state fair is Nina. The next are Bjørn and Tor. But Nina — she charges off to the pig house right away, because she knows what she wants and where to find it. So in the giant pig house we admire all the big pigs and the little piggies after which piggie banks are named.

Did you know that if you "sweat like a hog" you perspire out your nostrils? Well, we gotta see the biggest pig in America before we move on. I haven't seen any bigger than the one in 1993 that Nina said weighed in at 1350 pounds, a big boar. I note that all he does is lie on his side. Probably doesn't walk too far, either, dragging a 75-pound scrotum like a 300-pound NFL tackle.

Did you know that insulin comes from pigs? Their skin is used to protect the flesh of burn victims. Sonja likes pork chops better than any other meat. Anyways, she usta. Tor too.

The poultry barn has so many species it boggles the mind. Each and every one of the roosters seems to be crowing at each other and at us. Of course they are programmed to do this. They probably get higher marks from the invisible judges. But did you know that chickens have ear lobes? They don't got no lips, no.

Last year, Bjørn and I were in a constant state of wonderment in the cattle barn. Who in the world could imagine these Holsteins and Guernseys would be so huge? I am perhaps the only one who pronounces "Guerns-eye" correctly, but avoid doing this in public, for they will turn upon me. Or is the swine barn where one does not cast pearls? It's been so long.

Those wide bony hips on a cow are called "hooks," the bone above the tail is called the point. There is also the moo-booth where they have the large fiberglass-encased cow stomach. As I recall from Grace Holstad's freshman biology, they have four stomachs: the rumen, reticulum, omasum and obasum. (Gimme that blue book exam, Grace, I'll chew this stuff up and spit it out till the day I die.)

Over in the horse barn they have lots of horses, and some horsies. What they used to claim they had was a horse called a fox trotter that was trained to trot along without giving a bumpy ride. "I'm Sure!" says Lars III to that one. I say they ought to teach the Argo-sneak to the horses. When Argo the dog knows he did something he no shoulda done, such as sneak over to the neighbors, he lowers his belly and sneaks back to hide under a vehicle, usually the Bronco, another form of horse with a bumpy ride.

I enjoy the sheep and goats so much because it reminds me of Norway. My namesake, Lars Kindem the Elder, was the first to import the Cheviot lamb to Norway. Probably made a bundle on that as on everything else. Cut from the same cloth as Lars III. Knows where the money is.

But the beautiful goats! I just walk around there wondering how much gjeitost each could produce in a day. I bet it is a lot — almost as much as in Norway, be sure of that. Gjeitost is "Norwegian peanut butter," a strong, brown, sweet goat cheese with a touch of caramel and taste of goat milk.

But the sheep get more attention than the goats, because they have to be shorn so neatly and get their daily comb out. I should tell Gus in Portland that 150 yards of wool is used to make a baseball. Tor probably knows already that lanolin from sheep is used in his electrical work.

You don't want to miss the Children's Barnyard, especially when they have a new hatch of little chickies or duckies. My friend and colleague from Roosevelt High School, Clifford Luke, Norwegian-speaking former agriculture teacher there, started the children's barnyard in 1941. Cliff also supplied me with three whips taken out of his freezer which I planted. The three apple trees that resulted — the Honeygold in the Garden, and two Haralsons, one in the rips ("ribes" in Latin, currants in English), and one below the fence next to the woods. Got that?

When I used to go to the State Fair with the most marvelous company in the world, my kids, we always saw the animals first; then we hit the big milk truck for all you can drink (this year, I think it is 50 cents). Just because I took my kids there does not mean I was cheap. It always was and is my firm belief that the only money to be spent at the fair is for food, drink, and a souvenir of some kind; for me the souvenir is usually the WCCO Weather Calendar.

But there are lots of other things to buy. In recent years, I always gave the kids $20.00 each to start with for ga-ga-money. I dearly wish I could have done that 20 years ago. What is a fair for, if not free choice of what to do or what to buy?

You always gotta have a plan to meet each other periodically at the fair. The best place is the forestry watch tower for a couple of reasons. There is grass there, in addition to all the benches; and the coffee stand is right there on the street, which is also across the street from WCCO TV.

This year when I go, I will be alone, and not plan to meet anyone periodically. I will, of course, wear my famous "Northfield Milk" tee shirt, and the cap Lars III gave me: "Red Bluff Bull & Gelding Show." People get confused with that one.

I just have to skip some of the booths and displays to get over to the Agriculture-Horticulture show. This year, alone, I will just have to be smug and think to myself, rather than rely on the play-by-play comments of Bjørn who would remark, from time to time, "Pappa, your stuff is better than this." Nice boy.

In the old days we would look at the fruits and vegetables for a while then sit on the grass and look at the fruits and vegetables walking by. Man, is that corner the best in the whole world for people watching! I don't know, Karl Johann in Oslo may be as good for international variety. But if you want a huge collection of overweight people, sit there outside the AG-Hort building. They are all there, and all eating as they walk. In America, people forget to sit down to eat. They walk and eat, then do it some more.

The food building smells of deep fat frying. I can't stand that smell. Every church in the world has a restaurant around there. All that fried food on the sticks will kill you, eventually. I believe there are 18 different foods on a stick so people can walk while they eat and spill on the asphalt, not the floor of the dining room. The only food I really have to sample is the honey taffee.

The honeybee displays are among my favorites. The bees are our friends who make it all possible so I support them by buying their products. And it strikes me as interesting that they have a display of home-baked goods there, all baked with honey. The stuff looks good, and it is good to see there are still folks old fashioned enough to take the time to make things from scratch. I know I do, and the food is so much better.

But of course I have time on my hands, yes I do. Ask me about it sometime. When I am not getting the mail, or going out to get the paper, or going to the store, I have Bosnia, Iraq, Nato, The Republicans, and other things to divert my energies.

Yes, wise old, experienced Kindem takes along to the fair a rubber stamp with name and address to simplify the sign up procedures for the prizes. Some time I will win. I know darn well that if I had Sonja with me, she would win. She has a way about her. Perhaps inherited. Yes, she gets that from me, and her stunning good looks from her mama.

The Oshkosh giant overalls are gone. The giant tractors and farm machinery on machinery hill that wowed the heck out of Tor are also gone. What's with the farmers? Tor climbed up into the cab of every monster on the hill, and I loved to see him do it. Sometimes I did, too.

Then we used to follow Nina through the crafts and homemade stuff building to see folk art at its best. Always stop by at the dental society booth for free dental floss on the way, or go over to the U of M computer or League of Women Voters computer and take a survey meaning nothing to anyone in the world.

Then Pappa has to look at the new appliances in the Minnegasco booth, and over to view the photos at the WCCO radio booth, where they have free water, all you can drink, and self-congratulatory displays, including that nummy, Sid Hartmann.

Strange, we have never taken a ride on the elevated railroad or up to the top of the space needle. Too sedentary, I suppose. I do not like to go to the fair with people who cannot walk a lot. I sure remember when Nini and I carried and pushed kids around that place for hours on end. It was the right thing to do, and I would gladly do it again, frequently, but you need to be able to walk.

Maybe with grandkids. I know my starlet, Arianna, will want to take the tour with grandpa. That will be the finest, grandest tour the world has ever known. And she knows how to eat, yes. The heck of it is, with little girls, they have to wait a half hour in line to use the rest rooms.

I quit going to the auto races and trick stuff of Joey Chitwood. You can see all you want of that on I-35. I saw the gal riding on the top wing of a biplane that did the loop too close to the ground, lost power, and headed in. That was my last grandstand show.

Nowadays they have some show biz acts that draw lots of fans and curiosity seekers — Whoopee Wilfahrt and his 19 Nosepickers (playing, "Git that Bugger").

And if you think that's music, it snot.

Then there is Bill & Judy and the Rubber Duckies; Slim Slam and the Titties; Burt Snarl with Hoo Fung Dung; The Taxpayers Who Won't; Whiney Billy Joe Bob and the Counterfeit Confederates.

And Robert E. Lee, XIV; Old Hunt & Peck; The Cleavers, playing Meat; The Icemen playing Ice; The Tooth Fairy; Loco Motives; No Motives; Shabby Babbs; The Cowpokers; and the Gospels: Sin-no-Mo.

Music, anyone? Let's bring the Ole Choir to the grandstand at the Minnesota State Fair!

      Argo —

The Visit

Burnsville, March 11, 1995

Dear Donald,

There are a number of reasons why the elderly take up residence at the Northfield Retirement Center where my father lived and died. One has broken both hips and cannot walk; another is ninety-six and has broken an arm and shoulder; none is able to fulfill the requirements for living independently at home. It is the end of the road; someone has to care for them, and someone has to care about them.

Many of those whom I visit are former neighbors who had lived in comfortable homes with well-kept yards, former professors and others who have lived their entire adult lives as part of the St. Olaf family. These are Northfield folks. Two of them are mothers of gals who followed me through Longfellow School, Northfield High School and St. Olaf College, singing in the same choirs. They are my friends.

Today I joined two nonagenarians for coffee and cake in the dining room. Someone had made it to a hundred and one. I started with a couple of one-liners and we laughed. We brought up memories of "Ole" acquaintances and their foibles. More laughter followed, even some tears.

It was so much fun! We understood each other, and others in the room, though old, crippled and hard of hearing, knew that our table was having all the fun. This was some coffee time — loud, exuberant, even memorable! After about half an hour, we had nearly laughed ourselves sick. Then one lady left, pushing the walker which the attendant had located for her. Another, escorted by her daughter, returned to her room for her nap. I made one more short visit to one who was not able to leave her room for coffee. She was glad to get some homemade flatbrød — "Mamma's récipe." I wished her well, and left.

Just before reaching the door to the outside, I met the lady with the walker again. She was sitting on a bench, talking with another who also had a walker. Remembering how much fun we had enjoyed together about five minutes earlier, I said to my erstwhile table mate, "You should laugh as often as you can. It is good for you!"

She began laughing again and said to me, "Oh my! I have been laughing so much that my stomach is sore! We had so much fun at coffee; a nice man sat with us and told the funniest stories!" I smiled at her and walked out the door past a large sign which read: "IT IS COLD OUTSIDE TODAY, CORRINE. DO NOT GO OUT."

    Argo —

Too Easy

Dear Donny,

I found the following account, written on yellow notebook paper in my fishing map box dated July 29, 1993, Caribou Lake, Itasca County, one of your favorite spots.

Argo —

Argo and Argo made the trip. We stopped at Aitkin for rest and a cone. The middle spot at Caribou was taken by two quiet men. They have a female Lab. I threw doubles with the retrievers so Argo and new lady friend could have fun.

We chose the lowest site for the view and the convenience. I set everything up in an hour and twenty minutes. Some clouds, but warm and mostly sunny. Tried after supper of stew with five colors. Nearly a full moon.

July 30: Bob Saunders of Marcell arrived at 6:30 a.m. He tried for two hours. On July 28, he reported, a windy and cool day, caught five nice Splake, 16-18 inches long. He was very cordial. Told me where they hit, 7 colors. He gave me two flies he had tied, said they would work.

I started at 9:30, caught a 2 lb. 16-inch Lake Trout at 10:30 using 7 colors between large rock on NE side of Buckhorn Lodge over 62 ft. depth. I must have been down about 40 feet. Surface temp 67 degrees to 27 feet; 43' was 43 degrees.

At noon went to see Benson. None there. Argo and I did some target shooting off Graves road. Shot well. One .22 shoots left, the other, right (Marlin). Dog Argo assumes with each shot he will have a retrieve, so he did lots of running 50 yards and return.

My radio and tape deck work great! I have a Norwegian flag from the bow. I did a review in front of the Buckhorn where Hal and some guests were lounging on the dock. As we passed in review, we played "Pomp & Circumstance" and saluted the flag. Hal was pleased.

I boiled the Laker and served it with boiled potatoes and buttermilk to finish. This meal transcends the transcendent.

Dinner music was by Elgar: "Enigma Variations." Choice! The Laker was caught during a solunar major time frame: 9:30 - 11:30 am.

The next period was 3:30 - 5:00 pm, so I went out and caught two more Lakers (limit is 3 daily) and one Splake (also a limit since it was over 16 inches in length.) The Splake was 17" and 2 lbs. Good fight. (Splake is Speckled Trout [Brook] X with Lake Trout.) Two limits in one day is OK.

Couldn't fish this evening, however, so will gas up and ice up and sit around. Got hot today, in the eighties. It is 76 now at 8:15 p.m., with some cloud cover.

July 31. Awoke to warm sun, cloudless sky. The high today was 87 - no clouds, not much breeze. Fished the Solunar table advice: start at 10:15 a.m.

11:30 a.m. - Lake Trout, 14", one lb. caught on yellow fly given me by Bob Sanders (off east rock - 7 colors over 60' bottom.)

1:15 p.m. - Lake Trout, same size from Buckhorn toward N. rock. Next solunar "minor" starts 7:26 p.m.

7:30 p.m. - Caught Laker off north center ridge over 60 - 70 ft. bottom.

8:20 p.m. - Same.

8:25 p.m. - Same. I gave two Lake Trout to neighbor campers so I could fish tomorrow. I ate two. They were good.

August 1. Awoke to 68 degrees, clear sky except some high clouds in the East. Better breeze from NW. Started fishing at 12:45 p.m. over center sunken island. Boom! 1-2-3 Splake and one Laker. Splake 16+ inches (limit). Quit — too easy.

   Argo —

War on 'Coons

Dear Donny,

Your favorite correspondent has just returned from a visit with "Argo" and reports he is fighting mad.

Argo —

Headline: Show of Arms Rivals Custer Battle; Neighbors Applaud Argo's Proposal

(Northfield Exclusive)

Argo tells his favorite reporter what makes him so gosh darn mad today. "It's my grapes. You might call 'em the Grapes of Wrath. I calls 'em 'Swenson Red' and those 'coons are back at it again. Got five of them darned critters, last night I did, and thought that was the end of it, but no."

Argo takes a bite out of an apple he has just picked off a tree. "Looks like I am going to have to shoot instead of trap the sons of buggers," he goes on, taking another bite of an apple. "I got plenty of experience shootin' 'em out of trees, so I reckon that's what we're going to have to do, my faithful dog Argo and I. All he gots to do is chase one up a tree, and I sure as heck will dispatch the critter," says Argo, taking another bite of an apple.

Argo appears to have all his pants pockets filled with apples. Asked why, he responds, "Well, you see, I got these here Argo-cargo pants awhile back. Bought 'em because the name rhymes with Argo. Got to keep the pockets full, else they goes to waste.

Your correspondent asks, "You gonna skin 'em out?"

"Sure as heck am," says Argo, "Gonna skin 'em and roast 'em like a pig. Folks south of the Mason-Dixon line claim coon's as good as poke." "Poke?" "Yeah. That's what they calls it anyways, hogs, you know."

When asked if he planned to enlist the help of neighbors, Argo said, "Naw, they best stay outta the way so they don't get hurt."

Tell us, Argo, what kind of artillery are you going to use? "Well, it looks like as though it's gonna be my Ruger .22 with the red dot scope. It's the best one to use in limited light conditions."

Will you use artificial light? "Well, I usually do when it's dark out. And the darn 'coons don't exactly come out in the daytime. Sure, I use a 6-volt flashlight, hold it in my right hand, whilst I hold the fore stock. Then I aims, and bang, off we go! If'n I just wing 'em, then Argo gets to 'em right quick and then we have a heckuva squabble."

Afraid faithful Argo might get hurt? "It can happen, I suppose, but he has a powerful anger when it comes to 'coon critters, so they don't stand much of a chance."

How big is a 'coon? "Well, says Argo, the five I already got this year weighed in at about 25 pounds each on my bathroom scale. But you know how them bathroom scales are. Always weighs heavy. But Argo don't care none, he goes into the scrap at about 90 pounds. I'll bet on him."

Any advice for other 'coon hunters? "Well," says Argo, taking another apple out of his cargo pants pocket, "You gotta tell the dogs to stay away from the 'coon's saliva. It'll paralyze a dog's mouth. Don't go swappin' no spit, no."

Anything else you wish to pass on to our readers? "Yeah, what I really needs here is a field commander to sort of direct the fire and such."

Who do you have in mind? "Well, he should be an ex-marine. I know one who would be good at that. Shoots pretty good himself."

Care to reveal his name? "Yup. Name's Donald, was a Sergeant in the USMC, "Semper Fi," they say.

Well, good luck, Argo, hope you can bring your Semper Fi friend on board. "Why, luck's got nothin' to do with it, you should know that — it's all about Semper Fi."

Well, friendly reader, that's the latest from Dakota County, and a visit with one of the original types there. Till next time, your correspondent,

    Argo — (aka Isabella "Big Tits" Goliath)

Wednesay night fights

Dear Donald,

All manner of mischief could be created by the Ole men of the mid-fifties. It wasn't necessarily because they were naughty boys or bad men, but rather because the system at St. Olaf, the place we called the "Popstand," created an explosive atmosphere that from time to time required release.

These young men, "these boys," learned how to release tensions early on, these post-war Vikings who were mislabeled "The Quiet Generation." To state that they were quiet begs the question, not just a little.

I referred to men and boys, but remember, some of these troops at 'Olaf were military vets on the GI Bill and had been shot at — some in Korea, others during World War II — some even in Dundas. The vets were for the most part quiet, and even humble. To them, St. Olaf was a blessing, a refuge, and one heckuva lot more secure than the beaches of Normandy, Inchon, the Yalu, or some cold and lonely MASH outpost above the 38th parallel.

Most of the 'Olaf mischief makers in those days first learned much of their craft at the Ytterboe Training School as freshmen. The Red Wing State Reform School would have been shut down if some of these guys had been students there. The training ground for sophomores was known as Viking Court, a fine sanctuary for eccentrics and lunatics below Old Main!

It was thus, later in their junior year, that many Ole men earned their real stripes with initiation into Thorson Hall, while some of the nice guys became counselors at Ytterboe. It was there that they learned details of miscreant and aberrant behavior they had missed on their first pass through the halls of the greatest dormitory in the Lutheran World Federation.

Episodes of truly erratic behavior usually erupted in springtime, normally after a week of sustained high temperatures; the coming of new grass, leaves, and fragrant lilac blossoms; and the inevitable courting that took place in Norway Valley. Countless escapades originated in Ytterboe Hall and the Viking Court, the Ole Store and the Viking Lunch, the Lion's Den and the well-known Well downtown. Nothing really originated in Dundas, but lots of events ended there.

The onset of the dreaded final exams caused many to take leave of their senses after several sleepless nights making up for lost time and a life of sloth during the semester. We know, for example, of a friend who read his first Ibsen play three days before the final. Many fellows regretted whiling away so many carefree hours in the Lion's Den over a cup of coffee trying to psych out the new crop of frosh women. Others were rewarded for their efforts.

It is with this background and setting that we recall the episode known as the "Wednesday Night Fights" at Thorson hall, held in the basement lounge. The guys needed something radically refreshing to break up the monotony of the week — more specifically to provide a mid-week break in the routine. Someone had the bright idea to stage boxing matches, ala the Friday night fights sponsored by Gillette on TV.

We have to proceed with caution here, using anonymity wherever necessary to protect reputations established long after the student days at St. Olaf. Nobody knows, for example, who went over to the locker room in the gymnasium, sneaked into the towel room guarded by old "Pete" Pedersen who handed out towels in between puffs of Sir Walter Raleigh in his pipe, and "borrowed" four pair of 16-ounce boxing gloves from the barrel over in the rear of the towel room by the box of basketballs. Is that where they got the protective headgear too?

The advertising of the bouts for the Wednesday Night Fights was by word of mouth. Some must have felt that public advertising would have been a mistake. This establishes, conclusively, that "the boys" knew they were doing something wrong — at least something which would cause the authorities to check into things and investigate.

To launch the venture, certain appurtenances and support items were needed, to wit — a gong, a stop watch, and volunteer referees. The gong came from Ralph Haugen's storeroom behind the drama studio. Someone arranged for a stopwatch out of Ade Christiansen's desk drawer. Chet Mathison was one who wanted to be referee.

They tried to borrow a wrestling mat from the room above

Ade's office, but learned that "Tuffy" was using it for a bed; besides, it was too bulky to carry over to Thorson and was therefore a boxing mat was ruled to be "superfluous equipment." That turned out to be the biggest mistake, eventually leading to the downfall. More accurately, I suppose, some earlier downfalls led to the eventual downfall. More on that later.

The Thorson hall boxing commission decided a number of procedural questions early on. First, all bets would be final and the Marquis of Queensbury Rules, whatever they were, should be followed if possible. Second, there were to be three one-minute rounds, if needed, and winners were to be decided by acclamation and would thus advance in the Wednesday night competition. There were other rules and procedures as well.

To the extent possible, guys about the same size were matched up and in between rounds and bouts, commercials would be presented. A group of St. Olaf men in the Choir were commissioned to do the well-known Gillette commercial, singing, "Look sharp...feel sharp...be sharp...for the quickest slickest shave of all!" There would also be Pabst Beer commercials punctuated with the rolling of an empty Pabst can across the boxing ring floor between rounds, but it was considered risky to sell beer by the keg.

The matter of settling on the boxing card was solved by the boxers themselves who simply agreed to step into the ring with someone who challenged them from the floor. Of course, there were some grudge matches but for the most part the contestants merely agreed among themselves to fight for sport or by acclamation. It would be a gross understatement to state that the matches were uneven. But all the sources agree that for three weeks running during that January of 1954, all pandemonium broke loose on Wednesday nights in the Thorson Hall basement lounge!

Most boxing experts also agree that five fighters stood out as sterling examples of St. Olaf's best. We saw Frank Peterson knock out Roy Lindquist, star tennis buff, silly. The next time Frank fought was against Jack Aamodt, in what was generally thought to be the classiest bout of the season. The Pabst Beer people got in with a short commercial after round one, and the customary symbolic empty Pabst Beer can was rolled across the ring. The guys cheered more for the can than for the boxers. As it happened, there was such a crowd that there was precious little space remaining for the boxers in the boxing ring.

The boys, Frank and Jack, fought with hurricane speed, but were booed by a couple of die-hards for getting into a clinch or two. Nobody in the crowd wanted clinches, ever! The idea was to stand bravely, man-to-man, toe-to-toe, and slug it out till someone dropped, or ran, or the familiar drama studio gong sounded.

After round two came the official commercial sung by the Choir boys. Gillette could well have hired them on the spot, they were that good. Round three was the same as rounds one and two, a wild-swinging barroom brawl, with unbelievably rapid flurries which rarely landed effectively.

At the conclusion of this great bout, the combatants were played out, but good enough Lutherans to congratulate each other and politely acknowledge the cheers of the hysterical crowd. Since the winners were chosen by the crowd, there could be no doubt that this fight ended in a draw.

Boxer Del McCoy was a tough, relentless, plodding machine. No punch ever slowed him up. We told him to keep his guard up, but he was not one to follow instructions, so lots of punches got to him, but he never let on that they had any effect. Nobody beat Del, although T. "Rod" Peterson would like to have, and he tried hard. Rod later joined the Navy as a pilot and graduated some years later from 'Olaf. I wonder if John Strom could indeed have handled Rod?

We brought in a kid named Duane "Whitey" Brekken, a freshman, for an exhibition bout with his roommate, Al Lyng. It was a love feast, a waltz. They danced around and demonstrated various choreographed swings. It was terrible. We decided to sucker Whitey into a match with the much larger Bill Redman.

They went at it like the fight was for the world title. Both were very strong, but Whitey had Redman on speed. Even though Whitey clocked Redman a couple of good ones in the chops, Redman just shook them off, which made Whitey start to laugh. So Redman took the offensive but Whitey stood toe-to-toe with him, slugging and laughing.

Again, Pabst commercial authorities rolled an empty across the floor. Again, the Choir boys sang the Gillette ad to the delight of the thirsty crows. After the fight was over the jury mob had arrived at another draw.

The worst match pitted a rather roly-poly kid up against a tough kid from the Cities. It was a total mismatch, and Wendy claimed the fix was on. The roly-poly kid got whopped all over his body, and he went into a defensive stance covering his head and ears so he could absorb just about anything.

After three rounds, the tough kid had landed hundreds of punches. When the final gong came, the roly-poly kid straightened up as best he could and proudly proclaimed, "He only hit my back and shoulders! I'm all right!" Then his knees buckled and he decided to sit on the floor for a while.

It was generally thought that Jay Kinne had challenged Chuck Anonson, who outranked Kinne as a cadet in ROTC. Jay decided to straighten out Anonson and their fight was scheduled for the next Wednesday, but it was not to be, for the fights came to an abrupt end. Another grudge match was to be Wendy Miller vs. Marty Bunge. There was a suspicion in boxing circles that Marty was a head-butter, but the fight never materialized.

The only surviving photo of the boxing matches is found on page 223 of the 1954 Viking Annual. There we see Chet Mathison who refereed that evening. Boxing action shows two lightweights duking it out. From the caption: "...Rocky Braaten lands a right cross on the floating ribs of Kid Anderson."

Jim Braaten showed up to watch the fights and decided he would enjoy participating and so challenged Joel Anderson with a "Let's do it!" Jim did not tell Joel of his earlier boxing experience. It was a good fight and Jim, one of the five great boxers referred to above, was brought back for two more fights. The room was so overcrowded with fans that the boxers had to elbow their way through the crowd to get to the ring, which wasn't really a ring — merely a bit of floor space where boxers could "go at it."

Doc Pete's office was frequently filled with the walking wounded, more so on Thursday mornings. There were routine contusions, fat lips, a dislocated thumb, two injured noses and some concussions. Everybody lied, of course, about how they got banged up.

Analysis of the facts surrounding the events of 1954 reveal some interesting insights. First, in regard to the two concussions — they were not suffered in boxing matches. One guy leaned too far backward in his chair while sleeping in Political Science class and fell on his head.

Another slipped on the dance floor at the Dundas Dine and Dance (3-D) after the lights went out when the juke box was shoved out the emergency exit and shorted out the electrical system. A third concussion was reluctantly reported because of the bizarre circumstances surrounding the event.

A novice was ski jumping at night off the Pop Hill Slide when he "crashed and burned," hit by a ski on the noggin. One bloody nose supposedly happened when a guy got hit in the face by a snow ball while leaving the library. It was his first visit to the library.

Another broke his nose on a girl's head while diving into the swimming pool during a lights-out costume change at a Dolphin show. A tailbone injury purported to be the result of a knockdown while boxing was not true.

A guy fell asleep in Dr. Clausen's ancient history class and Clausen went back there, picked him up by his arms and slammed him back down in his desk chair without so much as a pause in his lecture on the Code of Hammurabi.

The worst injuries reported to Doc Pete were by a guy who claimed he was hit by an automobile in front of the Ole Store, when in reality he ran into the side of a parked car in the dark near the rear of the Corner Bar in Dundas while being chased after running off with a case of beer.

Doc Pete finally felt he could not keep up with the work load. He contacted the feared Dean of Men, Mark Almli. Together, they did a little checking around and found out about the fights. Almli gave as his reason for stopping the fights the risk of getting badly hurt on the hard tile floor, but most of us saw no risk at all.

What that cancellation did to ruin morale cannot be overstated. The bottom dropped out. We had going for us the premier sporting event of the century at 'Olaf. Heroes were made. The boys let off steam, bet lots of money, learned who not to cross or butt into the line ahead of in the cafeteria, or to cheat at cards. We had our heroes but no villains.

We lost the final showdown bout. Football star and Little All-American John Gustafson had been banned from the ring for fear he might kill someone. After young Whitey Brekken put on such a show, his brother Carol was very proud of his younger and smaller brother. He let it be known that he could handle his kid brother anytime, thus inadvertently setting himself up for a showdown to prove his stuff by taking on Gus.

Now that would have been a fight to remember! Too bad it did not come to pass. But some things at 'Olaf were just not meant to be, those amazing Wednesday night fights in the winter of 1954.

    Argo —

"Powah!"

Dear Donald,

It isn't often I get the impression that I have power. However, this evening's occurrence made me wonder just a little. Sitting in a chair in my living room watching TV, I reached for my thermos of coffee on the coffee table to my left. As I picked up the thermos, I banged it into a votive candle in a votive glass. The candle was burning.

Off the table it went and onto the carpet! When I looked to see the damage, there was none. The candle remained upright on the carpet and continued to burn. I picked it up, placed it back on the table and said aloud to myself, "Powah!"

This reminded me of one day about ten years ago when I left school with a hot cup of coffee for the road. Since both hands were full, I placed the cup of coffee on the roof of my car while I opened the car door. I got in the car and drove off, forgetting about the cup of coffee on the roof. It was a warm day, so I lowered the window.

When I got to the main intersection near school, 28th Avenue at 42nd Street, I saw some of my students standing on the corner waiting for a bus. As I stopped for the red light, one called out, "Hey, Kindem! Your coffee cooled off enough yet?" I nonchalantly reached out the window, grabbed the cup, called out "Thank you!" I took a sip and when the light changed, drove off. "Powah!"

In 1954, I was pole vaulting in a track meet against Carleton at St. Olaf's field on a windy day. I cleared the bar at eleven feet while vaulting into a strong head wind. My forward motion was such that I flew far into the pit. As I sat in the pit, I could see that the pole was perpendicular, but was about to follow me into the pit, and would have knocked off the crossbar.

However, the strong wind stopped the pole from its forward motion and there it stood — perpindiculaaaaar — for what seemed to be about five seconds. I cupped my hands to make a funnel and addressed the pole with a "Roogie-roogie!" followed by a "Whoosh!" The pole then fell back onto the runway. The

Carleton vaulters shook their heads in disbelief, confused. The year before I had defeated them following a choir concert and while still wearing a suit, white shirt and necktie. "Powah!"

Argo — March 27, 1996

Blabbermouth

Dear Donald,

An unexpected phone call this morning brought back some memories. I don't recall the man's name, except he had no first name, only a middle name and a last name.

The caller invited me to come over to his cafe one of these nights and regale the crowd with some funny stories about Northfield and "St. Olaf's." I told him I would think about it but really I won't. My blabbermouth days are over. Besides, my contract does not permit freelance appearances.

I used to partake in the so-called "Blabbermouth Night" at Lee & Eddy's Bar on 4th and Cedar, near Seven Corners back in 1959. There was no Lee, only Eddy, but he thought the bar would sound classier with two names. I didn't tell Eddy there was a famous bar on Broadway by the name of Lee & Eddy's. He may already have known that, since he was a North High grad, and those guys got around, I'll have you know.

Eddy tried to win me over as a potential speaker by treating me to some dried grasshopper munchies. They were OK right out of the can, but I never ordered them off the menu. I had come to listen to the Monday evening speeches, poetry and music. People used to do poetry in public back then. Sometimes it was good, but sometimes when the poet had too much beer, the banter was more like what you would hear at Mike & Al's in Dundas.

After the first night of listening, I figured I could do OK in that crowd. So the next Monday night after choir practice at Central Lutheran, I came prepared for some action. I brought a lemon, sliced in two, to deal with the lousy band. As soon as they started to play, I stood up directly before them and sucked on half a lemon, puckering and making faces from the bitter taste. In a second, the band members got all puckered up and had to quit playing, except for the drummer, who tried to continue until he was booed off the stage.

I then grabbed the microphone and started going after the four suits sitting in a booth who obviously were slumming and didn't belong in that place. I told them that the real beatniks all lived in Edina — they drove big cars, wore suits, had wives that only put out for the guy next door or the plumber. Because of large mortgages they were really more broke than they let on with their false fronts. I kept this up until they stormed out of the place in a huff. Everybody cheered, and I won the blabbermouth contest.

The first prize was five pitchers of beer. I was no dummy, so I said, "Gather 'round, good buddies, and have one on me!" This they did, and they liked me a lot. I knew right then that I was destined to become a sure winner in weeks to come whenever I spoke. I always shared my beer till it was gone.

One night, someone asked for a little Dylan Thomas, so I gave them "The Hunchback in the Park." There may not have been a dry eye in the place when I finished. The moment did not call for applause. Eddy came over with five pitchers of beer and after a while things got back to normal.

I had a following, to be sure. But after a few weeks of this blabbermouth routine, I got tired of it and did not return. It became difficult to determine whether the crowds liked me as much as they liked the free beer. So I said the heck with it and started going home Monday nights after choir practice instead of going to Lee & Eddy's.

There was another, more important reason why I did not hang out at Lee & Eddy's. I had a girlfriend. Her name was Nini. I "chased her around until she finally caught me." Nini had called me at my brother Ole's house and asked if I was that "su-weet thing" she met over at Donny and Linda's place in their Viking Court estate. I finally had to admit it, and she invited me over to her diggings in a south Minneapolis apartment that she shared with a gal from McGregor, Minnesota.

After a couple weeks of this, I knew we were in love and proposed marriage. She never hesitated an instant, so that was that. I knew I was a persuasive blabbermouth from my Lee & Eddy days, but this was different, for I was able to talk this babe into matrimony. I'm sure she probably had the whole thing mapped out anyway.

I'll have to ask her sometime — she's no blabbermouth.

Argo — April 10, 1996

Draw the Line

Dear Donald

Sometimes it becomes necessary to "draw the line" so I have taken to walking around with a roll of masking tape in my pocket. It's been three days now. But that is not the entire story.

I also have a roll of duct tape, a roll of scotch tape, a roll of electrical tape, some safety pins, and a quantity of rubber bands. My goal in filling full my pockets is fulfilled.

It all started in a logical way when I went to the wholesale house where I buy my gardening trousers. The pants of my dreams were hanging under a sign which read, "Cargo Pants - $17.00." Next to it was another sign, "Cargo Pants - $9.61."

They appealed to me because of all the pockets and especially because "Cargo" rhymes with "Argo." I chose the cheaper ones since they appeared to be the same as the others.

When I got to the checkout, $17.00 flashed on the screen. I did a "Hobo" with a firm, "Wait a minute. These pants are not $17.00, they are $9.61."

Well, the boyfriend of the cashier who was hanging around waiting for something useful to do to justify his presence, ran back to the pants department and returned with two pair — one for each price.

"What the heck is the difference?" I intoned, mimicking Hobo, my mentor in these matters — remember what you did at Cub Foods when you saw they were selling fish heads, fins and tails for $.89 a pound?

The clerk said, "You can see the cheaper ones are made in Singapore, the more expensive ones, in Arkansas."

After careful inspection, we discovered that the more expensive pants had a watch pocket. "Gimme the $17.00 pants," says I, "that watch pocket is worth at least $7.39 to me."

That threw them off a bit. They could see I wear a watch on my wrist and do not keep it in a watch pocket. I know that but I can fill the little pocket with quarters for the parking meters which no longer take nickels or dimes.

However, that's not the point. I now had real Argo-cargo pants to wear, with two extra pockets in front, a small jack knife pocket in the rear, zipper operated back pockets for preventing the loss of a handkerchief, and a small jack knife pocket, for a total of eight pockets — and cargo rhymes with Argo!

Imagine my joy at contemplating the prospects for success and happiness! You see, I have always gotten by with three of the four regular pants pockets. This man, Argo, is becoming a real operator.

Well I put on my new pants, didn't I? And I figured I couldn't very well walk around in cargo pants without some cargo, no. So I grabbed a roll of masking tape which was handy. Fine. But I was out of balance, so I put a roll of duct tape in the pocket on the other side. Now I was feeling good and my stride had a new spring in it.

So in the door walks my son, Tor. "You look happy, Pup, what's up?"

Being on a roll, I pulled out one, and flashed the duct tape. I told him I like to carry around duck tape.

He asked what I was going to use "duck" tape for. "I don't rightly know, says I, "Maybe I can tape up that decoy duck hanging by his neck out there by the bird bath.

"Why is he hanging there?" he asks. "I don't want him to hog up all the water in the bath," says I.

My son does a double take, then explains, "It isn't duck tape, Pup, it's duct tape — you know, like for wrapping furnace ducts and the like."

"Oh," I mumble and walk away, properly chastised. I have to let him win a few. He got me last week after I had proudly announced that I had a toilet that flushes blue, and he dismissed it with a "So do I."

Then it occurred to me that some jobs require neither type of tape, so I stuffed a roll each of scotch tape and electrical tape into the cargo pockets. Of course, some things require safety pins, not tape, to mend them.

And I never heard of someone hanging a picture with any kind of tape or with a safety pin, so I grabbed a tin of thumb tacks. I remember once using a stapler to hem my tuxedo pants, but I don't like to carry a stapler around, no. But I do take along fourteen rubber bands in my new Argo-cargo pants.

Down the basement stairs I go, straight over to the window by the back door which has a crack that was taped before we moved in 24 years ago. The tape is somewhat faded, but looks like it will hold another couple dozen years. (I learned that tactic from Gus).

Suddenly it dawns on me — I'm retired. I don't have to go around fixing, mending, repairing stuff if I don't feel like it. It's not as though I have a wife urging me on to greater heights. No, I just have to walk around, getting my money's worth out of these new Argo-cargo pants. I liked them so much after three days, I went and bought another pair. Now I have a tan pair and a green pair, real camo green.

The troublesome part came when I spilled chocolate ice cream all over my lap and had to change pants, moving money, keys, jack knives, tapes and all the rest to the new pair of cargo pants. I found this transfer process to be lots of fun, but very time consuming.

I began to think, as I sometimes do, and became partially inspired so I located a tackle box which I can easily use as a tool box and put all my cargo in that box. This can be placed near my bed, so that upon arising in the morning, I can pick up my tool box and walk around the house with that.

Now that part is easy. The difficult part is the decision I need to make concerning the cargo to carry in Argo-cargo pants. Should I transfer those items to my tool box and just carry that around the house?

Or should I add also carry pliers, hammer, screwdrivers (a "Phyllis" and a "regla"), tin snips and a few drill bits of varying size? I kinda like the tool box idea, but the little problems, such as how do I carry that around, plus a thermos and a cup of coffee, into the living room?

How do I open the back door with a bowl of dog food in hand, tool box in the other? Exactly. I'll have to keep setting it down, picking it up, or else spill a lot.

I am of the opinion, Donald, that you have wide experience in the wearing of cargo pants, and generally carrying lots of useful stuff in your pockets. This is why I consult you in this matter.

What should I do? Help me draw the line!

    Argo —

Day of Wine and Roses

Dear Donald,

In 1964, in a house on Lincoln Lane in Northfield, Rodney Swenson and I made 150 gallons of wine from apples we had picked at Hansen's orchard. You know the place. It was there that our friend Hans Hansen lived.

The apple varieties were Prairie Spy, Haralson, and Wolf River. We bottled up a quantity of wine in fifths and corked them. They are long gone. After testing one 30-gallon barrel at 4%, we decided that it was not wine and poured it down the floor drain. Of the remaining barrels of 9% apple wine, I laid down two Red Wing stone crock bottles, five gallons of wine in each.

The bottles have remained undisturbed since 1964. The beeswax and paraffin seals are intact; the bottles rest on their sides to keep the corks wet and to prevent contamination as well as leakage. They are in prime condition, and I have every reason to believe the wine is good.

I keep the bottles in the darkened well pump room, covered with gunny sacks. It is my intention to allow the wine to reach age 50, at least, which will occur in the year 2014. At that time, only one bottle will be opened. The other will be given to one of my children who will have to agree to allow it to age another 25 years at least.

At that time, when the bottle is opened in 2039, the first dram will be poured on Mother Earth — on my gravesite next to yours at Oaklawn in Northfield. In commemoration, a rose will be placed on the spot.

The second dram goes to Mother Earth on your gravesite. You get a rose too. We will have a good laugh, and our spirits will be at rest.

This day will be called the "Day of Wine and Roses."

    Argo — April 7, 1996

Down on the Farm

Dear Donald,

Now that you have gone federal, impulse shopping at places like CHAPS, Sally, and most importantly at garage sales, will be even more of a delightful possibility. You may have to charter one of the van lines to haul back to Portland some of the odds and ends to fill your bathtub again.

We often act on impulse, and that makes life more interesting and enjoyable. Take, for example, the old days in the thirties when my family would saddle up in whatever vehicle one of my brothers or Uncle Jacob happened to have and head on down the road, south toward Waseca where my mother had a couple of bachelor farmer cousins living with an unmarried sister.

The farm, as I recall, had a lot of things which bring back fond memories — free-ranging chickens, cows, hogs, a couple of dogs, many cats, horses, and of course a barn with a hay loft and a windmill in the yard. Climbing the windmill was what we could call an adventure.

Today, the windmill would be regarded as an "attractive nuisance" by OSHA and give rise to lawsuits should children climb and topple from the heights. I never heard of a kid falling off a windmill. The most common command I heard from anyone, anywhere, during my childhood years was, "Get down offa there!" It didn't matter to me — I liked climbing up on anything. Maybe that is why I became a pole vaulter and ski jumper. The challenge was the excitement, the prize, a cheap thrill.

It was in those days we had a German Shepherd dog named, "Fritz." From the time I was an infant dozing off to la-la-land in the happy sunshine of the 101 [Lincoln] Club, Fritz would diligently stand watch. More specifically, I suppose you could say he would lie down on the job. Fritz always rode along on our forays into the Waseca farm country until our next door neighbors, the Soviks, complained about his barking and we had to get rid of him. Fritz was always my protector, and any passerby on Lincoln Street who ventured a peek into my baby buggy would very quickly learn who was in charge of the "sitjiation."

On the way to Waseca, packed into whatever vehicle we had available at the time, the elements of impulse and intuition became apparent. Invariably, the driver would get lost on the dirt roads. And invariably, he would inquire of my mother, "Which way do we turn here?" She would reply either, "To the left," or "To the right." The driver would invariably turn the opposite direction and we invariably would arrive at the Johnsons' farm near Waseca.

It got to be a family joke: "Ask mamma, then turn the opposite direction from what she suggests." At the Johnson's, we met up with other relatives from town, the Sybilruds. One of them was later to become Captain of Waseca's state championship basketball team. They couldn't lose, having two 6'-5" players, the legendary Hambone Papke and Shyde Krause. No other team in the state had guys that tall.

We always played a lot, climbing the windmill, up into the haymow in the barn, and up the silo ladder. We slopped the hogs and scattered corn for the chickens. We used the three-tined pitchfork to throw hay down the trapdoor to the cows in their stanchions. Sometimes they got silage, too, but if it was too green, unfermented, the cows would go ahead with their projectile shots, spraying the whitewashed walls with liquid cow pies. We got a big charge out of that.

The big meal of the trip was always a triumph of Minnesota's best farm food. We usually had a couple of chickens which we butchered and plucked that day. The system used was this — first, catch the chickens. This could be difficult, but if you would do a quick feint to the left, then lunge to the right, you might catch one.

However, the best way was to use the six-foot iron rod with a hook on the end to snag their legs. What followed next was the execution. You held the chicken's head on the top of the chopping stump. If you wanted a neat job, you had to hypnotize the bird by stretching a length of grocery string from the beak across the stump. The bird would stare fixedly at the string and remain immobile.

Then the rest was fairly straightforward — a swift chop, then quickly jump back so you wouldn't get sprayed with blood as the chicken would run around like a chicken with its head cut off. I learned that technique from Hans' mom, Mrs. Hansen, out on Greenvale.

We also had plenty of fried pork chops. There was nothing better. By the way, on one of these trips mamma showed me the procedure for collecting pig blood for making blood sausage. Someone else always stuck the pig, often shooting it in the head with a .22 first. Then, working quickly, you had to hold a five gallon pail to catch the blood which gushed out. A couple handfuls of salt were stirred into the liquid to prevent coagulation. After about five minutes of stirring, it was ready to be poured off into gallon pails for further use in making blood sausage.

I never really enjoyed the blood-letting, but sure did like the finished sausage which we made in five pound cloth sugar sacks, adding diced chunks of beef belly fat (suet) to the mixture before filling the bags and quickly dropping them into a kettle of boiling water. Finished sausage, sliced a half inch thick and fried in butter was the best breakfast I knew. Everyone in the family was of the same opinion.

After a big feast prepared by womenfolk who all knew how to get around the kitchen, the men would go have a smoke and talk about grownup stuff. The women would clean up after dinner and the kids would run around the farm yard, playing on farm machinery, looking for rats in the corn crib.

And we all took turns cranking the ice cream maker. It was a four-gallon wood pail with a tin cylinder inside that contained thick cream and other ingredients. This cylinder was packed in chunks of ice surrounding it. The ice chunks came from a shed full of lake ice packed in sawdust. Salt was strewn over the top of the ice chunks in the churn, which was rotated by a crank that would spin the cylinder around, freezing the ice cream.

In those days, you couldn't have a meal without pie for dessert. One of the ladies made the best pie in the county. It was really something to behold, with fine small indentations around the edge which we would count. You could tell how big a piece of pie you got by the number of indentations: a large piece had at least two sets of indentations, a total of twelve.

One time I had occasion to come into the farmhouse to see if I could filch a snack in the kitchen. The pie lady was at work, and I saw how she got those neat little indentations around the edge of the crust.

She pulled out her false teeth and stamped the impressions in the dough all around the outer edge of the pie — that's life down on the farm.

       Argo — October 6, 1997

Duck Soup

Dear Donald,

My duck decoy is frozen in the bird bath. You have a photo I sent some time ago showing him (or her) cavorting in the puddle, so happy to be released from the leash I had around his (or her) neck.

Apparently the duck fell asleep during the night. We had a minus twenty wind chill, and I knew something was wrong this morning just before sunrise when I went to the living room windows to practice spotting deer. The duck was facing north in the midst of a combination of rain, sleet, and snow storm, and at a time when ducks normally face south. The duck did not respond to my duck call. None of them does.

A number of things crossed my mind when I discovered this dilemma. My first thought was that our duck had suffered a nervous breakdown waiting for the sky to fall so it could run and tell the king, but there was no turkey-lurkey in the neighborhood to pass on the report in the chain of command. I have been rather rigid in my requirements that my household staff and pets go through proper channels.

After ruling out the insanity diagnosis as being a bit premature, I had a fleeting thought that ducky lucky was merely steeling himself (or herself) against the snow and cold, preparatory to spending the winter here instead of Coral Gables. But then, after a half hour observation during which he (or she) did not move, I decided to look closer.

The duck, whom we shall call Beverly, since that name is commonly used in England for both male and female children, (at least until the males are about thirteen), had apparently fallen into a careless habit again, that of allowing a chunk of concrete to rest upon one of his webbed feet for ballast. I had advised against this practice earlier, but to no avail. Now what?

I made a passing reference, earlier, to practicing the spotting of deer. Therefore, early in the morning before dawn, I take up my position at my sit, not my stand, in a Lazy Boy recliner facing the woods, pipe and coffee at the ready, but no firearms, no. There is a deer path down the hill about 150 feet from my living room.

Each morning, early, five or six does and fawns pass by, followed a short while later by a great big buck. My practice sessions should help me up north this weekend, for I now can state without equivocation that my skill in picking up silhouettes and movements has improved considerably. Now all I need to do is figure out how to get my recliner up north and positioned in the woods along a deer path.

(Time out while I go outside to chip the ice away and free Beverly. I'll be right back!)

Back again. Well I did it, Donald — I mean I really screwed up. In the process of chipping away the ice, I chipped away Beverly's privates. Bev was a male. Now we have a eunuch or castrade, whatever you want to call it. I think he is either dead or dormant. Probably better off dead, since his brassy "quack-quack!" would now sound more like a mourning dove, which is exactly what happens when male ducks lose their private parts.

I am also withdrawing the name Beverly. You're not supposed to eat what you have named. Ever hear of someone eating a cat? I had a little kitty once and I gave her a bath. It took nearly an hour to get the fur out of my teeth, but that's another story.

At any rate, my plan is to make use of the duck before it sours. I know what — I'll make a nice pot of your favorite Peking duck soup!

    Argo —

Experts

Dear Donald,

An expert oftentimes becomes known as one because of his ability to convince others that the confusion is theirs. On occasion, we have found meaning and revelry by pulling someone's leg, jerking their chain, putting them on, and generally doing whatever is necessary to keep them just a little off balance. We were often good at that, as experts.

One Friday at Roosevelt High School, I furnished my friend, colleague and cohort, Fred Lundquist, with about 30 Latin expressions, none of which was ecclesiastical or church related Latin that common folks would quickly recognize. I asked Fred to take a corner chair in the second floor sassy lounge. I, in turn, would enter about 30 seconds later and sit in the opposite corner. Each of us would have the Star-Tribune spread out so our faces would be hidden. We had concealed, inside the paper, lists of Latin expressions.

I began somewhat arrogantly by announcing to the world in general, and specifically to the lackluster ladies who knit in the lounge, than an educated man is by definition one who knows another language. No response, of course — they always feared a trap when I started a conversation. So I looked over the top of my paper at Fred and said, rather loudly, "Frederico: Sic transit Gloria mundi." He turned down a corner of his paper, looked at me and responded, "Repetitio est mater studiorum."

The room fell silent. People were wondering if they heard what they were not sure they heard. I launched into the body of my report, "Ab usus non tollit usum!" to which he responded, turning a page in the paper, "Exceptio probat regulum de rebus non exceptis." I leaned forward and smiled as I pointed index finger skyward and exclaimed, "Forsan et haec olim meminisse juvabit!"

Fred and I were on a roll. They were at our feet. This banter went on for about four minutes, during which time we covered about 25 expressions each, and no one even thought of interrupting this Latinized intellectual discourse. Finally, I tapped out my pipe, he his, we stood and folded our papers. I nodded to him, "Exit, Homo?" To which he responded, "Exit."

We got about 25 feet down the corridor before the shrieks rang out. Fred and I paused briefly to listen. "What the heck was that?" and, "It sounded like Latin." We chuckled and went to our rooms. The experts pulled off another one.

    Argo —

Follow the Leader

Dear Donald,

Ordinarily I discuss musical matters with you that encompass "Songs of the West" and things such as show tunes. How the memory is jogged by familiar songs! It was you who introduced me to Norman Luboff's "Songs of the West." Your family had something to my liking that I found at only one other place, Marie's, and that was a nice phonograph. We never had one at our home. Now I know how Gus must feel.

Remember how we would play the favorites like "I Ride an Old Paint," and "Colorado Trail," and "Bury Me Not on the Lone Prairie" (I prefer Oaklawn, thank you), and the other tunes which stand the test, not only of time, but by any standard anyone could apply. The Norman Luboff Choir could sing these songs as no one else in the world. Listening to them transported us out among the Buckaroos, the tumbleweed, towns like Laredo, places and times when men were manly and often carried their manliness on their hip in a holster.

I still delight in "cowboy food" which you also enjoy — the beef stew with lots of stuff in it, and gravy that wants to be sopped up off the plate with a crust of bread. I'm going to have a nostalgic dinner party, alone with my stew, and the music will be "Songs of the West." And I will say a prayer that only God will hear about this feast, and God, too, will be pleased. For it pleaseth me to please Him and give thanks for these blessings and the simple truth — good music goes well with good food; and as Hobo said, "Hunger is the best sauce."

Speaking of sauce, I phoned the public music station I listen to at 4:00 daily, avoiding WCAL's NPR program, "All Things Considered." I like news, but I don't want that much at a time. I explained to the person answering the phone that I like to cook, and I had just caught the tail end of a blurb about calling such and such a number to get the "Public Music Sauce."

He responded, confused and apologetic that I was confused. His lame explanation was that the announcer, Stephanie Wendt, was from Australia, and she was plugging the purchase of music from the "Public Music Source." Oh well, let it pass, let it pass. Again,

I digress.

These Luboff guys had a nice bass section which is a necessity with such music. They were by and large the same crew that Roger Wagner and Robert Shaw had. There weren't that many basses around in Los Angeles (it is no Minneapolis) where most recordings were done. They would "close mike" the bass for emphasis.

Once, during a recording session with the St. Olaf Choir, I called out to the recording technician, "Move that mike up here by the bass section. We'll give some good low notes." Olaf intervened, "You guys don't need any help back there." We applauded that compliment. He liked us basses a lot, for he knew very well what a strong foundation can do for a choir. No other section came close to our "esprit de corps."

From time to time I turn on the music box and listen to favorites. It is no longer necessary to go out to the garage to listen, for I found the volume dial after a couple months, and I conduct. Argo enjoys conducting the choir or the orchestra, particularly the St. Olaf Choir or Robert Shaw's Festival Singers singing Rachmaninoff's "Vespers." I keep a stiff upper lip much as Olaf did, tilting my head to the side, pretending to hear a note that doesn't belong. Olaf never shed a tear in our presence but that doesn't prevent me from doing so, for I learned that one on my own.

I took the choral conducting class from Olaf. I learned a lot about conducting from him; he was a genius at conducting, that's for sure. He taught that rhythm is the pillar of musical expression, and when I led the class in an anthem or the Ole Choir bass section, I can gar-awn-tee you there was a beat-a pulse, if required, that kept the music on track.

As to orchestral conducting, I learned from Dmitri Mitropoulous, former Greek acrobat with the Minneapolis Symphony Orchestra which played once a year in the St. Olaf gymnasium. I also took lessons from Leonard Bernstein, who taught how to clasp hands around the baton, seemingly in prayer, to persuade the orchestra to feel deeply what they were playing with such emotion and beauty. I think I have the emotional traits of a conductor, sometimes.

Truly, I find myself calling out to the brass on a crescendo, and cheer loudly with a "NOW!" as I urge the orchestra on to heights they only dreamed of before I took the podium. Why only today, with Elgar's "Enigma Variations," we let it all out in the "Jaeger" (Hunter) variation. This crescendo is arguably the finest in 20th century music, and I worked the orchestra yesterday; yes, I drove them hard.

But no matter how I tried to get around the Montreal Symphony's ritardando in the final two measures near the climax, they wouldn't move with me. Sometimes they just won't follow the leader.

  Argo —

Frozen Rain

Dear Donald,

It was three years ago that I went to the largest funeral St. John's church ever had. I barely got a space on the stairs in the balcony. The deceased, an old friend and St. Olaf Choir bass, Don MacRae, died of a heart attack while attempting to free up his garage door which had frozen shut after a freezing rain.

The same frozen rain that day stuck my garage door shut. I took a gallon of anti-freeze and poured it all along the rubber base of the garage door, waited three minutes and hit the button. It opened. Maybe Don didn't think of that. Perhaps he was ready for such an event to help take him away from this life.

Well, that was the end of him, but not his memory. People loved him and said fine things about him at his funeral. Everyone was there. I remember him as a 25 year old Marine Corps veteran who came to 'Olaf with a very mature and heavy bass voice. Solid. He sang lots of barbershop quartette gigs and was the voice over the loudspeaker at the Jesse James Bank Raid events. The downtown guys liked him a lot.

He lay in the coffin in front of the church, his pipe in his hands. The funeral director, Benson, went for a pouch of Half & Half, his favorite brand, but Don's wife thought better of it. His grandchildren played tag around the pews after the service, not fully aware of what happened to their grandpa.

I walked around the church for some time after the service, seeing ghosts. There was Eddie Tripp in the can under the stairs. I sang at his father's funeral in 1956. Hans Hansen was there too. I saw my confirmation class lined up in the center aisle during public examination on Luther's Catechism. It was then that Bobby Seitz fainted, falling right on his face. None of us dared to pick him up, so his father did. They passed him anyway, I guess.

I went up to the balcony where I used to ring the bell before and after the services when I served as janitor my senior year at NHS, replacing Old Tendall who taught me how to ring the bell. The extra rope was there that he installed for the slow ding...ding...ding which I rang at the end of the service and at the end of funerals. I usually got $5.00 extra for funerals and sometimes $10.00 extra for cleanup after weddings. It depended on the generosity of Mr. Anderson, father of Fat Phil, or else the father of the bride.

Mr. Cassler, the organist, was a kick. I remember the time he played a beautiful fugue on the organ at the end of a service. Fred Schmidt was laughing and the rest of the choir caught on. I knew what the tune was — it sounded like Bach, but in reality, it was "Three Blind Mice" as a fugue with all sorts of runs and flourishes. They don't make them like G. Winston Cassler anymore. I also saw Boral Biorn and Marie today. The last time I saw both was this fall when he was laid out and later buried about 30 feet from Ingvald and Anna. Another ghost.

This night, during the freezing rain, I went out and raised the garage door up about six inches and left it there. I don't intend to get myself into a hassle tomorrow morning with a garage door frozen shut.

Experience is a good teacher. When we are young, we think that intelligence is a substitute for experience. Then, when we get old, we think experience is a substitute for intelligence. What we know from Will Rogers is, "Good judgment comes from experience, and a lot of that comes from bad judgment."

Well, Hobo, that's the way it is — beware the frozen rain.

Argo —

More Ghosts

Dear Donald,

In my house there are many ghosts. I do not, however, confer with them on a regular basis. Which is not to say they are not present or that I am not aware of their presence.

I was reminded of my propensity for sensing ghosts yesterday as I passed through St. John's Church while paying my respects to my departed friend, Don McRae. As I walked through the basement, there was "Kindy" cooking egg coffee with the other ladies who aid with funerals, weddings and the like.

In the room labeled "MEN" I saw the boys. You were there, and Eddie and Hans. It was a meeting of boys who laugh. As I walked up the stairs to the main floor, I thought of the many thousands who have walked here, and I remembered a few with fondness.

In the balcony, I saw the new organ but remembered the old, with G. Winston Cassler at the manuals, smiling and pleasant. Fred Schmidt stood before the choir he started in 1950 when the St. Olaf Choir moved to the campus at the time the student congregation was begun. Marie was in the front row.

I looked for the two bell ropes, one for continuous ringing, the other with a loop braided at the end for the individual gongs to signal the end of the service. A woman custodian had the rope in hand to perform her offices, but I saw the ghost of white-haired Old Tendall who cautioned me to resist the temptation to seize the main bell rope and make like Quasimodo again.

I wondered why there was a huge knot in the end. Is it possible the rope could get away again, possibly to slip up through the small round hole and into the belfry? I asked the woman if she ever was carried aloft by the rope. She told me she had not, but that her son had. "Good boy," I said.

Looking toward the altar I saw the ghost of Bernt J. Muus who founded the St. John's congregation about the time he founded St. Olaf's School. Then came Lawrence M. Stavig, who baptized me in the Norwegian language, of course.

There was Arne Nelson, who confirmed me (Ingvald said, "conformed"), followed by Boral Biorn and his assistant, Ivar

Ramseth. It was Ramseth, you recall, who was shown the door by Mrs. Leivestad who preferred to see "the head man."

The stained glass above the altar has lost its angel pointing skyward by the stone rolled away from the tomb of Jesus. It has been replaced by something red in color.

My confirmation class stood at attention under duress and great stress, one by each pew, waiting for the impossible questions which made even Bobby Seitz faint dead away. Kendall Paulson was there, Dick Jacobson, Donna Mae Reynolds, Alice Jean Olberg, Dean Tollefson, and other ghosts whose forms I could not distinguish.

My brother Roald's wedding was going on. I stood there as best man while my nervous brother hummed aloud, six notes off, the medley of hymns for the processional. My family all signaled me to get him to "shush" but I was having too much fun enjoying his show to interfere. I was adequate as best man.

I needed more time, Donald, more time to remember faces and events in that wonderful edifice which has been silent witness to so many confirmations and baptisms, weddings and funerals. Lots of young children were running around playing, not fully understanding that coming together at that time and in that place was because their grandpa lay there in the open coffin with a pipe in his folded hands.

It was here I first heard the St. Olaf Choir sing one Sunday. They sang in German, "Die Mit Tränen Säen," (Those Who Sew With Tears) and life for me took a turn down a path which has brought many changes for the good. In the Sunday School area of the parish house I saw my eighth grade teacher whose maiden name was McCornack, but was now Forsythe.

The place was not as ghostly as the old wood frame parish house, now gone, which stood where the North parking lot is now situated. That place had proper stairs of well-worn wood that made lots of noise as we thumped up and down, always going somewhere, but never anywhere. We didn't sit patiently and studiously in those days. We were coiled springs waiting for the bell to ring. No kid I ever knew took those stairs one at a time.

Lacking the time for more ghostly visitations, I returned home to more familiar haunts. On the piano and the wall behind the piano we see a number of noteworthy items — the Old Main, an Olympic poster, a St. Olaf Choir poster, ceramics by Nina, precious photos, other memorabilia and some of your non-memorabilia.

Next to a photo of my only granddaughter stands a trophy awarded to you and which I proudly display. The plate reads: "1981 MAC Peacekeeper Challenge Runner Up Team Member."

Over toward the fireplace, past the Hobo stereo I use as a "decoy" in the event we have a quick in and out burglary by kids, we find the china cabinet. Prominently displayed atop the cabinet we find a large wooden plaque with a wooden helmet. On the plate we read from your fadduh: "Presented to Donald M. Clark, Master Builder, 50th Anniversary, 1935 - 1985." Hoz said you received another one in Washington, DC for building The Pentagon subway.

Now I suppose, Donald, I could just as well display my awards in place of yours. But this I cannot do, no. Your awards deserve viewing by those who pass through my house, for it is my friend I honor.

Naturally, members of my family know who the heroes are. And if strangers inquire, they will be told. They will be told that I salute my friend, Donald, and I salute him smartly, for such he deserves.

So it is, with a quick glance to the left while coming or going between the kitchen and my room or the bathroom, I see a reminder of awards given you by others. The one is because of merit, the other, an expression of love from your father.

Their placement in my home is a reminder to me of ghosts that entertain, edify, spread joy and friendship and loyalty. These are friendly ghosts, reminders of my friend Donald.

    Lars —

Gifts

Dear Donald,

During the MIAC track meet held at St. Olaf last May, I took up a position alongside the college pastor who was standing near the curve on the West end of the track, the final turn, as it were. It was a strategic location. As each Ole runner passed before us, I shouted: "Encouragement! Encouragement! Words of encouragement! Words of encouragement!" The Reverend Benson smiled but did not join the incantations even though he doubtless recognized the value of such demonstrations of support.

Although no longer active in athletics, I still consider myself an athletic supporter. Arlen Erdahl, former congressman, Secretary of State, and Ole track man who has a son named Lars, revels in the memories we share each time we meet about the old days when he was a lonely distance runner. I was his personal cheerleader sent by God to encourage him, for he needed all the help he could get. Arlen would run the 880, mile, and two-mile on any given day, often winning one or all of these races.

What was his secret? To hear Arlen tell it, or have me tell it to his children, it goes like this. I was usually idling in the vicinity of the pole vault pit, often nursing hurts suffered by falling from a great height and landing hard on four inches of sand. As Arlen approached the curve, carrying the mail in his hand, I would stand by the curb and shout encouraging words to him in Norwegian: "Full fart i svingen!" (full speed on the curve) and "No mao du skunda deg!" (you better hurry up now). Arlen always raised his arm, fist clenched, in a return salute. He would smile broadly and turn up the tempo, leaving others behind. Always.

Arlen has never forgotten the words of encouragement that helped him along. He was doubly grateful that they were shouted in the Norwegian dialect of his forebears who came from Nordfjord, not far from Voss where Ingvald was born. I knew my words gave him a lift. It was our secret weapon. Ade never knew. Ade didn't have any arrows in his quiver for track and field coaching. No one coached me during my four seasons. My personal coaching formula was this — your first opponent is yourself; your next the environment; the third and last your competition.

As things have come to pass, I remember only two of my collegiate track performances. You know the first, when I won the pole vault event against Carleton and Macalester by jumping eleven feet in a white shirt, suit and tie. My encouragement came from Wendy Miller and company who shouted vociferous, strident, clamorous and blatantly partisan yelps of encouragement. I couldn't lose with all that support.

The second performance was more subdued. The only spectator was my father who happened by on his way home from Thorson Hall where he was the janitor. I was so glad to see him, for he had only seen me once before in an athletic contest — a football game in high school. No one could hold me back that night after I saw pappa and mamma in the crowd.

Pappa stood there in his green work clothes and sized up the situation just like a coach. He then gave the same advice he gave on all occasions, "Yust take your time." I did, for I knew I had better not miss.

There was no one in the world I would rather have seen at that time than my father. His simple presence was all the encouragement I needed. Then I said to him, "Watch this, pappa!" He did. I cleared the bar at twelve feet by such a great margin it was a giggle. It was over and I had won. In truth, I suppose it could be said that we had won.

There are times when you can go over the top with the support and encouragement of others. Some days it helps you get out of bed, put on your shoes and face the day when without encouragement you just don't feel that it is worthwhile. It has to do with motivation — what makes us do what we do.

Why do we seek the company of those who give us positive feedback? Why do we support those whose thinking is on the same frequency as ours? What moves people to go out and do things that are commendable and worthy?

More often than not, it is a kind word from someone. My father said it all in one sentence that gave meaning to my entire life. He waited until he was ninety-eight to tell me, but this is what he said, "Lars, you have gifts."

And so it is with you, Donald. You have gifts. Not only your personal gifts of good humor, loyalty, generosity and many talents. You give your friendship. You will recall that you and I, last June, visited our mutual friend, Inez Frayseth, in the Northfield

Retirement Center. I was there yesterday with some Christmas cookies I baked for Inez and her friends. When I told her I was going to visit you in Portland after Christmas, she went to her desk and pulled out a newsletter published by the Retirement Center.

Inez was featured in a biographical sketch which reads, in part, "Inez graduated from St. Olaf College in 1935 with a teaching degree in English and Latin. She spent the next 40 years guiding many students through their college years by working nine years in the Treasurer's office and thirty-one years as the Registrar at St. Olaf. Many students told Inez that they would never have made it through their four years at St. Olaf without her advice and support.

A perfect example of her great concern and care for the students was when she asked a student, who was somewhat of a rascal, to refinish the stock and forearm of her favorite .22 rifle. This student stopped at the Retirement Center this last year to let her know how much he appreciated what she did for him at a time in his life when he needed encouragement."

Aye, Donald, but here's the rub: Inez told me it was remembering her during your visit in June that was so important to her. The fact that you considered her effort worthy of remembrance in the gun stock episode made a lasting impression on her. It is safe to say you and Inez are fast friends for life.

Your kind words of encouragement made all the difference. That's a good thing to remember this Christmas season.

You have gifts to give that are worth more than gifts of silver and gold.

    Argo— December 19, 1996

Gunfight at the OK Corral

Dear Donald,

On this date we commemorate the Gunfight at the OK Corral which took place in 1881 on the afternoon of the 26th of October. You are familiar with the principals in this most famous shootout — the three Earp brothers, Doc Holliday and the Clanton-McLaury cowboy faction.

The gunfight lasted about 30 seconds — the Northfield bank robbery in 1876 took seven minutes. When the Earp shooting stopped, three of the Clanton-McLaury party were dead, and Virgil and Morgan Earp were seriously wounded. Bad blood had been brewing for some time between the Earps and the cowboys. Virgil Earp was the town marshal and Wyatt had his eye on the post of county sheriff, then held by John Behan.

The brothers Ike and Billy Clanton and Tom and Frank McLaury (sometimes spelled McLowery or McLawry) were known as cattle rustlers. The feud between the two factions reached its climax at about two o'clock in the afternoon, the approximate time of this writing while waiting for a new bread to rise that I created for the fishing trip up north, — my new "Log House Bread."

According to notes I made in the basement of the US Supreme Court Marshals' display in 1991, the gunfight did not occur in the OK Corral, but in the alley leading from the corral and on Fremont Street. This report is based on the pencil sketch done by Wyatt Earp who diagrammed the locale. The map he made of the scene was in the display case. The Earps and Holliday marched along Fremont Street toward the gathering of the Clanton and McLaury brothers and their drinking buddy, Billy Claibourne.

Intent on a showdown, Virgil Earp had taken the precaution of deputizing his brothers and Holliday. Sheriff Behan tried to stop the fight but was brushed aside by the Earps who told him to get out of there if he knew what was good for him. Doc Holliday punctuated the order by placing his hand on one of the two revolvers he always carried. Behan probably knew that the former dentist had drilled more torsos than teeth, sixteen by that time.

So the "shef" got the heck out of there. Eyewitness accounts of the fight differ in many ways, including the most famous version put out by Hollywood and starring Kirk Douglas as Holliday and Burt Lancaster as Wyatt Earp. All that is certain is that both sides opened fire at close range and that the McLaury brothers and Billy Clanton were shot dead.

Virgil Earp was wounded in the leg and Morgan in the shoulder. Holliday suffered a slight wound and Wyatt emerged unscathed. Ike Clanton and Billy Claibourne ran away from the fight at the start.

Some said that the Earps opened fire without just cause. Others claim that the lawmen were defending themselves. Wyatt Earp and Doc Holliday were arrested on murder warrants made out by Sheriff Behan and Ike Clanton.

At the conclusion of the preliminary hearing in Tombstone, Judge Spicer absolved the defendants of all blame and discharged them. "They had," said Spicer, "been fully justified in committing these homicides; that it was a necessary act done in the discharge of official duty."

Further note: Doc Holliday had an affair in 1877 with a prostitute named Kate "Big Nose" Elder. You recall the name was incorrectly used in a John Wayne horse opera called, "The Sons of Katie Elder."

Doc and Wyatt were firm friends, like Hobo and Argo. Wyatt once said of Doc: "He was the nerviest, speediest and deadliest man with a six gun I ever knew." Compare that with what Argo once said about Hobo: "He could shoot fastern a frog can lick flies."

From: Doc Holliday by J.M. Myers (London, 1957); The Earps of Tombstone by D.D. Martin (Tombstone, 1959); It All Happened in Tombstone by J.P. Clum (Flagstaff, 1965); "Personal Notes" from the Supreme Court U.S. Marshals' display (Argo, 1991).

Argo —

Hershey Bars

Dear Donald,

It is unalterably the province of the farmer, the gardener, indeed, the landowner, to establish to his own satisfaction prerogatives pertaining to a priori threats to his stables, his creatures, his crops, his stores, his structures and his kinfolk which he determines to be inimical to their health, well-being, prosperity, safety and quiet enjoyment of the premises. There are a number of firewalls and stratagems used by the enterprising and vigilant tactician toward these ends, such as Hershey bars.

Marauding insects which seek to invade and defoliate and infest need to be hindered in their nefarious purpose. To do this, we combined our talents to manufacture attractant devices which entrap the unsuspecting eight-leggers on yellow sticky plaques, four of which are suspended in each fruit tree, resembling giant pheromones. In addition, Tanglefoot-coated red spheres are strategically placed to monitor insect activity. Various sprays to manage certain insects and fungi are applied in an efficient, not willy-nilly pattern.

Creatures of the day, the tree rat and his striped cousin, the ground squirrel, are trapped and destroyed. Tails are chopped off, and saved for recycling as fishing lures. The moles are trapped, skinned, and their cured hides are painted and used to make ersatz Indian totems and charms to be sold at flea markets throughout Dakota County.

Creatures of the night, raccoons (known as "'coons" in the suburbs) are trapped, or sometimes treed by faithful watchdog Argo who retains a propriety interest in the property as long as he wants to be fed on a daily basis. The 'coons are then shot.

There have been instances of furious battles between dog Argo and wounded 'coons which thus far have resulted in slight wounds to Argo and death, usually by lead poisoning, of the 'coons. Some 'coons have been unable to swim the Minnesota River while in a cage tethered and thrown far into the deep.

An undeniable fact is that additional creatures of the night, the skunks, whose odors are an annoyance, have made certain incursions onto the property recently. Two of these polecats have been trapped while stealing peanut butter sandwiches intended for the 'coons, drowned in an adventure that must be characterized as one fraught with great risk.

The total population of skunks in the neighborhood is unknown. They are extremely difficult to count at night, appearing as they do at various places and at unpredictable times. Shooting them is problematic, for their eyes do not reflect the flashlight beam as do the 'coon critters and wild cats. In addition, the older bucks will spray, given half the chance, and sometimes just for the heck of it.

Which brings us to the plan of attack to get him, her or it, with Hershey bars. To this end, I have purchased a quantity of large, 7-ounce female Hershey chocolate bars at $1.49 each in order to test my theory which posits these assumptions: (1) The skunk is attracted to the aroma of chocolate just as he, she or it is attracted to peanut butter. (2) The skunk will eat its fill of chocolate because of its high fat content and besides, it tastes good. (3) Just as the canine cannot tolerate the ingestion of a large quantity of chocolate, the skunk, likewise, will eat, then go somewhere else and die.

Preliminary estimates indicate that a typical large Hershey chocolate bar selling for $1.49 weighs seven ounces. The average skunk in my yard weighs between 14 and 21 ounces, meaning the skunk will eat variously, a third to a half its own body weight in chocolate.

I ask, how would you feel, Donald, if you ate at one sitting between 60 and 90 pounds of chocolate? And you may respond, but what causes death?

I say probably the caffeine, silly, but how should I know if it was the Hershey bar?

    Argo — Aug. 29, 1995

Humility

Burnsville, Monday, Nov. 26 or 27, 1995

Dear Donald,

I want to talk to you about humility and the struggle it entails. By the time you get to be my age, you will have had ample opportunity to learn a lot about the subject. For once this year, I remember the day of the week even though I have not been able to agree with myself as to the date. Today I know the day because a "post it" note on the kitchen table informs that tomorrow is Tuesday.

That means I have a dental appointment at eleven bells. Say farewell to Argo, dear old friend. They mean to do me in, says I. I skipped my last appointment for cleaning, and that cost them a bundle. They don't forget, no. Whenever I sit in the dentist's chair, I lose all sense of bravado, humor and equilibrium. I am the ultimate picture of humility. One cannot, for example, charm with witticisms or sage commentary, for one's mouth is open and someone's hands and tools are in there wreaking havoc.

They always ask a question when you can't possibly answer them. They do that on purpose, to be sure. It's a power play. I have discovered that the most ominous sound in the world is the long, low hum of the dental assistant when she looks into my mouth. But the gal at the front desk, the receptionist, is always very sweet and cheerful. She doesn't make me feel humble, no. She doesn't hate me. But the other one in the back room, look out! I address her as "the cleaning lady" much to her consternation.

This feeble attempt at humor is usually a mistake because she has at her disposal for the next hour or so the means by which to get even. Perhaps this woman chose the wrong career. She could have been a warden at Sing Sing or in another era run a torture chamber for the Gestapo. This woman could make a midget grow tall or a tall man shrink while she digs around in the mouth. She teaches humility to one and all.

But I had earned a dose of that a half century ago. Dr. Aamodt, our neighbor, was of the opinion that a molar in the back of my ten-year-old mouth was crowding the others out of alignment. I didn't concur, but did not want that tooth to grow sideways, straight out of the side of my cheek as my brother, Roald, told me it would. So they agreed I was to have a tooth pulled. Dr. Aamodt assured me I would be asleep and not feel a thing. I did not, of course, believe him.

I knew right off that something was radically wrong when they strapped my arms down and put another strap across my chest. I was in the electric chair and I knew it. Matters got worse when he said to my mom, "Anna, you can sit out in the waiting room. Close the door." Now why close the door, I wondered, getting more and more scared. Then he opened the valve on a tank of laughing gas and sneaked up on me and held a mask over my face, covering my nose and mouth. I shook it off once and bit his hand, but he was persistent.

He said, "Breath deep, Lars," but I held my breath after getting a whiff of that God-awful gas for as long as I could. I was about to explode and had to gasp. That was a big mistake, for soon my head was spinning like yours was that night at the ski resort in Wisconsin ten years later. He tried to smooth-talk me and I could hear him counting. He got all the way to 25, but then lost count when I delivered a kick to his instrument tray. He picked up his tools, rinsed them off in the sink, and counted some more.

The Doc was ready, I knew I was not. But I could only talk like Woody Woodpecker, which alarmed me more. Now I knew I was a goner for sure. He said, "Gap opp!" which is Norwegian for "Open your yap."

Now why would he say that if he thought I was out? He had a tool that looked to me like a small tin snips, about the size of a pair of pliers. When he yanked that tooth out after a monumental struggle, I felt it, real bad. He held it up and said, "I got the whole thing, all right." He didn't notice I was choking on blood running down my throat.

Ma soon came in to comfort me. I lay down on a couch with a thing like a tampax in my mouth, my head resting on ma's lap. She gently rubbed her hand over my face again and again, and did her best to comfort me.

After about a half hour, we left the office. On the way home in a 777 taxi, since we had no car, my mother said, "Lars, I didn't know you knew all those swear words you hollered at Dr. Aamodt while you were unconscious."

I was boxed into a corner. There was no retreat, no escape, no credible defense. I thought I could jump out of the taxi and get all skinned up so ma would feel sorry for me, but I ruled that out.

I remember staring out the window of the taxi not seeing anything but a blur. My mouth hurt like the dickens, but not as bad as my feelings.

On that ride home from the dentist's I learned all there is to know about humility.

Argo —

Humility, Part II

Donald,

Eddie Tripp and I had a run-in with a lady the same week as the dentist episode with Dr. Aamodt. We were out riding bikes at a time when Lincoln Lane was still a pasture and the surface of Lincoln Street was gravel.

As we rode up Lincoln Street toward St. Olaf Avenue — the intersection of the world — a lady's hat blew off in a strong March wind. It got caught in Eddie Tripp's rear spokes just as we passed in front of Squint and Moose Howard's house. Moose was a butcher at Armstrong's Locker Plant at the rear of the Ole Store. I don't know what Squint did after he lost an eye to a pitchfork while haying, except hang out on the west side downtown.

Eddie's hat went bup-bup-bup-bup! and Eddie kept on riding fast. The lady was really squawking and yelled at Eddie to stop. He yelled back at her, "Up your gee-gee with a meat hook, grandma!" And like a fool, I repeated the expletive because it rolled off the tongue so smoothly. Besides, it sounded more authoritative and grown up than the usual "Pass on you!"

I had no idea that she knew me. After taking out the crumpled hat and throwing it at her, we got out of there. How was I to know she would call 595-L and report the incident to my family? Why did she pick on me? Well, she probably didn't know who Eddie Tripp was. They had no phone anyway.

My sister, Andi, who was then about eighteen, took the phone call. She took all the phone calls, hoping for a date. Besides, she was snoopy, and wanted to know who was calling for my older brothers. But I always had love and affection for Andi. She treated me right, most of the time.

Well, that evening at supper Andi was carrying the daily mail as usual. I sat humbly on my stool as a good ten year old was supposed to do back then in 1943 with a war on. I was the youngest of six boys in the family, and there was no goofing off tolerated at the supper table.

Andi, devilish as she always was, moved quickly into the topic of the day occasioned by her conversation with Mrs. So-and-So who was the lady that lost her hat on Lincoln Street. Andi posed a really tough question in the presence of the whole family: "Lars, what's a gee-gee?"

I spilled my rice porridge on my lap and got slapped by my brother, Roald, because I got his lap too. Alf and Erling, my other brothers still at home before enlisting, looked at each other and rolled their eyes at the ceiling.

Andi was on a roll, as usual. She said, "Well, I don't know what a gee-gee is!" Then she asked, "What did you mean when you said, 'Up your gee-gee with a meat hook!' to Mrs. So-and-So?" That was too much for Erling who delivered a sharp kick to her shins under the table. "Who's kicking me?" squawked Andi, making matters worse.

At that moment I wanted God to part the earth or at least cave in the whole house to make an end of me and Andi too. Boy was I scared!

My dad didn't do anything but eat when he sat down to supper, and Ma didn't let on that she knew anything, so it passed by, but not quickly enough to suit me.

That was my second lesson in humility.

  Argo — Humility II written Tues., Nov. 27 or 28, 1995

You Are What You Eat

Dear Donald,

Sometimes you have to be careful about what you eat. I found that out yesterday. Starting the day with a nutritious breakfast of steel-cut oats and bulgur cooked in a double boiler was the plan. To this, I added a large handful each of wheat bran and oat bran. I remembered that oat bran makes me gas up like a race horse, but paid little heed, for a little gas around the house isn't so bad. Bjørn does it all the time.

Actually, if you want to get attention while waiting in line at the checkout, a loud harmonious one does wonders, perhaps even thin out the line ahead and behind. I'll have to keep that tactic on the front burner. Besides, blowing a good one while squeezing tomatoes in a crowded produce section is quite enjoyable if you can keep a straight face — better yet, turn quickly and give a startled look at the person behind, the way we did in the classroom as kids or bombing out. I think Wendy still does that one. But I digress.

For our first lunch, Bjørn and I had tacos that were very tasty. I wonder if they produce gas? For the second lunch, we had homemade tomato soup which I had frozen last August. For our later snack time, we feasted on fruits, particularly dried Turkish apricots. I ate a prodigious amount. That, together with the oat bran, is what contributed to my feeling of being overly full and bloated, so I went to bed early.

After all these years I have learned a lot about the mechanics of letting gas in bed. The required procedures are: sleep with a single coverlet, not in a sleeping bag. Farts, as you know, are gas bubbles generated in the intestines. They want to get out the rear door, but often the journey through the labyrinth of small and large intestines is one fraught with difficulties and internal engineering problems.

Normally, I lie on my right side upon retiring, and remain thus until a rumble occurs. I then lift the coverlet from my backside so the odor, if any, may be allowed to drift harmlessly away. Then I turn over to the other side and wait for the gas bubbles to round the curve in the intestines and float or work their way to the top of the guts on the other side. I then follow the same procedure and the methane gas, deadly perhaps, or at least sickly, goes away.

Last night was quite problematic for me. Over a 3-4 hour period there was lots of tossing, turning, and farting. I lost count after 40 of what could be termed "significant blasts." It then occurred to me that if I dozed off and did not flip the coverlet back, I stood a good chance of becoming asphyxiated in my sleep. The medical examiner would have quite a field day coming up with a cause of death, so I devised a plan.

Get up, drink four glasses of water in rapid succession like Wendy, and in time create an overpowering urge to go to the passeur. To make the effort so worthwhile, I would then have a lengthy pee as satisfying as Hoz' on the Brenner Pass. I would drink four more glasses of water and go through the same routine again, and so on, and anon. I was certain to awaken at intervals frequent enough to preclude my being gassed to death in my sleep by what was the most potent methane gas produced since the days of Homer's fiery beer-cabooms in Ytterboe or while pheasant hunting with Wendy Miller and Paul Holtan in 1956.

Well, Donald, I am happy to report that my plan worked. My analytical thinking, honed with your assistance during undergraduate days at 'Olaf to meet extraordinary challenges in everyday life prevented the demise of your old friend.

It remains to be seen whether I will never again eat oat bran and Turkish apricots on the same day, but if I do...have care for what you eat Donald, don't blow it out the wrong way — we are what we eat!

Argo—7umpo (how's that for secret hieroglyphics?)—April 15, 1996

Huntin' and Fishin'

Dear Donald,

There was a time, long ago, when I would issue edicts, dicta and claptrap for the purpose of engendering within the populace some sense of meaningful values and virtues which could lead them into Renaissance II.

I devised a useful slogan to assist me in overcoming apathy, duncehood and snarking as the predominant engagements of our society. The slogan: "Fishing...the only thing that counts." I regret that I cannot properly score that statement musically for your use. Gus would undoubtedly read it correctly were I to insert after the word, "Fishing," two quarter rests in a musical notation. This gives the slogan the proper pause for emphasis, thus: "Fishing, (rest... rest) the only thing that counts." But I digress, as usual.

This new slogan of mine, taken verbatim from my first fishing record book, a three-inch spiral notebook kept for recording fishing successes, expresses a truism for the masses. It is a clarion call to the wild as well as the tame — to young and old in equal measure.

This statement of truth transcends most of those advisories committed to memory by youth who aspire, such as, "A stitch in time..." or "A penny saved..." or even "It is better to be rich and happy than to be poor and unhappy." It becomes at once inspiration, comfort, and blessing to the weary of work and those heavy laden by eternal problems with bill collectors, empty-headed dullards as supervisors, NATO, The United Nations, and Bosnia. Of necessity, a revision is indicated: hunting and fishing, or contractions thereof. So we now have just plain "huntin' and fishin'."

It is with huntin' and fishin' that my present commentary is concerned. More specifically, a single expedition to the far north on the Gunflint Trail in the company of my first-born son, Lars, III — called "III" or "Larsemann" (diminutive form for Lars). The year was 1974 and his age, thirteen; my age, unknown, just as today.

I owed Larsemann III this trip because of our rather harsh outing in Mahoney's woods in Scott County the previous winter when I thought for sure he had suffered frostbite in about a half-dozen places. He hung in there, even though he could have done what twelve-year olds sometimes do — complain about the cold. He did not, and so it was that the following year, his thirteenth, he was ready for the big time. He had fished the Hood Canal, gotten lost with me in a squall on Priest Lake, outfished me catching Kokanee on Emerald Lake, and caught more rainbows and salmon than any other kid in Minnesota, to be sure.

We decided to travel light, so left the tent and most of the duffel at home. All we took was a mattress for the rear of the 1970 Ford wagon, sleeping bags, guns, fishing tackle, and a small amount of groceries, hedging our bets, as it were. I had a surprise for Larsemann: a portable TV which we could plug into the cigar lighter. We placed the TV in the rear of the vehicle so Larsemann could recline on the mattress, resting his head on a pillow by the front seat. I could view the TV picture in the rear view mirror.

We drove all the way to Grand Marais with only one stop, arriving about eight o'clock in the evening. After stocking up on milk, candy bars and fuel, we drove to Kimball Lake Campground, some eleven miles up the trail. One spot remained, and that pleased us greatly. We built a roaring campfire, placed the TV on the hood of the car and tuned in four different channels. This gave rise to raucous laughter at our good fortune. We were sure the other campers thought we were nuts, but that didn't matter to father and son who were having a banquet of roast wieners and later cherry pie made in the coals of the fire with our pie maker. We did some channel switching, from two Duluth channels to Superior and one from Thunder Bay, Ontario for the weather.

We resolved to get an early start the next morning, a very important day — opening of grouse season. Our strategy was simple: head on up the tote roads toward the Greenwood Lake area. This we did. However, we found the driving slow at first, as we were behind an elderly pair of road hunters. We beeped them aside, took the lead, and immediately spotted a grouse. Getting out of the car, loading the guns and slamming car doors was too much racket for the grouse who flew off to the left. I explained to Larsemann that we might see only one grouse and so had to find this one.

After a short while, Larsemann found the grouse roosting high in a poppel (poplar) tree — original Norwegian spelling here. He asked if he should throw a stick to make it fly. I responded, "Don't bother. I'll 'Arkansas' him where he is." I did. We stripped and gutted the bird and placed it in a plastic bag inside the camping cooler. Just then, I spotted a grouse in the middle of the road some forty yards distant. I said to Larsemann, "Watch this!" His response was, "Why don't you shoot these two first?" (Indicating two grouse, frozen in mid-stride, a car length away.)

I prepared to shoot, but then Larsemann again broke in: "Do you have enough shells to shoot those other two?" (Indicating two more, on the left side of the road!) Again, I said, "Watch this!" I lit off four shots "fastern a frog can lick flies," so that only the fourth bird had time to fly. I winged that one too.

"What about that one down the road?" asked young eagle-eye Larsemann. "You have a gun. You shoot it," said I. He aimed the 12-gauge single shot Spanish tube and fired. The gun kicked so hard that Larsemann nearly fell over backward. The wounded bird fluttered off into the weeds. I said, "I'll find mine, you go find yours." He ran to the spot. I found mine first.

Then Larsemann called out, "Pappa! He's standing on my foot! What should I do?" I hollered, "Reach down, grab him, and wring his neck!" Larsemann countered, "Will he hurt me?" "No," said I to assure him. He grabbed the grouse by the head and twirled it furiously in a circle until the head and body separated. Now we had six grouse in the cooler. "Let's go fishin'," I suggested, "this is too easy!"

We drove north on the Gunflint Trail, past Fiddle Creek where we usually see moose, and pulled in to my secret place. I said to Larsemann, "You must never reveal the name of this lake to others, agreed?" He agreed. We took a rod and reel each, the 12-gauge single shot gun, and a carton of night crawlers, traveling light, because the hike over the trail to the lake is steep and hard going.

We used the worm-blower to inflate the ends of the crawlers and a three-foot leader behind a Lindy Rig sinker of a half-ounce. Soon we caught two fine Rainbow Trout, about two pounds each. They signaled being hooked by clearing the surface of the water in several two-foot high leaps. "Did we bring a stringer?" "No."

We cut a forked stick and put the Rainbows on one fork of the stick. Again, we decided it was too easy — we had enough for us to eat so we left. On the way up and over the steep hill, we saw a grouse before us, head sticking up above a rod. Might as well, we figured, so I shot the only part visible — the head. No lead shot in that bird, no. Now we had seven grouse and two fine Rainbows.

Larsemann had never before eaten grouse, so that was on the

menu for the evening meal. During and after dinner, we tuned in on the TV and laughed and laughed. We weren't sure why, and to this day I am not sure. Could it have been just pure, spontaneous joy?

After a good night's sleep and a huge breakfast, we decided to return home. We had taken our share and were satisfied. It was the best huntin' and fishin' trip of our lives, Larsemann's for sure.

Father and son — huntin' and fishin' — they go well together, don't they?

Argo —

Dundas Justice

Dear Donny,

Hoz found his notes from the great Dundas trial on January 21, 1958.

Argo – Midsommer, 1998

The Village of Dundas versus defendants Lars G. Kindem, Donald M. Clark, and David J. Martinson, convened before Justice of the Peace Arthur Terry for the Village of Dundas at 10:10 am January 21, 1958 in the Village Fire Hall downtown Dundas before an overflowing crowd of spectators seated on the fire engine and standing around the single jail cell next to the fire truck. Attorneys Robert G. Lampe and Burton R. Sawyer from the Northfield law firm Sawyer & Lampe represented the Village of Dundas and Northfield attorney James O. Caulfield represented the defendants in a 4.5 hour trial.

Mr. Robert G. Lampe called Al Anthony, co-owner of Mike & Al's Bar in Dundas, to the witness stand before Justice of the Peace Arthur Terry for sworn testimony on behalf of the Village of Dundas. Mr. Anthony stated the following under oath:

"On the night of Friday December 21, 1957 [corrected to Saturday], at about 10:00-10:15 pm Martinson and Clark, they come into my place when I was workin'. Troublemakers. I told 'em, get the hell out, I ain't servin' you. Martinson called me goddamn son-of-a-bitch. I went out to call the cop, Lehman, we got trouble. I went next door to the café to use the phone to tell Lehman the cop I got trouble. I told John Kes [café owner] and he come outside with me, out there in front of John and Lil's, and then we fought 'em, mostly Clark and Kes, after Clark snapped his suspenders. All I did was shove Martinson a little. Martinson done the swearin' and Clark too. Martinson tried to help Clark, ran away to a car, then he come back. I think Kindem was with 'em, and he tried to help Clark. Lehman come up and he took 'em to jail. I went back to the bar, Kindem never come in."

James O. Caulfield, attorney for the defendants, cross-examined Anthony under oath:

Anthony repeated his previous statement saying that when he

saw Clark and Martinson come into his bar he hurried over to them, told them to leave, then left the bar immediately to find the cop, and was followed outside by Martinson and Clark. Anthony said that he did not push, shove or assault anyone. Caulfield asked Anthony why he didn't use the phone in the bar to call the cop, "Why did you go next door to call?" No reason provided by Anthony, said he didn't know why. Caulfield asked why Kes came out of the café and Anthony said, "Cause he wanted to see what was goin' on." Anthony said Clark hit Kes first when they decided to place Martinson and Clark under citizen's arrest. Caulfield asked if he announced to Clark or Martinson that they were being placed under citizen's arrest and charged with a misdemeanor. Anthony said he couldn't remember and that all he knew was that Clark swung first. Anthony provided the following additional testimony in response to Caulfield's direct questioning:

"Then Lehman come up and I asked him to arrest them two boys. I told the cop to arrest 'em for bein' a nuisance, disturbing the peace, and swearin'. Lehman took them by the arm; no, I didn't hear Kes say he was arrestin' the boys. I don't think Kindem was with 'em at that time. No, Lehman didn't ask me on what grounds I wanted 'em arrested. One of 'em was swearing and that was the complaint. I also signed a typed paper and I signed nothing else. Yes, I guess it was Saturday that the trouble took place. I was not present or nearby when the shot was fired. I didn't see no shooting. I don't know nothin' about Kindem. I never saw Kindem. Martinson never got a blow on the head. No, I don't know how he got cut. I remember I never saw Martinson hit anyone. I pushed him away so he wouldn't help Clark and he fell down the curb, that's all. I had physical contact with Martinson, not Clark. No, I did not attempt to break up the fight between Kes and Clark.

At 10:40 am John Kes, owner of John & Lil's Café in Dundas, was called to the witness stand by attorney Lampe and provided the following sworn testimony:

"Anthony come into my place Saturday December 21, 1957 about 10 pm. I come outside with Anthony and told that guy [Clark] to shut up and Clark and I scuffled. Then Martinson come at me with my back to the wall and Martinson he pulled my shirt and suspenders and swore terribly."

Defense attorney Caulfield cross-examined John Kes, witness for the Village of Dundas, who stated the following under oath in response to Caulfield's direct questions:

"When men get excited we use bad language. Well, someone come into my place and said to shut up the kid standing outside on the street. I'm a businessman operating my business, so I step outta my café and told Clark to shut up, get outta here. I kept going toward Clark and he kept backing up, he snaps my suspenders first once, and again. Martinson come, not in a threatening manner. Now remember, I was outta my place of business, they had never come in my café, I never said I was placing them under arrest, no. I don't know who threw the first punch, not me. Yes, I had no business out on the street. I had no past history of fighting or trouble. Yes, I was under bond for six months for fighting. I had no right to boss or handle those men. Yes, they were on a public street when I told them to keep quiet. No, we weren't wrestling; yes my shirt was torn and my suspenders. When Martinson come up, Martinson never hit at me, I didn't use any bad language, nor Al. No, I never saw Martinson hit anyone. The reason I went outside my café was to shut Clark up but I never heard Clark myself, what he said, just what Anthony told me, then I fought him. I was going to hold the boys till the cop come, well maybe I overstepped a little, but bad language was addressed to me and Al. I never said to the boys that I was going to hold them under arrest. I never saw Kindem. I signed a paper December 21, 1957 and I signed no other paper. The paper said I wanted Martinson and Clark arrested. Al and me never told the cop to arrest those men during the scuffle or even after. Al told Lehman he wanted those boys arrested."

Recess was called until 11:10 am when attorney Lampe called George Butterfield to the witness stand for the Village of Dundas. Butterfield testified the following under oath:

"I was in Mike & Al's Bar, I saw 'em there at 10 pm, Martinson and Clark, and he went to a booth. Al told 'em to leave. Al said if you don't go I'll call the cop. The boys said they didn't want any beer and I stayed inside and then went outside by the café when Kes and Anthony come outta the café and there's a scuffle, I never heard anything said except Al told Lehman the cop to arrest the boys for cussin' bad. Al said he'd sign the complaint cause they swore. Lehman took 'em to jail. No, I don't know Kindem, but he ran in, pushed Lehman when he was taking the boys in to jail, told Martinson "go, get outta here," that's when the cop Lehman said to "stop or I'll shoot." Lehman said to come, but he didn't, that's when he shot, then he put Martinson and Clark in the jail next to Mike & Al's, that's when Martinson ran away, going into the jail."

Defense attorney Caulfield cross-examined George Butterfield, witness for the Village:

"I do not know Kindem. The boys left the bar 2-3 minutes after Al did, Clark stopped to talk with someone in the bar, don't know who. Al said, "I'll call the cop. No, he never gave a reason for calling the cop. I came outside and saw the scuffle, Kes and maybe Clark, then Lehman came, Al told Lehman to arrest the boys for trouble in the bar, Lehman asked which one, Al said arrest both of them. I do not know Kindem but then there was a shot; after the shot Martinson stopped running, I am positive it was Martinson that ran. Yes, it is possible I am mixed up in the facts; yes, a shot was fired down at Kindem, Kindem in the street. I don't know Kindem, no I can't point him out now. I heard Kindem say nothing; one boy stopped after the shooting with his hands up. At the café I never heard anyone say anything about the arrest. I saw no pushing, shoving or assault in the bar, no blows." Caulfield said that was all the questions for George Butterfield.

At 11:25 pm William "Buster" McKinnon testified for the Village of Dundas under oath:

"I came downtown at the time of the scuffle, I was in front of Mike & Al's Bar and saw the scuffle between Clark and Kes. Martinson did not fight, I am sure, but I couldn't say if Martinson said anything profane or who said the profane language, don't know where it came from. Kes and Clark were fighting and Kes got his clothes torn off, suspenders first. Al told the cop to arrest those two boys and I know Martinson did not struggle, but I didn't follow them up to the jail.

Caulfield's witness, Buster McKinnon's testimony under oath:

"I saw the scuffle, Kes and Clark. Martinson did not take part in the scuffle, made no trouble for the cop. I can't say who used profane language. Anthony said to arrest those boys. I knew it was Clark. George Butterfield was near the fracas, on the street. I heard the shot but didn't go outside."

Constable Jim Lehman testified for the Village of Dundas, under oath:

"I am the village cop, received a call from Al Anthony at 10:15 pm, went uptown, Kes and Clark were scuffling, Anthony was pushing Martinson away. I broke up the fight, took them by the arm, put them under arrest. Anthony and Kes said they would sign warrants for the arrest. Martinson gave no trouble but Clark did.

I took them to the jail, unlocked the door, then someone pushed me from behind and Clark ran away but Martinson didn't. I don't know who pushed me but I saw Kindem and Clark going down the road and I said, "Stop or I'll shoot." I pulled my gun. Clark turned around and came back, Kindem didn't stop. I put George Butterfield in charge of Martinson and Clark. Kindem was backing up, said he never broke the law, that's when my gun was out – I shot, Kindem swore.

Defense Attorney Caulfield questioned Constable Jim Lehman in sworn testimony:

"I had never been a peace officer before, was a constable in 1937 for a few months when I was 28 years old, never went to any police school, no law training. Yes. I typed these papers I see before me that night, December 21 1957 and I alone signed the formal complaint. I did have some doubts afterward if Martinson was guilty but I left the official complaint stand. Martinson had been a good boy and I told Caulfield and Marty's father that I had some misgivings about Martinson's complaint. I got a phone call from Anthony that night, said Kes and Clark and Al and Martinson were pushing and fighting. When I got there I found four men fighting and I took the two young men in and held them before anyone said arrest them. I did not want to treat all four alike. Clark scuffled with me and the two young men were aggravating the fight. I had assumed who the aggressors were before I got there, that's when Al told me there was trouble. I took the two young ones in knowing that police officers are only permitted only to make an arrest if they had seen it happen or have a formal complaint, but it was a mutual fight, and I didn't know who started the fight, so I took the two young ones in and said they were under arrest, but I didn't tell them on what grounds they were under arrest, I did not state the grounds for arrest. Martinson had been a good boy but as I was unlocking the door to get into the jail I was pushed from behind and I saw Kindem and Clark, they were off the sidewalk. Martinson halted and asked me why he was under arrest and I said I would tell them later what it was all about, just get in jail where you belong. Then I turned around and saw Kindem and Clark running away, but Clark came back, Kindem kept going, backing away. I told Kindem to come back, that I would arrest him for interfering with the law, Kindem swore and said there was no reason to arrest him, then I shot at his feet. Later I said, "I almost shot your buddy in the leg." I also told Kindem I would shoot Kindem in the leg. After I shot Kindem walked backward, away. No I do not know the FBI rule for shooting, I have never been trained in those rules. Martinson was in no way aggressive, did not attempt to run." Kindem said he had broken no law when pursued by me."

Jim Lehman was excused pending recall; Court recessed 1.5 hours for lunch; reconvened at 1:30 pm; defense attorney Caulfield called Constable Lehman to the witness stand:

"I had my blackjack in hand and said I would hit Clark. The grounds for apprehending Martinson were for fighting, but I only took two of the four fighters. When I went after Kindem in my mind the grounds for arrest were interfering with the law, striking a peace officer (Caulfield submitted papers of evidence to the Court); I never saw Martinson assault Anthony or Kes, he never swung." [Lehman dismissed]

Mrs. Kes was called by attorney Lampe to testify under oath for the Village of Dundas:

"I saw Martinson and Clark, I was in the cafe and heard some foul language, a customer said some foul language was used outside, Clark and Martinson used profanity, I heard Martinson and Clark say some profanities, I heard them from Martinson and Clark."

The Village of Dundas rested its case and the Court ordered a 5-minute recess. Defense Attorney James Caulfield then called David Martinson to the witness stand.

"I am David J. Martinson and am 21 years of age, my father and mother live in Northfield; my record is good. I was at the Quist home before I came downtown [Dundas] and rode with Lars Kindem. We arrived at Mike & Al's after Quist and company. We entered around 10 pm, to mid-bar, and Al said "I will not serve you." He said it belligerently. Mr. Anthony started the obscenities and was not self-controlled. Clark and I left immediately after Anthony. Clark was on the sidewalk and I was on the street. Anthony told Kes to get in. We were then proceeding to the cars. Clark said, "So this is two against one?" Lehman appeared and Anthony said, "Take them, Jim." Then Mr. Kindem came up and asked why they were arrested. Lehman remarked that he almost shot Kindem. Neither Anthony, Kes or Lehman said anything about being arrested. Lehman stated no grounds for arrest, never asked any questions, merely took Anthony's word. Clark demanded to make a phone call but was denied. We were then taken to Rice County jail but never had any idea why we were locked up. We were released from jail and went to Mr. Sawyer's house and up to December 26, 1957 had no arrest papers served on us. I never resisted any arrest and no one pushed Lehman. The closest Kindem and Lehman were ever together was five feet. Clark and I were inside [the jail] when the shot was fired. Mr. Sawyer told me to "sit tight" and it'll all blow over. I received no papers until one week after Christmas. Anthony and Kes attacked Clark first. They rushed out and fought."

Attorney Lampe from the Northfield law firm Sawyer & Lampe questioned the witness, David Martinson, on behalf of the Village of Dundas:

"I was at the Quist house in Dundas on the night in question. I left the Quist house with Mr. Kindem, three cars left the Quist house. In downtown Dundas, Nelson's car was two door-lengths north of Kes' café; Kindem's was across the street. I went into Mike & Al's Bar with Clark; Quist, Nelson, Wilson, and Ellefson were sitting in a booth. Clark talked with them. Clark and I were refused a drink by Anthony. I went to the bar to talk with Anthony. There was some swearing by me in retaliation. The second time I saw Anthony he was coming out of the Kes café next door. Kes and Anthony started the assault. Clark was passing in front of the café. I never said anything after I left the bar. There was a verbal exchange and Kes and Anthony assaulted Clark. We went out of the bar after Anthony. Kes and Anthony assaulted Clark. Anthony swung at me. Then Lehman came. Lehman arrested us for no apparent reason. I never saw Lehman pushed."

The Village of Dundas rested its case. Defense Attorney James Caulfield called Donald M. Clark to the witness stand for sworn testimony:

"I am 22 years old. On the evening of December 21, 1957 I went to the Quist home. I never saw Lars Kindem in Mike & Al's Bar. In the bar I talked with Quist. Martinson was at the center of the bar. I told Anthony not to holler at me. We left and I walked in front of the café next door. Kes tried to grab me. I took him by the shoulders. Kes and Anthony came after me. David Martinson tried to stop the fight and then Anthony took after me. I did not see Anthony hit David Martinson. Lehman came; he raised his arm with a blackjack and Collison deflected the blow. Lars Kindem was in the street all the time. Lars was not antagonizing the officer. We went to the jail, I broke, Lars never pushed, I ran, stopped, went back in [the jail]. Then there was a shot. Lehman came back and said, "I missed your buddy by a few inches." Marty was quiet and peaceable. We were never informed of grounds of arrest. I requested to use a phone but was denied. "

Attorney Lampe questioned defendant Clark:

"Kes grabbed for me when he came out of the café. Al Anthony left the bar immediately before me. For no apparent reason Kes grabbed for me. Lehman let go. The nearest Kindem ever came to Lehman was a car width."

Attorney Lampe called defendant Lars G. Kindem to the witness stand who provided the following sworn testimony in response to Lampe's questioning:

"When the shot was fired I was in the street. I never came off the street. For no reason at all, Lehman pulled out his gun. Martinson was slapped by Anthony and Martinson did not strike back. Anthony tried to strike Clark several times. On Sunday, December 22, 1957 I went to Burton R. Sawyer's home and then to Faribault and got the boys out of the Rice County jail. We went back to Sawyer and Sawyer said he represented the Village of Dundas. I never assaulted anyone. The cop [Lehman] said, "I'll shoot you in the leg." He never said anything about arrest. The policeman shot at my legs. He threatened to shoot again. The cop left and I went to my car. I didn't see any papers until the preliminary hearing. I went to my car and waited. I always felt I was in my rights. I never swore at the cop. Clark came out [of Mike & Al's Bar] and the two of them, Kes and Anthony, went after Clark. Martinson went up to the fight, got slapped. Lehman came, slammed into Clark and Martinson, pulled out his blackjack. Collison warded off the blow. No one stated anything about arrest. It was a fracas involving four men. Lehman took Clark and Martinson away; I said you got the wrong guys."

Wayne Quist testified [no notes were recorded]. Lars Kindem was cross-examined by attorney Caulfield:

"I am a graduate of St. Olaf College, insurance business, post graduate work to be a high school teacher and coach; drove over to downtown Dundas, went into Mike & Al's Bar, went out, Al Anthony ran out and went into the Kes café, then Clark and Martinson ran out."

At 3:15 pm attorney Caulfield rested the case for the defendants — Not Guilty! So ordered by Justice of the Peace Arthur Terry the following Saturday— Not Guilty!

IBM 1604 & the Marriage of Tor

Dear Donny,

Tor's getting married! Here's my email to Bjorn, subject: "Old Stuff" —

Argo —

Date: Monday, Sep 28, 1998 at 9:46 AM

To: bkindem@emerald.tufts.edu

Bjorn,

Back in 1961, the year after I married your mother, I was approached by the author of several books on the Norwegian language, a Mr. (for sure) Einar Haugen, to discuss several items of mutual interest.

He first referred to my book reviews of his "Beginning Norwegian" and "Reading Norwegian" texts in the "Modern Language Journal." I had been critical of his procedures and various elements of what I perceived to be flawed approaches to language learning. His approach was the old-fashioned grammar-translation method used by most schools at all levels, including St. Olaf. We used his texts there.

I learned Norwegian grammar thoroughly. However, had it not been for oral language at home and through visits to Norway, my facility in the language would not have been much, since they did not teach speaking and understanding and very little writing in any language course at 'Olaf. I politely but firmly informed Mr. Haugen that the days of his old approach were numbered, and my articles gained wide acceptance.

That is why he invited me to the University of Wisconsin to discuss the "dictionary project" which was to begin in June 1961. He was going to be off-campus, doing some linguistics work in Finland. A government grant of $48,000 would be lost if the work on the dictionary did not start by June. That was a lot of money at that time — 12 times my annual teaching salary!

So I became the project director on the very first dictionary to be written "by computer." More accurately, I suppose, with the assistance of the computer for doing most of the alphabetical interpreting, adding inflections, diacritics, endings, tenses and so on. I was given an office in the basement of the venerable grand structure on top of the hill at Madison, in Bascom Hall.

It was a prestigious location where the Scandinavian Department was housed. In addition, I rented office space off campus about a mile away, across the street from the Primate Research Center, in a new apartment building. I scrounged up a pair of desks, some filing cabinets, book shelves and lamps — typical office furniture needed. So now I had two offices.

I was given an assistant who was paid a rather paltry hourly rate. He was a graduate of Wayne State University, a Ph.D. candidate for something or other at Wisconsin, and knew no Norwegian. His only languages were some German for the MA degree and whatever he picked up in the Talmud Torah school he attended in Hamtramck, Michigan, an inner "burb" of Dee-troit.

Just behind Bascom Hall toward the West and lower down the hill was a rather imposing modern structure occupied by the US Navy. This building housed the mammoth IBM 1604 main frame computer. We were to use this computer for word processing, cataloguing and so on.

Each entry prepared by my assistant and me was by means of IBM punch card. Approximately 300,000 cards were the final product, although we only had time for perhaps 20,000, since the 1604 was not always available for our use and it crashed frequently, red lights flashing, alarms ringing; cacophony and scary business.

The IBM 1604 was a valve unit with old-fashioned vacuum tubes. There were thousands of vacuum tubes in the innards of the beast that generated lots of heat that had to be controlled with some sort of heat pump system and cooling radiators, perhaps with freon, I do not know. It was too scary for me to blunder about behind the panels.

The machine was built in a rectangle, with a fancy face in front where there were various inputs and outputs and hundreds of buttons and switches. The entire unit was about twice the size of our living room, stacks about eight feet high. There was a constant hum and some buzzing, lots of clicks and clacks and some klunks.

My job was to bring in stacks of punched IBM cards and place the stacks in a receptacle in front of the "alphabetical interpreter." Each card was whisked off the bottom and passed through a series of lights that penetrated through the slots punched in the card, almost like a primitive sort of bar code reader, but there were no bars, just rectangular holes — anywhere from a half dozen to perhaps 75 holes, depending upon the material typed on the top strip which looked like primitive type script, with dots forming letters.

The product of the processing was the old-fashioned folded computer print-out paper with alternately green and white bars across the page. These printouts were used by me for proofreading and correction with red ink. The corrections and additions were then retyped by my assistant after some mild scolding for what seemed to be obvious mental screw ups from a PhD candidate. I devised a system for separating Nynorsk from Bokmål in language membership and for those words which were used in both, a systematic procedure for listing endings and inflections. I did nothing with pronunciation.

But there was one problem — our IBM typewriter did not do Norsk. So I used a code: number 6 was typed in place of the digraph AE; number 7 was for the ø as in Bjørn; and number 8 was for the a with circle above it, the aa. After a few hours, my assistant seemed to catch on to the system, although it was a little confusing at first. I was given a large bookshelf of dictionaries, Norwegian and Danish to use as source material. So I had them laid out on desks, sometimes on the floor, weighting the pages open with other books, ash trays and whatever. I could have used a large magnifying glass but that would have slowed down the work.

It got lonely for your mother so I drove back to Minneapolis to fetch Larsemann and your mom. We stopped at our first McDonald's in a suburb of Madison. I think it was the second one in existence, after California. The sign read, "Over 1 million sold." I had rented a room upstairs at the home of Ron Henrichs' mother. This hot, poorly ventilated room was to be our residence for the next two months. It was not pleasant. Lars III got lots of rashes, food was a problem, and it was a rough time for all, especially your mother and our III.

I get a kick out of various references in the magazines to the early days of Jobs, Microscrap, and the Internet. They are talking basically about the seventies — in garages and such. I got my computer baptism early — in 1961 — been there, done that. But wait, this G3 I'm using today has considerably more to offer in computing. It cannot process the tons of paper each day, but it sure can outperform the old 1604 and spelling correction is a bit easier too.

Oh well, just thought you might be interested. I know you are interested in the early days of rock, and I will bet a malted milk that the most interesting fact above is the one about McDonald's. This is the first time I ever bothered to refresh my memory about my early computer experience, probably the last, too. The memories of that summer of slavery are not pleasant. It was darn hard work, and I still remember that we all suffered. But the work ultimately had something to do with my getting a Fulbright award a year later. Didn't hurt none, no.

Hey, by the way, Tor's getting married. Can you believe it? Wow!

    Love, Pappa22222

Interview

Dear Donald,

Our favorite interviewer corners a door-to-door interviewer and asks, "What do you do when you do what you do?"

"Ask questions and write down answers," comes the first response.

"Is that all?'

"No, sometimes I have to shield myself from menacing gestures, occasionally physical contact. Verbal abuse is fairly common. Sometimes I find it necessary to run away."

"Well, now, there, then," asks our interviewer, "What seems to be the problem?"

"Well, the people don't always sometimes like the questions; sometimes they don't like to give answers to questions they like. Sometimes they feel non-communicative, verbally, that is."

"I see."

It is then our interviewer does a double-take and says to the other interviewer, whom we shall call Willie, "Say, Willie, will you please show me a profile?"

He does.

Then our interviewer, Max, turns his back toward Willie and looks over his right shoulder. "Aha! Now I got it! You're Willie! Used to run the mile for Faribault!"

"That's correct," says Willie. "I was the crooked boy with the crooked foot that ran the crooked mile."

"You sure as heck did," says Max, "I was there, running ahead of you in every race since the ninth grade. How come you ran so crooked, Willie?"

"I don't know. I think I just tried too hard, got tensed up."

"But," says Max, "you only ran real hard as you passed the grandstand. Were you grandstanding?"

"Yes, I was. The mile is boring enough to watch so I sort of sweetened it up a bit by turning on the jets for about fifty yards on the straightaway. I always led at the end of that sprint, but sagged badly for the remainder of the laps."

"You never did win a race, Willie, did you?"

"No."

"I remember every time you finished the crooked mile you would say you were going to go out for golf. Did you do that?"

"No."

"What was your best time in the mile run?"

"10:02."

"Well, Willie," says Max, "I kinda hate to ask, but how come you ran so many times after so many failures?"

"Persistence," responds Willie, firmly, "that's why I got into this door-to-door stuff. I am persistent. I always get shown the door"

"Mind if I tag along while you make some calls, Willie?"

"No, of course not, Max. Come along, but stand an arm's length away so they can't reach you with a quick slap to the head."

Down the street they go in Northfield, stop at the second house from the opposite corner, one with green trim around the windows, Mrs. Gustafson's place.

"Hello, Mrs. Gustafson," says Willie in his most friendly manner, "May I call you Mrs. Gustafson?"

"Yes, you may."

"Now then, Mrs. Gustafson, I'm taking a survey and need to ask you some questions. Is that all right?"

"Sure. Won't you boys come in?"

"Thank you. Now, Mrs. Gustafson, what kind of rags do you use for cleaning around the house?"

"Look in this drawer, Mr. ah," "Willie. My name's Willie."

"Ah yes, Willie, of course. I went to high school with a Willie. We called him Willie-nilly because he ran the mile and ran in every lane before he finished each race."

"I bet he was last in every race, Mrs. Gustafson."

"Why yes, he was! How did you know?"

"I'm persistent."

"Well, here are the rags. You see I use old jockey shorts with holes. I won't let Harold, my husband, wear them. What if he got in a car accident and had to go the hospital and they saw underwear with holes? It would be a shame for the family!"

"Yes, of course," says Persistent Willie. "What do you use these particular rags for?"

"I do the furniture with these. For windows, I use old tee shirts. I do the piano keys with my old bloomers. Harold likes that. He plays the piano."

"Have you any brooms and dustpans?"

"Yes, I have one of each."

"May I see them?"

"Yes. Here you see I have gone over to plastic instead of straw for the broom. We believe in buying American, besides, it's beveled."

"Beveled?"

"Beveled?" "Oh, I get it, beveled."

"Have you ever measured the handle, Mrs. Gustafson?"

"Yes, I have. It's a 44-incher. Suits me just fine for reaching behind the refrigerator and under the table. Harold has to choke up on it, though."

"Why is that?"

"Well, Harold is six inches shorter than I am, and I am five feet and six inches so you can just about figure how tall he is, or how little he is."

"Is your husband little?"

"No, silly, he wears a size fourteen shoe.

"Would you like to look under my kitchen sink, Willie?"

"Yes, that would be nice," replies Willie, turning a page in his 3-ring binder notebook.

"Ah yes, I see. You have most, if not all the standard cleaners. Let me see here now. Tide, Electrosol, Dawn, sponges, Ajax (the foaming cleanser), scrubbers, stainless steel cleaner. Looks like you have it all, Mrs. Gustafson, but I don't see any Lysol. Don't you use Lysol?"

"No, Mr. Willie. This isn't Greenvale Avenue!"

"Greenvale Avenue? What's that got to do with it?"

"Well, Willie, when I was a child, I used to live in Northfield, city of cows, colleges and contentment, and I used to play with Rose, a neighbor. Her house always smelled like Lysol because her mom used it a lot. Can't stand the smell to this day."

"Tell me, Mrs. Gustafson, did Rose have a brother named Hans?" "Yes, that's the one. He swore some, but otherwise was a nice boy."

"Tell me, Mrs. Gustafson, do you vacuum?"

"No, I don't. Harold does."

"I see you have a variety of costumes there in the closet where you keep the vacuum cleaner. Do you go out much to costume balls?"

"Actually, Willie, we enjoy dressing up in costumes and staying at home for dinner. We program our entertainment to include appropriate historical meals, music, dancing, and the like. It's a lot of fun for us."

"I see you have some nice pictures on the wall there," says Willie.

"Tell us about them."

"Well, here's my daughter, Dawn. She went to St. Olaf, you know. These twins are my sons, Frank and Ernest. They are both frank and earnest."

"Both?"

"Well, he's Frank and he's Ernest, and they are both frank and earnest."

"I get it."

"I bet you do, too."

"I didn't graduate from St. Olaf, although I went there awhile. Partied too much," says Mrs. Gustafson, "But here's my high school diploma, see?"

"Ah yes," says Willie. "I see. So your maiden name was Ruth?"

"Yes, Ruth Lidecka."

"Oh. Is that the doorbell, Mrs?"

"Yes it is. I'll get it. Come in!" she calls.

Mrs. Gustafson turns to the two interviewers and says, "It's been real nice, boys, but you'll have to leave now. The plumber is here, and he has to fix something. He was here yesterday but said he needed to come again. 'Bye 'bye, boys, see you!"

The interviewers leave and continue up the street. Our interviewer, Max, asks Willie, "What are you going to do next?"

"I need to gather data on things such as living room wall paper, refrigerator contents, canned goods in the pantry, chairs. Want to come along?"

"Why not, but let's go over to the Ole Store for a cup of coffee first."

"You're on. I'll buy."

In the Ole Store Restaurant, our interviewer, Max, asks Willie, "What did you do before you did this?"

"I was a garden inspector," replies Willie.

"Did you excel in that endeavor?"

"Only too well. Folks got a mite out of joint because I had to pull up root crops to look them over. Got pelted often with rutabagas and such."

"What are your plans when you reach retirement age, Willie?

"That'll be next year. I've thought a lot about that. I have a proposal before the Northfield City Council that I expect them to take action on before long."

"What's that?"

"Well, I think they need to have someone sit on one of the "Squint" Hower Memorial benches and rail at passersby, especially Oles, saying "Scandinavian Cattle."

"What if they don't buy that?"

"Plan B is to count cars at the Intersection of the World."

"Intersection of the World?"

"Yes. Lincoln Street and St. Olaf Avenue. Everyone gets there sooner or later so join us, we are called Fubar."

Argo — by Max Goliath, pseudonym, no relation to "Isabella BT"

Jens Speaks

Dear Donald,

When my daughter, Nina, lived at home, or whenever she visited, I would ask her to give me a haircut. She never charged for the service, but I always tipped her $20.00.

Now that she lives in Spokane, I find it necessary to go to the Dan Patch Barbers, otherwise called "Savage Barbers" in the town of Savage, home of the great Dan Patch, world record holder at 1:55, fastest mile for a harness horse, fastest pacer ever who broke world speed records 14 times.

Anyway, these Savage barbers cut hair for $15.00, amounting to the same hourly rate one would pay for a good defense attorney, but not nearly as fast as Dan Patch, nor as liberal. You see, I never met a barber who wasn't a conservative. Fancy salons, on the other hand, are different, for most are gay, or liberal, or both. But conversation with the Savage barbers is usually uninteresting, the participants dull and uninformed, except for their prejudices which tend to generate interesting responses from customers.

I decided this time to start it off with a new slant, for I was aware that the Savage barbers very likely considered me a loose cannon on deck, and I was not in the mood to sit around and insult the dummies who normally carried on indelicately and ineloquently in the same tired discourse of conservative sloganism and bumper sticker phrases that make no sense.

I placed my St. Olaf baseball cap on the rack next to a baseball cap with the "Pheasants Unlimited" logo. That gave me an opening for some hearty conversation, possibly with the owner of the cap on one of my favorite subjects, the pheasant. "Whose cap is that?" I asked in a loud voice. The number two barber said it had been there on the coat rack for two weeks and he didn't know who the owner was. End of conversation.

I tried again. "Where the devil is Jens?" (the owner, whose chair was empty). "He's out back," said the barber, "concentrating on a 'razor cut' where concentration counts a great deal." End of conversation. I figured I had better start on a new tack. Just then, Jens emerged from hiding out back where I suspect he was sneaking a smoke.

Pointing at a large picture on the wall, I said, "That's a nice picture of Dan Patch. How tall was he anyway?" "Sixteen hands," comes the reply from the other barber. Well, we wore out that topic, and I didn't mention that Dan Patch was a liberal. No sense running it into the ground.

I took my seat and said to Jens for openers, "I'm glad I'm not a Carleton man." Just then the phone rang, and that was that. "Will you please put down that phone and cut my hair!" I bawled at Jens. I figured it was his wife on the phone and she was calling from the beauty salon on the other side of the wall.

I wanted him to know that I was a busy man in my free agency, not one to be trifled with when I was on a schedule. "You know," I began anew, "I am sick and tired of people complaining about politicians. Those guys aren't so bad. It's the common man that really rips me off. They are the ones that go around robbing, raping and killing. We have to pay for all that through our taxes." I figured someone in the shop would pick up on that last bit.

Jens nods toward the other chair where the customer sits smiling from ear to ear at my outburst. "He's a politician," says the other barber. I knew right off that he must have been a conservative, or he wouldn't be in a barber shop. Liberal politicians get clipped at fancy salons, where no self-respecting conservative man would go except to pick up his wife. The really liberal liberals get clipped at home by someone or else they do it to themselves.

Jens makes short work of my baldie trim, as quick as a Dan Patch mile, and I am ready to get out of the chair. I know he won't give me the baldie discount I deserve, but it doesn't hurt to ask, again. He smiles and shakes his head, something he does very well and often.

Shaking off the coverlet, I remark that he found some gray hair or else it was from the guy before who sat here. He smiles. No talk. "You know, Jens," I joke with him, "the hair roots grow down in the scalp. If they hit gray matter, they turn gray. If they hit nothing, they fall out." Jens smiles and nods approvingly.

Another customer takes my place in the first chair. I remain standing before him, determined to get a little conversation on this visit to Jens, the Savage barber. I sure as heck don't get my money's worth in just a two-minute haircut.

"Yeah, it's the ordinary citizen who ain't worth a you-know-what," I state firmly, escalating the front-end loading of a proposed topic. "Take that darn Rastafarian that raped and shot a girl the other night over here in the River Park."

"You mean," asks the other barber, getting technical on me, "The guy with the dreadlocks?"

"Precisely!" I respond. "Look at what that gonad does. He comes out from the Cities, picks up a woman, takes her down to the river park, rapes her, then shoots her in the hip when she runs away. Look what he does in one night to the crime statistics for our community — kidnapping, rape, attempted murder, assault with a deadly weapon — you got four felonies that raise the percentages in our crime statistics and the values of our homes drop. What's the world coming to, what are decent people to think? Then the guy has the gall to commit suicide instead of facing justice."

At this point, someone wonders what the girl was thinking about when she got into the car with this obscenity of a man. My conclusion was that he probably offered to do some coke with her, and she went along with it, looking for a freebie. He was the other one looking for a freebie.

Now we've got the pump primed. The other barber puts in, "He woulda cost us a fortune in court costs, attorney's fees and hundreds of thousands of dollars to try him and keep him locked up for forty years!"

Even Jens almost starts to talk now, "Ummhmm." His new customer interrupts and eagerly enters the conversation with, "He shoulda stayed in the Cities!" Jens nodded. I suppose the new customer was a little off his pace because the conversation wasn't the one for which he had made advance preparations, as we'll see later.

In walks the beautician from next door and I haven't even put my St. Olaf baseball cap back on yet. She is Jens' wife. She knows I once was a teacher, so wants to make me feel at home.

"Did you hear about the teachers' union over at Burnsville?" she announces to the room at large. She had probably waited all morning for a full barbershop so she could stride in, make her play, and move on. "Would you believe they scheduled a meeting to endorse candidates for the school board and it's a closed meeting. No citizens, no press, no city officials, nuthin' but the union. What's going on here with free speech?"

I detect a slight bias, so I move quickly to ease her fears. I sense she is obliquely directing her complaint to the city councilman still sitting in the second chair, getting far more for his money than I got at an hourly rate of $450 an hour for a two-minute haircut, unless of course the conversation is prolonged.

"They are," I explain, "not a public group. They have membership dues and are entitled to meet anywhere, anytime, and do not have to let observers in to spy on their deliberations."

"But," she protests, "They're meeting in the basement of our City Hall!" The city council guy puts in, "The hockey parents meet there too. It's a public room for private meetings."

That was the end of her performance, or nearly so. "Well, I don't think they are going to endorse any of our candidates," she says on the way out, blue hair and all.

I quickly gave her, "I guess they have a right to endorse whomsoever they choose — you might be pleasantly surprised."

Jens nods approval which I quickly accept with, "I guess it boils down to whose ox is being gored." He nods again. No talk.

Well, the new guy sitting in the chair recently vacated by me finally sees his opening —the one he probably uses every time he sits down in the barber's chair, or at the Legion Club, or at one of the animal clubs such as the Moose, Elks, Lions or the bird sanctuary Eagles. He's the type that phones in to the conservative radio talk shows. It's always and ever the same. Even a close friend of mine does it.

The guy looks at me, unsure, to be sure, but he's got to get the line out that he's been waiting all morning to let out: "It's those liberals again."

That's all he said. It's the standard conversation initiator or concluding remark for this type of silly nitwit. It was just about enough to make me want to slap his mouth. Those guys always know when they are saying something stupid, for they say it out of the sides of their mouths.

I decided to quell the uprising quickly and roared with my booming St. Olaf Choir bass voice: "What are you talking about? You should be back in second grade!" He was surprised and speechless.

I head for the door, picking up my St. Olaf cap. "Remember what I said when I got into your chair, Jens." He smiles and nods.

As I walk out, I overhear Jens telling his mouthy customer, "He's real smart. He's a retired teacher from St. Olaf."

Argo —

Kid Stuff

Dear Donald,

Every boy should have a number of items in his room, or else in the basement, if there isn't enough room in his private room. And remember, you can always hide stuff under the bed. Here's my list for Boys of America, please send me yours.

Argo —

ARGO'S LIST

    Candy

    .22 & lots of shells

    BB gun & sling shot

    Leather sling for heaving rocks

    Cap gun & caps

    Standard deck of cards

    Deck of cards (naughty pictures)

    Cigarette papers

    Tobacco& matches

    Cigar box for different junk

    Compass & flashlight

    Chrome signal mirror

    Gyroscope

    Kaleidoscope

    Jack knife (with can opener)

    Huntin' knife, large

    Jar for captured bugs

    Army surplus canteen

    Some rope

    Marbles & steelies

    Old coins

Slugs, different sizes
Feeler gauge
Church key
Skeleton key
Other keys
Corset stay
Pup tent & pegs
Sleeping bag
Scout camping cook set
Firecrackers
Railroad fuses
Padlock & key
Crow call
Screwdriver
Jacket, cap & other shoes
Comic books: Superman, Captain Marvel, Batman, Dick Tracy

Hobo, you may wish to add to this preliminary list and I encourage you to do so. It is important that boys today have an idea of what is needed in life. Please send me your ideas so that I may incorporate them into the body of my report to the Boys of America.

Argo, — February 9, 1996

Dear Donny,

I have the pleasure of recording your additions to Argo's list and thank you most sincerely for your valuable contribution.

Argo — February 16, 1996

HOBO'S LIST

Flare gun
Axe
Flint/steel
Magnifying glass

- Bug juice
- Fish hooks & line
- Dehydrated water pills
- Brandy or Rum
- Bible & lip ice
- Suntan lotion
- Whistle
- Plastic tarp
- Clothes line & soap
- Mink oil
- Hobo walking stick
- Bandanna
- Sun glasses
- Awl
- Sewing kit
- Rubber bands
- Safety pins
- Water proof alarm clock
- Wool socks, 3 pair
- Norwegian mesh underwear
- Camera
- First aid kit
- 10 candles
- Reversible jacket
- Shock cords
- Sierra cup
- Primus stove
- Folding saw
- Hammock
- Rubber ball
- Rubbers, used or new

Um! Yah! Yah! flag
Various pennants
Salt & pepper
Nails & thumb tacks
Scissors
Duffel bag
Swim suit (optional)
Wool sweater - heavy
Nail clipper
Tooth brush & tweezers
Block & tackle to hoist food up
Sketch pad, soft lead pencil
Liquid paper correction fluid

P.S. This should do it for now, Donald, and if there are no additions, I can complete my report to Boys of America with these suggestions as to what they need in their room or somewhere. They may well have to borrow some items, perhaps purchase under the five-finger discount option. Please sign and certify:

I hereby sign and certify that this list is complete, and hereto have affixed my official seal of approval, thereby:

Signed: _____

Donald McCornack Clark (Most Revered Hobo)

Argo — Feb. 16, 1996

Man's Best Friend

Dear Donald,

There comes a time in our lives when we must sit back, relax, and have a good laugh. Normally such occasions do not occur during "60 Minutes" or similar programs.

That is, until this evening, when much to my relief, my son, Lars III arrived home with my Ford limo earlier than planned. That in itself is not humorous, merely a relief, for the weather reports cautioned people to avoid travel this evening, issuing the standard "travelers' advisory" so common this season of the year in Minnesota.

I was glad to see him, not just because he arrived home safe and sound, but also because it meant that my vehicle was safe for another day. It happened in the garage, he reports, summoning all the drama at his disposal. Lars III was barely able to comprehend what had happened when he opened the car door.

Argo, my faithful dog, burst through the opened door, hopped up onto III's lap and into the back seat with lightning speed, coming to rest in a sitting position in the back seat, ready and raring to go pheasant hunting. It should be noted here that III was wearing white jeans and Argo had dirty, wet paws. No, this has never before happened in recorded history.

Perhaps some background will assist in understanding Argo's aberrant behavior this evening. When it became apparent that the Ford limo was going to become the main mode of transportation for people around here this week, I removed Argo's custom-made back seat compartment.

This meant, of course, that Argo-the-dog and Argo-the-man could not team up for drives to Cub Foods, or Sam's, or Holiday or anywhere else. Each time the vehicle left the premises, Argo was left behind. This had gone on all week since before Thanksgiving.

I suppose the last straw was pulled when I made a quick trip to Cub Foods this morning. Not wanting Argo to dirty up the back seat, and not taking the time to install Argo's compartment, I drove off without him, issuing the command, "Stay!" He stayed all right, but I could sense he did not like what had happened, no.

They say dogs have good memories, or at least remember well. This must be true. So when he saw two relative strangers make off with his vehicle, it became too much for him to bear, and thus he needed to take drastic action.

Faithful Argo may see himself in the role of supervisor, or at least back seat driver when it comes to riding in the car. Day after day, he hops into the back seat where he belongs. However, we use the back door for entrance and exit. The ride anywhere is his big event of the day. Tor takes him along in the Bronco from time to time. He has also traveled with Bjørn on occasion. But he expects, always, to accompany me, whenever and wherever I go.

It all goes back to the theory that once a dog learns something that is pleasing or satisfying, he spends the rest of his life waiting for the same experience. Remember the dog who watched a squirrel jump from the garage to a tree and miss, falling directly into the dog's mouth? That dog, as you know, spent every day for the rest of his remaining eleven years sitting by the garage, waiting for another squirrel to fall. But none ever did again — how disappointing.

With Argo, it probably goes back to the first time we went hunting near Union Lake. He never got over that, it seems, and every time he gets into the car, he thinks we are going hunting again, to Union Lake. It's always the same, just like Fubar. Faithful Argo never cares that we take side trips, say to Northfield, specifically to St. Olaf — visits he enjoys immensely. He has his favorite trees for pass call behind Agnes Mellby Hall. Well, that's not so preposterous. I probably did the same at one time or another.

There are other places Argo habitually likes to visit for a good pass — the bushes at Holiday, the big rock near the parking lot at Cub Foods, the fence at Knox Lumber, the fine bushes at Burnsville Center near Dayton's, the oak trees at Oaklawn Cemetery, the horse chestnut trees at the Northfield Retirement Center, and of course in the woods and fields.

The most satisfying pass calls for him are always in the weeds behind the car when we pull into a public hunting area. On those occasions he relishes the good pass so much he scratches the ground afterward as if to urge me to hurry up and get the shotgun out of the case. He impatiently waits while I relieve myself. As you know, I enjoy passing outside, especially in the woods, and do not rush myself, no.

So it is, Donald, I fear Argo-the-dog has learned a lesson about vehicle travel that is indelibly imprinted upon his memory. The travel ritual is very important to him. That must be why he broke all rules of deportment and leaped onto III's lap today, soiling a pair of white jeans and sitting ready to go and be limoed about in the back seat. Someone owed him a trip in the car this day, and he was not about to miss out for a second time.

After all my Thanksgiving guests are gone on Tuesday and I have had my dental appointment, Argo-the-dog and I will go for the pheasant. There is a fresh snowfall tonight which should assist me in noting whether there are any birds out and about. But Argo doesn't need any tracks in the snow to find birds, no.

The compartment goes back in the limo under Argo's very close supervision. We will load up the duffel and the gun and faithful Argo will once again return to the happy rhythms of routine. He knows he is Man's Best Friend and wants to prove it day after day, year after year.

You gotta love that faithful Argo dog.

Argo —

Maynard's Duck

Dear Donald,

Thank you for your entertaining and informative letter about the Long Island ducklings. Bizarre!

Taking into use my stitching awl and a piece of canvas left over from an old boat cover, and further, using my acute memory of days gone by when I worked at Sam Haugen's turkey farm on the back road to Dundas, I fashioned a jacket my Merganser decoy similar to those we slipped onto the backs of turkey hens to prevent the Toms from successfully mounting and impregnating them. This jacket I slipped onto my liberated decoy which today had finally become free from the ice-bound prison of the frozen bird bath. It was a celebration!

All of which means, of course, that the prevert (a Milwaukee term) from Long Island you described will not disturb my duck; further, the species has undergone a change. I now have a Canvasback. We must use a modicum of caution here — it is entirely possible that the Canvasback will suffer identity crisis, yes, perhaps suffer even a nervous breakdown. I know a few things about ducks and their mental breakdowns, for I participated in the Maynard Study.

I studied the subject during the winter of 1963-64 with Maynard, the Minneapolis Park Board Keeper of ducks, geese, and swans during the winter months. I was fortunate that the waterfowl were housed in Theodore Wirth Park's Eloise Butler Flower Gardens where I skied and coached cross country skiing on a daily basis.

Maynard had an impressive array of coops and pens for the fowl he kept and managed. Our study centered on the issue of a duck that had apparently suffered a nervous breakdown. Of course, the senior park authorities pooh-poohed the diagnosis for a time until they saw the scientific evidence.

Our staff set up a one-way viewing glass mirror similar to those in many nut-houses and police interrogation rooms for observation of the subjects. The tape recorder was operated by remote control and utilized, together with an 8-mm color film camera, to record occurrences in this observation cell.

We tried many avenues of approach, changing the wallpaper, the recipe for feed, the ambient "elevator" music, and so forth. Each time birds of different species and sex were placed in the room alone with our subject, whom we labeled 006 for confidentiality purposes, our bird would demonstrate some sort of weird behavior.

One behavior was to limp alternately, first on one leg, then the other — sort of like a limping duck. Another was to walk backward while quacking willy-nilly at anyone and anything. A third was to hop up onto a perch and affect the mannerisms of a squawking parrot, mouthing nonsense syllables for a period of about 20 seconds, after which the duck would place his head under his left wing. He would then refuse to eat or drink for the better part of a day. No normal sex activities were observed.

At first we assumed he was perhaps dieting or was on some sort of weight loss regimen, which would be acceptable, though borderline behavior for a duck. But then, after a time, Maynard suggested that there must have been a traumatic experience during his early life. I had no choice but to concur.

Examination of the charts indicated that at one time, due to crowded conditions, from the age of two weeks to ten weeks, the duck had as a pen mate an old parrot which the Minneapolis Park Board received in exchange for six snapping turtles as part of a trade with the Como Park Zoo.

Maynard had some explaining to do here. The charts indicated that all the female ducks had indeed been molested — used sexually by the parrot who had a sperm count of zero. Those facts would tend to explain why there were no offspring from the ducks while consigned to Maynard's care.

Our duck wanted, of course, to communicate this fact to Maynard, but you know how some gamekeepers are. He just didn't get it. That explains the bizarre behavior which was diagnosed as a duck mental breakdown.

At my insistence, Maynard got tough with the parrot, threatening to pluck out all the parrot's beautiful head plumage and place the reprobate in an isolation ward if he mounted one more duck. Well, the prevert (Sic!) parrot could not leave them alone, so Maynard in fact plucked the parrot bald and locked him in the basement.

I suggested we have roast parrot for supper, but Maynard would have none of it. I told him they should have kept the six snapping turtles they had exchanged for this wily, troublesome parrot. Maynard took the parrot home for one-on-one therapy and personalized language instruction. In the absence of the parrot, our duck recovered fully, no longer exhibiting behaviors that one might associate with a duck who had gone south. In short, he was adjudged normal and released into the general population.

Maynard was short-handed at home for his 25th wedding anniversary on April first, that year, so he hit upon the novel plan of using the bald parrot, whom we named "Studley," to entertain at his April Fool's party.

Studley was placed on a coat rack perch just inside the front door to receive the thirty or so guests who were expected to show up for the celebration. His instructions were simple — as each couple entered the front door, he was to recite: "Awrrk! Ladies to the right, gentlemen to the left!" This would direct the guests to the two bedrooms which served as coat rooms.

We stood in line at the front door marveling at this phenomenon, when Studley cried out in a loud parrot voice to the couple in front of me, "Awrrk! Ladies to the right, gentlemen to the left!"

He then spotted a bald gentleman next and called out, "Awrrk! Ladies to the right — bald-headed duck fackers to the basement!" True story.

    Argo —

The Minnesota Dwarf Trout Lilly

Dear Donny,

You are being officially notified that the Minnesota dwarf trout lily is an endangered species and you need to get back here to give me a hand. Many endangered species are animals and plants that are in danger of becoming extinct. Identifying, protecting, and restoring endangered and threatened species is the primary objective of the US Fish and Wildlife Service's endangered species program, but they're too slow, so Argo has taken this on as a special mission — a self-appointed deputy-in-charge of the dwarf trout lily on some of Howard Hong's property in rural Rice County.

Quite a lot has already started because the Minnesota dwarf trout lily now resides on about 600 acres of woodland habitat dominated by maple and basswood and adjoining floodplains dominated by elm and cottonwood. A boardwalk at the Nerstrand Woods State Park was constructed to allow visitors to observe and photograph the Minnesota dwarf trout lily without disturbing colonies of this endangered plant. And a retaining wall was constructed to stabilize the bank of Prairie Creek in the Nerstrand Woods where spring flood waters were undermining dwarf trout lily colonies.

The rarity of the dwarf trout lily is probably best explained by its unusual mode of reproduction. Unlike many flowering plants, the dwarf trout lily almost never produces seed. Instead, it grows from an underground bulb that renews itself annually. Population is only increased when the underground stem of flowering plants produces a single offshoot runner bearing a new bulb. Because only a small proportion of all plants flower in any given year, only about one-tenth of all plants produce new offspring in a given season. Like spring beauties and Dutchman's breeches, trout lilies are spring ephemerals, adapted to flower and grow before the deciduous trees develop their leaves. When summer shade darkens the forest floor these plants have already bloomed and generated food reserves for the coming year and they lose their leaves.

The origin of the Minnesota dwarf trout lily is unknown,

but genetic research suggests it evolved from the white trout lily shortly after the last glaciation period. Because it does not produce seeds, it is likely that the plants were spread by floodwaters uprooting them from an original location somewhere along the Cannon River. Torn loose from the original habitat, these plants would have been redeposited on slopes and floodplains downstream toward the Carleton arboretum. Perhaps this mode of dispersion explains the plant's limited geographic distribution at elevations of 960 to 1000 feet within the Cannon River watershed and its tributaries.

You might ask, "Why is the Minnesota Dwarf Trout Lily endangered? The dwarf trout lily was listed as a federally endangered species because of the possibility of extinction. This is a plant that has always been rare, but housing developments, logging, and corporate farming have destroyed the few remaining plants. In addition to direct destruction of plants by human activities, increased conversion of floodplains to cropland has reduced the probability that plants dislodged by upstream floodwaters can find suitable downstream habitat. Disturbance of uphill areas causes erosion and siltation in areas where the lilies occur.

Like all native species, the Minnesota dwarf trout lily has its own niche in relationship to other plants and animals. Some conservationist said, "The first rule of intelligent tinkering is to save all the parts." The Minnesota dwarf trout lily possesses a genetic and chemical makeup unlike that of any other plant. It is known to be most genetically similar to the closely related white trout lily from which it is believed to have evolved no more than 9,000 years ago. The unique genetic information in each species is potentially valuable to all of us. Alkaloids from many wild plants are active ingredients in medicines and other useful products. Loss of the dwarf trout lily would eliminate the potential for such benefits forever.

There are three species of trout lily in Minnesota: the Minnesota dwarf trout lily, the white trout lily (Erythronium albidum), and the yellow trout lily (Erythronium americanum). All are spring ephemerals. All have tapering green leaves lightly mottled with a greyish-white pattern. Huge patches of leaves with very few flowers are characteristic of trout lilies and are common in all three species. The Minnesota dwarf trout lily is distinguished from other trout lilies by its underground vegetative runner, from which the species takes its name propullans or "sprouting forth." The blooming plant is readily identified by the very small size of its flowers. Flowers of the dwarf trout lily are about the size of a dime or less, pale pink, with a variable number of perianth parts. Most members of the lily family have six, but dwarf trout lilies may have four, five or six.

Approximately half of the known dwarf trout lily sites are in state Scientific and Natural Areas, state or county parks or private preserves such as those of The Nature Conservancy. A large number of dwarf trout lily populations occur on private land where farmers or other landowners have maintained the species by protecting its woodland habitat. Howard Hong's land by Nerstrand and interest in The Nature Conservancy stimulated my interest in this effort to help save the Minnesota dwarf trout lily.

Argo —

Mixed Signals

Dear Donald,

This morning as I walked past my vaulting pole which lies at the rear of the house behind Hobo's Smoking Lounge, I was reminded of a time long ago when I took such a pole into daily use in order to scale the heights.

After all is said and done, I now conclude that the reason I became and remained a pole vaulter was simply because it was so much fun to do. There came a time when I was a senior in high school and captain of the track team that I received mixed signals.

You see, I also thought singing was fun. The mixed signals directed me to two venues on the same day — a district music contest in Waseca where the choir and the madrigals were to perform and the Faribault Relays, where I was scheduled to defend my championship in the pole vault.

With my athletic bag packed to include track shoes, choir robe and suit, I boarded the bus one Saturday morning with the choir, bound for Waseca. I had told Coach Ed Byhre not to worry; I would be present for the pole-vault event scheduled for 1:00 pm in Faribault. There was some risk involved, but what is life without risks? The question was, could I find the means to travel from Waseca to Faribault in time to compete?

The choir and madrigals were flattered that I had chosen to be with them. They did not know of my scheme to return to Faribault that morning. After singing with the choir and the madrigals, I ran to the highway leading to Owatonna from Waseca. You may remember that old highway where the concrete set into a continuous stretch of humps that tended to give kids riding in a bus motion sickness.

I got a ride immediately from a picture post card salesman. The ride though short was enjoyable, for I looked at lots of picture post cards free of charge. He was kind enough to drop me off in Owatonna where the highway to Faribault intersects the Waseca road. Again my luck was good, and I got a ride with the father of an Owatonna track man whose son was in the shot put and discus events. He drove me straight to the Faribault track by the fair grounds.

I changed into my track suit. The pole vault had already started but the bar was only at 10'- 6" and I determined to wait until the bar was at 11'- 0" to conserve energy for my assault on the record I set a year earlier. When my name was called, I took up my pole and barreled down the runway. About half way to the pit, a Faribault vaulter, Tom Ulvenes, pretended to blunder accidentally into my path.

He was later to do that twice again, meaning he would thus earn himself three thrashings for his troubles. I won, setting the new record at 11' - 5 1/2" and was too jubilant to go over and punch Ulvenes. He later became a classmate at St. Olaf, but I did not associate much with his kind.

Coach Byhre had another use for me that day as lead-off runner in the 4 x 100 yard relay. I had a very quick start and so the choice was a good one. It was good, that is, until after the starting pistol was fired. I was carrying the baton in my left hand, running in the inside lane, when a curious onlooker leaned forward into my lane.

We did not exactly collide. However, my baton went into his jacket pocket, out of my hand and onto the track. After retrieving the baton, I ran like heck in a vain attempt to catch up with the others.

We finished third, and coach Byhre caught the entire episode on his new 8-mm movie camera. I wonder whatever happened to that film of the mixed signals.

     Argo —

Poems for Hobo

Dear Donald,

Here are some of Argo's poems to go with your colorful Portland oils.

    Lars —

Relationships
If you have a friend
You have someone who will listen.
A friend will also talk to you
So you, too, have the chance to listen,
And learn.

Those who learn
Also can teach others who learn.
And those who teach
Learn from those who learn,
Who also teach.

The singer needs the song
Just as the song needs the singer.
As the song is sung
It becomes known,
And so does the singer.

A brother helps a brother
And helps himself,
For the brother helped
Becomes a helper who also
Will help his brother.

The man yearns for the woman
Who will yearn for the man.
The woman brings joy and pleasure
To the man,
But then so does a fine cigar.

Secrets
People like to tell the truth
To others,
Not to themselves.
For it is said, the truth hurts.
And people would rather hurt others
Than themselves.
A secret told
Satisfies the teller
And often the one told,
Unless it is about something
Best kept secret.
Secrets may be written, whispered,
Or spoken aloud.
It doesn't matter.
There will always be those
Who delight in telling on someone.

Accent on New York
Do gulls fly or do gulls dance?
That depends on where you are,
Minnesota or Brooklyn.
To settle the question,
Give a gull a peck on the cheek.
If the gull returns the kiss,
You are probably in Brooklyn.
If the gull flies away
Find another gull.

For Bob Rose

Dear Donald,

Where do we find the stone precious enough on which to carve the name of Bob Rose? Who can rise to the task of providing an understanding of the worth of this man who is at once beloved husband, father, colleague, teacher, and friend? These questions, as do all such complex inquiries, challenge our ability to solve the enigma of a complex man whose professional career has been dedicated to the valued service of this community; of men and women, boys and girls. So we have to settle on certain basic truths which we all can readily understand — speaking these truths from the heart, which does not lie. This was my recent tribute to my friend from school, Bob Rose.

Argo —

FOR BOB ROSE

Bob, you spoke at my retirement so this one's for you, good friend, for you earned the highest respect of all the people in your life to which you have chosen to give of your talents, your deep understanding and love. You have elevated them to a higher state of being. You challenged your students and compelled them to think. You have always provided students and colleagues with an understanding of the meaning of justice for all. Fairness has been a hallmark in your conduct of affairs that colleagues and children alike have found at your desk on your watch. You have been the most innovative and imaginative teacher I have known. You could write the book on teaching strategies — those that work and those that need some work. Later generations of teachers may little note nor understand the positive results of the Great Strike for the benefit of teachers that you led in 1970. But they will always benefit from what you did for all of us. It was a difficult time for the striking teachers, but so necessary to assure the future security of all teachers. We thank you for that leadership. You have always been willing to fight for democracy and fairness. Your colleagues have from time to time disagreed with you on certain elements, but sooner or later have come to the realization that you were probably on the right track, traveling in the right direction. A good teacher needs to be energetic. You were that. Teaching requires more than just intelligence. When we were young, we sometimes thought that intelligence was a substitute for experience. Then when we got older, we sometimes thought experience was a substitute for intelligence. That was never the case with you, Bob. Teaching has been elevated as a profession because you have been its standard bearer. You never were indifferent. You were a good teacher. Now look what that has gotten you.

    Lars Kindem — April, 1996

Primlefse

Dear Donald,

I know you like lefse and I know how you like to eat good things, for as you say, "eating stimulates the appetite." Well, here you go — Anna Kindem's secret lefse recipe, never before revealed in print. I learned from her to make flatbrød first, baking it only on one side first. Then when it is turned over, smear it with the prim mixture. I use a stainless steel measuring cup to "ause," and then the bottom of the cup to spread the mixture.
— Lars

Flatbrød
4 cups white all-purpose flour
2 cups graham flour
1/2 cup butter, melted
1 cup water
1 teaspoon salt
1 cup buttermilk, warm
1/2 cup sugar
1 teaspoon soda
2 teaspoons baking powder

(In Norway, they use "Horn Salt" — calcium carbonate. I have some I smuggled in.)

METHOD: HEAT WATER AND BUTTERMILK, ADD BUTTER AND STIR INTO DRY INGREDIENTS. MIX WELL. ROLL OUT THIN.

****

Double Boiler

It is a good idea to have a double boiler to keep the prim mixture below warm and not scorched. However, the recipe may be too large for your double boiler. If so, get it started elsewhere and transfer half at a time into the double boiler. You will be a lot happier if you do. First, the ingredients:

2 cans evaporated milk. (Use Northfield Milk, which is the best.)

Primlefse

> 1 lb. primost, shaved (use a gjeitost høvel)*
> 9 oz. brown sugar
> 5 oz. syrup (karo, light or dark)
> 3 heaping tablespoons flour
> 5 oz. heavy cream, such as whipping cream
> 9 oz. butter (no substitutes!)

*If you cannot find primost, then make your own: Buy powdered whey (at health food Co-op such as Valley Natural Foods Co-op in Burnsville).

Mix it in a double boiler with the evaporated milk. Add enough powder to make primost liquid. Not too thick, now. This will yield 1/2 recipe for prim lefse topping.

You May Now Proceed:
> Combine primost, milk, syrup, and sugar.
> Simmer and stir until all is melted.

Then:
> Melt butter in a pan, add white flour to melted butter and stir until blended.
> Add this to the warm milk and primost mixture above.

(You know what? I use a heaping tablespoon potato flour blended in 1/4 cup cold water to add to the mixture. But if you have no potato flour, you "can might yust so vell skip dot," per Ingvald).

Next:
> Let the whole thing simmer a few minutes.
> Remove from heat.
> Then add the cream.

****

Watch out, this can get to be a mess if you are not careful. When you smear onto the unbaked side of the flatbread, check to see if the mixture is too thick. If it is, then just add some cream. Naturally, the prim mixture gets thicker as it sits in the double boiler so it is good to thin it out either with cream or evaporated mjølk.

Also, if you slip over the outside edge in your enthusiasm, you will get a scorched grill. So go ahead and smear the prim mix on, working fairly fast. It doesn't take long. Then, using all the skill you can muster, fold one half over the other and remove from the grill.

Cut it the way you want with a pizza wheel or whatever while it is still warm. Cool on racks. Then get back to work and don't eat it all right away. "Verk kom forst!" (per Ingvald). Now you are ready to proceed.

Knowing you, of course, I would imagine you will stick your finger in for a taste. That's all right. It's yours.

  Lars — who learned how to cook from Anna Sekse Kindem

Caribou Fishing, '84

Dear Donald,

I found this fishing report written on graph paper in my map case today, Oct. 22, 1995.

    Argo —

I am sitting in my folding lawn chair in the camp site nearest the boat landing. Before I started writing, I poured myself a cup of coffee freshly brewed on the Coleman stove while in the boat on the east side of the lake. As I sat in the beautiful seventy-two degree sunny weather looking at the lake, I sang, "Praise God From Whom All Blessings Flow," with more fervor than ever before.

Someday I'll read this memo and remember one of the finest moments a man could ever have. But it didn't start out right, did it? We had looked forward to this trip, Bjørn and I, for about a week. We had what is called "cabin fever" and needed to get away from 2608 County Road 34 for a while. Friday came; Bjørn reported in — sick. I have a feeling his tummy ache went away when I told him he did not get to go along. He really needs the company of his friends.

So I left alone at 4:30, Friday, July 6, with a certain reluctance about making the trip alone. Not because I don't enjoy solitude — but because I wanted Bjørn to share the wonderful experience at Caribou that Tor and I did alone, that Nina, Lars III and I did together over Memorial Day weekend.

I expected the trip here to take less than four and one-half hours, the usual time, if we stop at the Aitkin Dairy Queen and the Holiday station in Grand Rapids, as we usually do. But traffic was stop and go all the way on I-494 and even worse on Highway 101 from I-94 to Highway 169. I was already about one hour behind schedule.

About ten miles south of Milaca, the Ford Limo coughed, rattled, lost power and nearly quit. I made it to Milaca after most stations were closed. A kid at a station said I needed plugs. He could help me, but he had no plugs. So I went to the Holiday station, got the last set of suitable plugs. Then he looked all over for a 5/8 inch socket to fit the plugs. I went to Holiday again and bought him one.

Then he had no tool to gap the plugs. I got him one out of my tackle box. Then he said he was in a hurry, could we call Jim's in Onamia? His buddy pretended to call Jim's in Onamia on the pay phone. It supposedly rang several times with no answer. But when he replaced the receiver, he did not get a quarter back — obviously he had not put one in and was faking the call. So I left.

At Onamia, Jim's mechanic was gone. Everyone leaves early on Friday evening, so I went to Anderson Bros Standard. He finished working on a pick-up parking light, waited on eight gasoline customers, then got around to my car. During the spark plug installation, he waited on some more people and finished about 9:00 pm. I had now been on the road over four hours, still had nearly three to go.

Discouraged but determined, I kept hoping I would find a camping spot at Caribou, but no luck. So I went on to the parking lot at the North Star boat landing where overnight camping is prohibited. I put on a mosquito net, gloves, insect repellent, and slept not very well in the back seat from midnight until 5:30 am — might as well get an early start fishing.

I launched the boat and started fishing, and immediately started catching fish. I caught three nice rainbow trout, one lake trout and two rock bass by noon, but still wondered where I was going to spend the night. Using the Coleman stove, I cooked coffee on the boat, boiled potatoes, and was about to prepare a meal of fish and potatoes on the boat.

I went ashore to use the outhouse and the Lord be praised, the tent that was at the best site was gone! I rushed to the boat for my stuff, pitched our new $20.00 Camel 2-man tent and said, "The Lord is good, he takes care of his own." So here I am, as tired and happy as can be, working up a powerful appetite. Soon one of the rainbows goes into the frying pan.

I gave two bass to a couple of young fellas camped at the turn-around by the boat landing. They had no fish and were very grateful. They have beer, firecrackers and marijuana. I don't think any of that will help them catch fish. A guy in a canoe with a woman was smoking dope while paddling. The wind blew the "funny smoke" right at where I was fishing. They caught nothing and soon left.

I tried the outrigger ("oter") and it made me laugh. It was fun and interesting, but that's all. I caught no fish with it. There were more boats than usual. One water skiing group, I think from the A-frame and four or five boats, trolling too close to shore and catching nothing.

The Lord is great and the Lord is good. Blest be the Name of the Lord — Caribou fishing.

   Argo — (verbatim account)

Cannon River Carp

Dear Donald Clark,

When we are young, we sometimes say something profound by accident. As we become older, we enjoy making profound statements all of the time, and never by accident. I would like to repeat Edna Hong's gem from long ago: "All the Cannon River needs is a poet." And why not?

Just think of the legendary rivers memorialized by poets and their collaborators. We have the Shannon, the Volga, the Mississippi, the Danube, the Rhein, the Missouri, the Yukon, Dawson Creek, the Shenandoah, the Pecos, the Rio Grande, and many more. This is the stuff of imagination — of war and peace, of travel and discovery, and of course, of romance, as we know.

It is the discovery of the Cannon River that has been largely overlooked. We do not know where the name comes from, maybe Cannon Lake near Faribault or from some lost French explorer. We do know that every student who ever went to St. Olaf or Carleton has seen the river's downtown section, and some have discovered its beauty as it meanders through the arboretum or followed its magnificent course from Faribault, through the Dundas oasis to Northfield, then on to Lake Byllesby, Cannon Falls and the Mississippi at Red Wing. One of the top canoe trails in Minnesota is that section starting from Cannon Falls — from the falls of the Cannon to the great father of waters.

The Cannon has supplied power for flour milling in Dundas, a favorite stopover on the way to Faribault, and for Northfield, plus electrical power generators at Cannon Falls. And it has carried away run-off from sewers and city dumps along its entire length. The men's room at Mike & Al's had a direct pipe straight down to the Cannon near Archibald's mill until just a few years ago when Dundas finally got its first sewer, complements of Northfield. Many have drowned face-down in those fragrant waters.

But history does not record a single example of someone intentionally drinking Cannon River water. Fishermen have caught Walleyes, Northerns, and other game fish; they have also caught carp, Sheepshead, Buffalo, Suckers, Red Horse, Bullheads, and some fish with sores. You will notice that "carp" does not deserve capitalization because it is clear that the carp-infested tail waters at the Northfield dam have done much to damage the Cannon's reputation.

Once the city dump was moved and the blight of Hungry Hollow was converted to highway and park lands, a remarkable transformation of the river's image began. And numerous sewage treatment plants have had beneficial effects. Now some smart Oles need to remove the dam by the old Ames Mill and return the river to its natural state, the sort of river people can really admire. When we were kids, we rented canoes just north of the Fifth Street Bridge. Can that happen again? Of course it can.

The river will always become angry in springtime. It has risen above the stone walls in downtown Northfield several times in history and this will continue. Perhaps you recall how we paraphrased Shakespeare on these occasions, "Rivah, rivah, whyfore overflowest thee, thy banks?" This question, posed often, has never been answered. Should we ask the authorities if removal of the dam would make any difference?

But the most vexatious problem is also the most difficult to remedy, namely the high population of carp in the river. Anyone who has ever lived in Northfield will tell you it's the catholic carp that give the Cannon River its bad reputation. People around Northfield just plain do not like carp, or any crap for that matter. I fear no public relations plan could ever reverse that opinion. There is probably no point in having an annual carp festival. No one would come, who would eat them?

Carp management by the Minnesota DNR has been somewhat effective in cleaning up lakes. The DNR poison the water with rotenone, then pick up the dead carp as they float ashore. From Lake Marion one year in the mid-sixties, they hauled away 110 tons of carp. When they poison the water of a lake they erect fish barriers to prevent the carp from re-entry. I don't think that trick is possible in the Cannon River, but they never have tried, have they?

A note: The ubiquitous "they" refers to some guys in Duluth who phoned a Minneapolis radio station late one night while in their cups to settle once and for all the issue of who "they" are, so often quoted by common folk. The answer to the question came with the announcement, "We are they." But I digress again.

"They" won't do anything unless enough people demand it and are willing to pay for it; but as we all know this is a democracy where nothing gets done without votes and money. So that leaves us where we started, living with our nemesis, the carp, but they don't vote. And they may stay out of the way if we ignore them and not let them bother us. That seems to work fine with children.

Which brings us back to the notion of the Cannon River needing a poet such as Hobo. We don't have a Mark Twain, we have no equivalent of the Volga Boatmen or of the American version, the Erie Canal, and we don't have an "Ol' Man River." There seems to be only one solution. We need a song such as those that glorified the Shenandoah and the wide, wide Missouri. Who will write it and who will sing it? I suppose you and I can reluctantly take on the assignments. There probably won't be any money in it. Johnny Western is a possibility as a singer, or perhaps the St. Olaf Viking Male Chorus, if the motif is somewhat religious in nature, but that is a long shot, and the lyrics must address pass-time in the Dundas jail.

Our poem could benefit from memorializing a local personality such as Carl "Squint" Hower who can be linked to the Cannon as a source of unbounded energy and heroic status. Or Johnny Olson and his river escapades. Why not? We could make an even bigger legend of "Squint" than he already is. I have decided, Donald, at this point to put off the writing of a serious work memorializing the Cannon River. I offer instead this bit of drivel as a draft with which you and I can have some fun. Feel free to revise, criticize, and recite verse in song.

Cannon River Carp

Down at the Cannon, by the dam
The carp do swim and that's no sham
We kill them off, both great and small
Don't mind the smell, no not at all.

We throw them up upon the shore
And there they rot, don't swim no more.
As weapons we use rocks and guns
To kill them on their spawning runs.

There's plenty there for one and all
In Summer, Winter, Spring, or Fall.
I knew a guy who once jumped in
To save his dog called Rin-Sin-Sin.

The dog could swim, the man could not
And that is why they marked the spot
"Here lies our friend who took a dare:
He's heaven bound, but we don't care."

In days of old when men were bold
And guns ran out of lead,
They'd snag a carp and do him in
By biting off his head.

Then spit the eyeballs in their hand
And put 'em on a hook.
Their ladies always glanced away,
They couldn't stand to look.

"Fish on!" they cried, when they got one
And dragged it to the shore.
They'd put it in a gunny sack
And then return for more.

And when the gunny sack was full
So it stood perpendicular,
They'd take 'em home and fry 'em up
'Cause they weren't too particular.

Now Kindem, Clark, and Company
With reverence for this river
Would take away the carp it has,
A thought that makes some quiver.

To New York they would send them all
In trains that leave each day.
Freshwater fish are needed there,
Just watch the people pay.

The wise men say it's good to plan
Ahead in each endeavor,
And kill two birds with just one stone,
Our move is now or never.

The money we will not reject,
With Northfield we will share
Our profits for their river dear

For which we also care.

Argo — end of poem, thank goodness, Edna excuses me.

P.S. Enough carping about the carp; here's something important — the Citation for my state record Kokanee Salmon. The record still stands — check it out at MN DNR:

CERTIFICATE OF AUTHENTICITY
RECORD OF LARGEST FISH TAKEN BY ANGLING IN MINNESOTA

MINNESOTA DEPARTMENT OF NATURAL RESOURCES

Angler: Lars G. Kindem, Bloomington, MN; 8/6/1971

Salmon, Kokanee: 2 lbs., 15 oz.; 20" length, 11.5" girth

Caribou Lake, Itasca County, Minnesota, USA

Button... Button

Dear Donald,

It isn't often that I sew on a button, but it happens, particularly as autumn approaches each year and we ready for winter and the cold.

I save buttons during the course of the year on my dresser top. That way I will have a daily reminder, for months on end, that there is a small task to take into consideration in planning the day's activities. Plans change, of course, and the buttons remain.

In a sense, this brings on a slight, temporary attack of humility, and we have discussed that before. Humility is at once bothersome as well as easily dismissed. Some people enjoy humility. They have, throughout the ages, done great harm to themselves physically as well as mentally to induce a state of humility. More than a few have tried flagellation; some, in parts of the world, prostrate themselves before icons. But I never heard of anyone doing something dumb like that over a button. So I quickly dismiss any thoughts of being humble as soon as I leave my bedroom.

This morning then, I decided to take care of my annual button-sewing task. This is not to claim that I embarked on this mission with total confidence. I had before me four buttons of different sizes and colors. The hunt was on — the quarry, all the clothes with missing buttons. I should add here that I am not always successful. I have in my rosemaled sewing box an assembly of buttons dating back to 1957 when I became a man and put away my childish ways of having my mother sew on my buttons.

But it does not pay to be over confident. One must assume that the search will be far and wide, high and low, in and out, up and down, under and over. You understand the complexity of the issue. I have plenty of thread in various colors; I have many needles stuck into an object that is improperly called a "pincushion." No pins are stuck in the pincushion. They just disappear, especially at times when they are needed.

As a pragmatist, I have on occasion used safety pins in place of broken pajama snaps since I do not own a riveting tool. I have stapled tuxedo pants to hem them to proper length. There are those who use the word "button" in strange ways, such as, "Button your lip," when they really mean, "Close your mouth." I never heard anyone say, "Button the door," or "Button the window." But again, as you know, I tend to digress.

Into the closet I go, determined to get it over with quickly. Right off the bat I find two shirts. Easy. Then I find the suit pants. I go find a London Fog jacket, and there we have it. All buttons sewn in the time it takes to listen to chapel exercises from St. Olaf on WCAL, which I do, and did, and wish I once more could.

But an even weightier problem emerges. As I search the closet, I admire all those suits and sport coats, fourteen in all — and those white shirts and neckties that have fallen into desuetude during the years of my retirement. If I am to get my money's worth, I should wear a suit and tie daily, as my father did for years, for the same reason. Of course he lived to be ninety-eight, so he made out all right on that.

But I'm not about to forsake my new Argo-cargo pants for the sake of walking around in a three-piece suit. Neighbors would think I was a bit balmy and I would hate it. Worse, I could be mistaken, what with pipe and all as an English gentleman for I only wear suits at funerals and when I pole vault. I can hear it now — a car full of teenagers speeds past the house while I am raising the colors and one shouts out from the rear window, "Blimey, a Limey!" What would he say if he saw a well-suited pole vaulter in shirt and tie?

Right now I guess the only use I would have for a suit or sport jacket would be to conceal a shoulder holster, which I lack and couldn't use except when pole vaulting. I suppose I should have one, because I shoot well. The Governor of Minnesota in all haste signed a new conservative-sponsored "Conceal & Carry" law permitting just about anyone who is otherwise normal to walk about with a concealed handgun on their person for protection from evil-doers.

Yes, there are dilemmas all over the place. But we cannot solve them all, these dilemmas which we face daily here on my farm — raccoons, opossums, rabbits, squirrels, and deer munching on the crops; passersby swiping apples at will, buttons on the dresser, suits unused, cargo pants that require decisions to be made as to what to keep in the large pockets, a toilet that tips over at a most inopportune time, so on and so forth.

But we work at it. Required is a cup of coffee, a pull on the pipe, and some good old twisted logic from time to time that only one raised as a kid in Northfield could understand.

Hobo, as somebody said on your twelfth night, you may not have had the privilege of being born in Northfield, but you were raised there, and remember, "some are born great, some achieve greatness, and some have greatness thrust upon them." Donald, you have buttoned up all three.

    Lars — "date unknown"

By the Fire

Dear Donald,

I like to sit by the fire and I know you do too. It doesn't matter if it's a small fire down by Heath Creek or a larger one at a lake like Caribou.

And there were fires we didn't sit around, like giant bonfires at keg parties in the Carleton arboretum along the river, or homecoming bonfires at St. Olaf, and the Carleton ones lit by Oles. Whether you sit by an outdoor fire or one in an indoor fireplace, it seems that sooner or later you will stare, eyes out of focus, into the glowing red coals and ponder life and the day's activities. Perhaps life's journeys are brought to mind at these times.

You have seen me take a small stick from the fire and light my pipe with the burning ember. Perhaps it was because my mother told me that was what her father did that I, too, began the ritual. I will observe that same ritual whenever and wherever I sit by the fire. It is one more link to the past, to a grandfather I never knew but realize now that I would have admired, respected, and loved.

You remember our early camping forays out by Heath Creek when the first thing we would do was to build a fire. It was always thus at BAB (Bare Ass Beach) by the Cannon too. We never had any cooking utensils along on those expeditions. We took whatever was handy out of the kitchen.

The favorite, of course, was Campbell's pork and beans. These we would cook in the can right in the coals of the fire. Opening the lid was a safety precaution to prevent explosions, as well as providing a handle for lifting the hot simmering can from the fire.

Then all we had to do was take turns spooning the beans out — unless there was a can for each happy camper. I don't remember a single time on our trips when we roasted wieners on a stick. We would have had to buy the wieners but never had money for that. After all, kids don't spend money on food.

When we got to boy scout camps we performed the normal

rituals, making fire with flint and steel (I still have mine) or making a small bow and stick for rotating in a hole in a log. I always thought that was a stupid way. The one I liked the most was a magnifying glass. However, in scouts no one built fires on a sunshiny day.

Once, during a winter scout outing at Heath Creek, we had to scoop out a hole in the side of a snow drift and build a fire in that small cave. It worked fine, but made no sense to me, because on that cold winter's day I wanted a big fire out there in the open so we could get warm. Well, we warmed some snow in a snow bank, and the troop leader was satisfied; we passed a merit badge test. I loved merit tests.

When we came of age there were occasional fires by the Cannon River in the arboretum where Hoz and Gus provided the first 16-gallon wooden keg of beer from Fleckenstein's in Faribault-on-the-Cannon.

I went to a few of those, and remember meeting a half dozen Carleton and St. Olaf's finest who were interested in some sort of competitive beer guzzling. I don't recall which team won, perhaps it was a tie, but Homer certainly deserved a medal for his efforts.

I caught one Carl, later a U.S. District Judge, intentionally spilling his beer while taking a leak in the bushes. I yelled at him and told him that was unacceptable behavior. He understood, drank up, but later passed out. We left him there with a big cupful in case he wanted refreshment upon awakening, and we left the bonfire going to keep warm.

Another memorable bonfire was the Fubar gathering at Union Lake, the famous floating keg blast. We built a roaring fire and started a huge log and dead tree ablaze, then went out on the lake in homemade rafts and inner tubes for the floating keg blast. There was no keg, we just called it that, but it sure was a blast.

I think each participant had a 12-pack, perhaps two cases or more of the new Schlitz 16-ouncers. The water was cold and we ended up gallivanting and cavorting around the fire, laughing a lot. Hobo and Hooper had a tent and one of our number fell off a log and got skinned up. Another, preaching in his cups, maintained that Fubar was headed for posterity or extinction. We told him to shut up and drink his beer. He did, and we named him Scuba.

We cleaned up our mess and some returned to the campus. Three or four of us did not, for we lived at home. We surely enjoyed our camaraderie there by the fire. These friends knew how to be friendly and also how to be Fubars. It comes natural with people of high quality.

The St. Olaf homecoming bonfires were a ritual. I remember from the time I was two and a half years old. Most people associate the Ole bonfires only with the homecoming of alumni. Actually, alumni have nothing to do with it. They usually gather in Dundas that Friday night. I suppose part of the origin of the bonfire has to do with homecoming.

But it should be remembered that in Norway people light huge bonfires on Midsummer Eve in June; others celebrate St. Olaf's Day, July 29, with a huge bonfire. The word for bonfire in Norwegian is bål (pronounced "ball"), and people would say "Let's have a ball." Sweet.

The Oles and Carls often assumed it was their duty to fire up each other's pile of wood before the scheduled time. On one occasion, my freshman year, the Carls took an old Chevy and filled it with their suicide squad. We saw them speed around the stalag barracks of the Viking Court and head straight up Old Main Hill. Someone hollered, "Her de kom, boys!" in Norwegian, of course.

We armed ourselves with bats, 2 x 4s and other weapons, and stood ready for battle. The Carl vehicle could not quite make it up the crest of the hill because the wheels were spinning for lack of purchase. We blasted their vehicle, bashing everything inside and out, and sent the Carl delegation over to Ytterboe with an armed escort of about 30 Oles for special homecoming haircuts.

It didn't take a genius to figure out that in addition to the campus junk assembled by John Berntsen's crew, there were additional items gathered by students to throw onto the fire pile that didn't really fit into the category of scrap wood and building materials.

The largest bonfires were always those built during or immediately after new building construction. No one tried to roast wieners in these blazes, at least until after midnight. Didn't you and I set off a huge mortar rocket there one year? I know I did. It had a 2-foot tube, dug into the ground and a fuse about two feet in length. It went up and exploded with a powerful

"Ca-Boom!"

It is nice to have a fire in the fireplace at home, but not nearly as pleasant as those campfires in the woods while on fishing or hunting trips. A memorable fire was the one Bjørn and I built at North Star Campground. We had been hunting the grouse on a cold day with no success. I shot a rabbit for supper. We set two forked sticks by the fire and put the skinned rabbit on the rotisserie spit for proper roasting.

At that time, cold and hungry, I felt like a mountain man and devoured most of the rabbit. Bjørn took a few polite bites, but had an awful stomach ache and was unsure about that particular meal. To me, it was wonderful! Sitting by that fire, eating rabbit, was better than any banquet I had ever attended.

During our family camping trips, the longest of which was a western expedition lasting seven weeks, Nini as head chef worked wonders with her campfire cookery. She usually had a black cast iron Dutch oven on the fire, and our meals included everything from deep fried oysters on Mt. Rainier to trout on the shores of Swiftcurrent Lake in Glacier Park. There was no such thing in our family as a fussy eater with the high quality fare we enjoyed. Nini once prepared roast turkey with all the accompaniments.

For a late supper, the kids loved to bake pies in the coals and roast marshmallows in the fire. After all the food was gone, they enjoyed poking sticks into the coals, rearranging the structures until sack time.

That is the way it can be with a campfire. You should have some good vittles and good friends for company. The talk is always good, the companionship unequaled anywhere in this world. Isn't that right, Donald! — by the fire!

Argo — March 1, 1996

Books & Bookmaking

Dear Donald,

Back in 1955 when I was a student at St. Olaf and poor, I had good company. My best friend and classmate, Wendy Miller, was in the same boat.

There was some question as to whether we would make it to the end of our senior year with the few bucks at hand. So it was that we formed a partnership to see if we could make some money. We did not want to work, no. The idea, rather, was to live by our wits.

So we set up a betting operation outside the bookstore in the post office lobby. It wasn't long before Homer Robinson and Marty Fossum of the bookstore became curious about our operation. However, their investigation led them to conclude that we were not in direct competition with the bookstore, and so they left us alone.

Our betting proposition was this: we set up a chart on which the suckers could place their five or ten cent bets. We had a real handle on things. The game was as follows: they could choose any three hitters in the major leagues who would, on any given day, collect a total of five hits among them. Little did they know they had only a slim chance, if any.

President Granskou looked us over once, but when he saw me there, just winked and walked on by. We never saw "Lumli." Clarence Carlson, professor of math who taught statistics, just rolled his eyes toward the ceiling when he stumbled onto our operation on his way to the Lion's Den for coffee.

Billy Benson, who knew ball, having followed it since 1895 and captained the 1905 ball team at St. Olaf, concurred that the suckers had no chance. (You will doubtless recall the trouble we got into in Benson's Political Science class when Dick Werdahl quoted our hero Michael Mantle as a reputed expert on European Power Politics during one of our famous episodes when we used the "avslav" or "bluff" theory while standing to recite. Benson woke up upon hearing the name Michael Mantle and asked, rhetorically, "You don't by any chance mean the baseball player

Mickey Mantle, do you?") But I digress.

It was true. The Oles didn't really have much of a chance to win. We got as many bets as we could handle during the short period after chapel when we set up shop daily on the table reserved for student activities. Well, as you can imagine, the boys finally caught on and complained about the fairness of the five hit deal. Dick Werdahl and some of his baseball teammates protested, and insisted we lower the odds. So we did. Now, under the new rules, the bettors could choose any three hitters to collect four hits among them. Such a deal! We loved it so much we could hardly concentrate on our studies this final month before graduation.

A clarification is useful here: remember, Mickey Mantle, Willie Mays and Roger Maris were really hot hitters. Also, Al Kaline, Detroit, was batting about 340; Richie Ashburn, of the Phillies, was close to that. Ray Boone and Jack Jensen and Duke Snider led the entire world in RBIs and were obvious choices in the betting. But remember — even if each hitter got one hit, that meant, if he was at bat four times, it would be a .250 average. Not bad, but not good enough. Most guys fully expected better of their favorite hitters. But most guys didn't understand ball odds as we did.

We came out way ahead, and had ready cash for any type of sandwich "Lightning" could serve up in the Lion's Den. We even had enough for study sessions downtown at our favorite watering hole, the "Well." But after about one month of prosperity, we became too cocky. We decided to expand our operation and take on bookmaking for the Kentucky Derby. That was a mistake.

We were convinced that Nashua would be a walk-away and so we jiggled the odds a little to entice the guys to place their sucker bets on the long shots. The biggest mistake was to give Swaps, the gray from California, a 4 - 1 spread. (We did not know that Swaps was a "mudder," and we also did not know it was going to rain all morning of the race.)

"They're off!" cried the announcer as the horses left the gate. Saratoga (8 - 1) immediately took the pole and our horse, Nashua, (3 - 2) under the famed Eddie Arcaro, was on his shoulder. Down the backstretch, Blazing Count (10 - 1) gave us a near heart attack by taking the lead; and in the final turn it was Nashua, followed by Blazing Count, Saratoga, and back in the pack was Swaps, under the indomitable Willie Shoemaker.

We had it in the bag! Pandemonium reigned in the Thorson Hall TV lounge as the crowd of over 100 rabid fans rose to their feet, cheering for Swaps. Then it happened: Willie Whipped, and Swaps answered the call. Blazing Count faded in the stretch along with Saratoga, but Nashua hung on. He was valiant until the final dash when Swaps, the dirty rat dream-killer and home-wrecker horse from hell nailed Nashua by a nose. He won, as I recall, $108,400 for his time of 2:01.4.

Napoleon had his Waterloo, Paul Holtan had his biology final, and we had our Kentucky Derby. It was all over for us. Everyone in the world now knows that Nashua was king of the three-year olds that year, winning the Preakness and Belmont Stakes. He won three quarters of a million that year.

Wendy really knew a lot about horses and he was basically responsible for giving Nashua the nod. Wendy and I huddled. What were we going to do, laugh it off? Smile a lot and slap our buddies on their backs and say we were just kidding?

Not a chance! All the guys remembered their baseball betting losses of the past month and showed no pity. Some had lost over a dollar, all told. So we signed IOUs — a lot of them, dozens or more — and developed a profound hatred for Swaps and all his ancestors. It has been forty-eight years and six months since I last spoke his name.

To be sure, there are guys who have had a million bucks riding on a deal that later fell through. I know the feeling, and Wendy does too. We tried in vain to explain away this unfortunate derby which we contended must have been on a Mafia fix.

Well, there's no getting around it. We had to dine on a two-course meal: crow and humble pie. Suffice it to say we lost our shirts and went back to Lightning's 15-cent peanut butter sandwiches. Prior to that Kentucky Derby, I was a strapping six-foot son of a gun. I shrank, almost immediately, to my present 5' and 9".

My nature being what it was, I had to have a little fun with this episode. I went down to Burt Sawyer, City Attorney, and asked for a blank subpoena form. I filled out the subpoena something like this:

> Wendell Donald Miller, laying aside all excuses, you are hereby commanded to appear before the Honorable Urban Steinmann, Judge

of Rice County District Court, to answer at a preliminary hearing charges, that you solicited wager subscriptions, contrary to the laws of the State of Minnesota, to wit: The Kentucky Derby.

I mailed the subpoena from Faribault, but Wendy was not fooled. He incorrectly determined that St. Olaf was in Dakota County and so assumed the subpoena must be bogus. He threw it away.

I had screwed up again, just as the devil did in Ibsen's Peer Gynt: "Se, det fikk fanden fordi han var dumm og ikke beregnet sitt publikum!" or, we can put the quote in nynorsk, which I prefer: "Sjå, det fekk faen for han var dumm og ikkje rekna med publikummet sitt!" ("See, that's what the devil got because he was dumb and did not understand his public.")

Wendy and I embarked on a few cleverly devised diversionary tactics to take the boys' minds off any notion they might harbor about collecting their winnings. That's when we took our famous "Argo" walks as members of the "Argo Walking Club."

As luck would have it, most of the guys got caught up in a combination of these nefarious activities; the remainder of track and field and ball schedules, and of course, the final exams. We managed to slip out of the net, as it were, although we paid off a couple of guys.

But it was tough. Wendy developed a habit as a result of this incident that he has continued to this day: He still finds it very hard to "pull the trigger on a dollar." We graduated from St. Olaf absolutely penniless, and that, my friend, is a rather inauspicious way to head out into the world.

We learned some lessons that were not in the books on bookmaking.

    Argo —

Carleton Lake

Dear Donald,

The only places to go for a swim in Northfield when we were kids were Carleton Lake and BAB (Bare Ass Beach on the Cannon River). You remember, of course, that on occasion in the winter we climbed in the window at the St. Olaf pool for a swim. But we discussed that in an earlier letter. We also covered the drowning I witnessed in Carleton Lake, so we won't get into that either.

You remember that there was only one "beach," the grassy slope on the West side of the lake by the Carleton arboretum. John Westerlund, our high school phy-ed teacher, was lifeguard from 2:00 to 5:00 daily. We called him "Wes," and his son was "Johnny Western" of "Paladin" fame on TV — "Have Gun, Will Travel."

The other side of the lake by the dam was reserved for those who proved they could swim across the lake. Dog paddling was acceptable, so that's what I did to pass the test. The lake over on that side was deeper, perhaps seven feet deep. There was a diving board, now long gone, although the cement footings remain. But we liked to jump or dive out of the big tree. The real sport was to do the "Cannon Ball." Now and then one would cannon ball into a school of unseen bullhead minnows and get stung all over.

Wes would dab the wounds with a cotton swab dipped in alcohol. I only heard of one guy making a bad dive. That was my brother, Erling, who bears a scar on his temple where he hit his head on the edge of the dam. My brother, Olaf, who weighed in excess of 270 pounds, liked to float around the middle of the lake, smoking, with cigarettes and Zippo resting on his belly.

My brother Alf, wounded and veteran of four major sea campaigns in the South Pacific, was the strongest swimmer in town before he volunteered for the Navy in 1944 at age seventeen. He could swim the "figure 8" which consisted of swimming around both islands, a feat we all thought stupendous.

Wes was really well-built and had an unusual swimming

stroke. It was done on his side, with his left arm extending up and over and out front. It reminded us of a shark fin going through the water. He always got water in his ears and would do several kicks with each leg after he got on shore to shake his body and head. We liked to talk with Wes because he was always friendly and nice, and he stuttered when he spoke. He had a very powerful build which he developed in two ways. First, he had been a lumber jack until he started ninth grade at age twenty-nine, and he liked phy-ed.

Second, he followed the Charles Atlas "Dynamic Tension" exercises advertised in popular magazines. Nobody ever kicked sand in his face. Wes had also played the piano for silent movies and could play anything you wanted from ear, but he couldn't read notes. Remember how he used to play lively piano tunes during lunch?

We had no bath house so we changed clothes in a grove of lilac bushes. The girls had sentries to watch their grove when one of them was changing. We never tried to peek. Dog days came in August and nobody wanted to swim when that thick green scum was on the water. I remember when the city physician, Dr. Nielsen, closed the lake to swimming because of outbreaks of bacterial infections, mainly in the ears. The lake was also closed to swimming during the polio epidemic in the early '50s. Then we had to swim at the BAB. We played lots of catch with a football on the level ground behind the beach. Our coach, Ed Byhre, encouraged us to work out, and we would get together at Carleton Lake almost every day, especially Saturday and Sunday afternoons.

This was a typical swimming outing for Argo from age nine through age twelve: Get my suit and a towel and on my bike; cut through the back yard toward Madison Street, passing Briddia Vallem's apple trees. Swipe a few green ones, then ride down Second Street and out to the Carleton heating plant. Pick up a couple of rock salt crystals, drink out of the hose, and head for Carleton Lake. Hide the apples so I would have a snack available later. Swim and laugh. Pick on some kid by saying he urinated underwater (we all did, I think) and laugh. After the swim, ride home, stopping off at John Sawyer's or Dick Jacobson's 916 Club to read comics and listen to "Jack Armstrong," "Superman," or "Batman," then home for supper and back out again.

Once a year, my family had a picnic on the far eastern shore of the lake. We had no car, so we took a 777 taxi for a quarter. These picnics were a delight, with lots of good things to eat. Olaf would float and smoke and Alf would swim the figure eight. I would sit on the blanket and eat their share before they got back. We usually had lefse, potato salad, lime Jell-O with pears, and sandwiches. Mamma and pappa had coffee and the kids had nectar. The 777 taxi would pick us up at the agreed time and we would go home.

Last summer I walked along the shores of Carleton Lake and it seemed much smaller than before. The bushes are gone, new ones are in different places. It has changed some but still is quite recognizable as the place where we had so much fun as kids.

The next time you visit, Donald, we can go for a walk and we will see ghosts: Eddie, Wes, and the others, but no one swims there now, yet still a pleasant walk, for sure, at Carleton Lake.

    Argo —

Cause and Effect

Dear Donald,

Today, April 9, is the anniversary of a date that lives in infamy — the attack on Norway by Nazi German military forces in 1940. Outside my kitchen hangs a Norwegian wind sock flag, as always. On the pole near the street flies the Norwegian flag in silent tribute to the memory of those people who suffered the greatest of indignities that can befall a nation, the forceful occupation by another nation's killers. The Nazis attacked early in the morning with blitzkrieg effectiveness by land, sea, and air.

Particularly horrifying and frightening to the Norwegian citizenry, my relatives, were the Stuka dive bomber raids. All strategic locations were bombed. It so happened that my mother's youngest sister, Marita Midttun, lived with her husband and three young children in a house close to the rail lines at Voss, the Aspen of Norway. A Stuka-delivered bomb landed just outside their living room and that was the end of most of their house. It was also the end of innocence for a peaceful family.

My cousin, Andi, said to me when she told of this in 1953 on the occasion of my first visit to Norway: "Du sko ha sett stovo oukan etter tyskane hadde bombet. Det saog ut nett so eit potagjerde!" ("You should have seen our place after the Germans had bombed. It looked just like a potato patch!") The family fled to temporary housing with friends on the other side of the valley, a region known as "the gray side."

My mother's older sister, Gunnhild Sekse, also lived at Voss, the birthplace of papa Ingvald Kindem. She was an elementary school teacher who never married and dedicated her life to serving children. The German occupation forces decreed certain Nazi changes in the curriculum and teaching which she declined. Her punishment was to lose her job, income, and contact with her beloved children. She lived under house arrest for the duration of the war, getting out for her first walk around the neighborhood on May 7, 1945, the day of liberation from the Nazis. What food she got was from friends and relatives who had little enough for themselves.

Aunt Gunnhild was here for a visit in 1950. We decided to

take her for a ride up Nicollet Avenue on a street car and do some shopping. On the street car happened to be a drunk who was singing loudly in German the national anthem sung by Germans occupying Norway. She stood up, cried aloud, "NEI!" ("No"!) and bashed the fellow full in the face with her purse. Passengers on the street car cheered and applauded her action.

All during the war, my family and others worried about their families in Norway. My oldest two brothers, Olaf and Halvor, both born in Norway, joined the Norwegian Ski Troopers of the American 99th Infantry Battalion (detached), a unit that trained in mountain operations in Colorado. All of my first cousins, aunts and uncles, and my grandma suffered loss of income and shortages of food and clothing during the occupation. But they suffered most of all from loss of freedom and the heavy weight of indignities they had to bear.

Some physical remnants of the war exist today. I could show you a couple of deteriorating gun emplacements, guns removed, and a machine gun nest just outside the museum donated by my father's uncle, Lars Kindem, to the city of Voss. But most of the physical evidence of the war has long since disappeared.

The emotional hurt is not entirely gone, however. I recall vividly the reaction my cousin, Knut Midttun, had when he saw older German tourists and heard them speak. He always became livid and was of the opinion that former occupation troops were now taking vacations to Norway, pointing out to their families where they were stationed — an eerie thought.

I know the following to be true from a personal encounter in Norway last year. Wendy and Marlene Miller and I were visiting Holmenkollen ski jump in Oslo. I was explaining the elements of scoring jumping events when I noticed an elderly man listening intently.

I asked if he agreed with my presentation. He leaned forward and whispered that he was a German tourist and didn't want others to hear. I asked him where he was stationed during the war, and he told me that he was a Luftwaffe pilot ferrying men and supplies into Gardermoen Military Airport. Not wishing to offend Marlene, I quietly whispered to the Kraut some solid advice on what he had better do immediately. He quickly left, taking his wife with him. That's what we do with Krauts.

I cannot write all the incidents and episodes from the war

that directly or indirectly involved my family. To do so would require more time and patience than I have, and would go beyond the message of this morning, April 9th. Suffice it to state, Donald, that I harbor ill will and bad feelings toward the so-called "Master Race." I don't like those guys and I never will.

Now comes the hard part. I have been a member of Bethlehem Lutheran Church in Minneapolis since 1957 and was married there. All our children were baptized there, except Nina. She was baptized in the same church at Voss as my father and his ancestors. Ingvald and Anna and Aunt Gunnhild were sponsors. They wore national costumes, of course. It was Easter Sunday, April 14, 1963.

Some years ago, perhaps the early eighties, my son, Tor, and I attended a church service at Bethlehem Lutheran. The organist struck up a tune that Tor quickly recognized as Haydn's 1797 composition, "Old Austria" — "Gott erhalte Franz den Kaiser" — Germany's national anthem adopted by Hitler. Tor jabbed me with his elbow and said, "We're walkin' out."

We walked out. I stayed out for one year. Tor is still out. Later, in November, 1994, the organist struck up the same tune for the first hymn. I said to the woman next to me, Phyllis Brynestad, whose husband Larry graduated from St. Olaf in 1958, and sings in the church choir, "I'm walking out!" I did. I have remained out because I cannot stand the thought of that German organist's insensitively playing that tune in a church founded by Norwegians and visited by Norwegians and supported by Norwegians.

Trouble is, I see no way to confront her and secure her promise not to do it again. It is a hymn tune in our hymnal, one we inherited from the Missouri Synod before they backed out of a union with our synod.

When I sought advice from my brother, Roald, the minister, he merely asked whether it was a hymn printed in our hymnal. I began to wonder what planet he was living on.

So I decided to consult a higher authority, my son, Bjørn. He is also a St. Olaf man and understands me and our family history. He said, "You did the right thing, Pappa."

The problem is — what next? We know the cause and effect, but that's as far as it goes I guess.

    Argo — April 9, date to remember, 1996

Changed by Chance

Dear Donald,

The Pupil Said: "Master, I read somewhere that we should not believe things will happen by chance; we should see to it that they do happen."

The Master Replied: "I am glad you read that, even though the idea is flawed. In reality, much of life is a chance. That is often why fighting men die. They cannot change what happens by chance. I can think of many examples of the element of chance affecting the outcome. The draft lottery was one. Getting on the wrong subway and getting shot could be another. In a film, "Dirty Harry" posed the element to a would-be robber, a punk, saying, 'I know you are wondering whether I fired five shots or six. Come to think about it...but this is a .44 Magnum... head clean off...do you wanna take a chance, punk?' He aims at the punk's head, pulls the trigger and 'click!' — Chance?"

Well there now, Donald, I have some illustrative material to add in support of the Master's thesis: everyone has been affected by chance. There are countless examples of chance that the Missouri Synod people would deny, but they nevertheless have lifelong effects on us.

Take the case of the boy throwing a chunk of frozen dirt into my right eye. This was the most significant event in my life, and it changed many things. When he threw the clump at me, I was rounding the Northeast corner of our house at 101 Lincoln; he was rounding the Southeast corner at the same time. He threw on the run. I was on the run. The clump could hit one inch off in any direction and many chapters in my life would have been different.

A number of difficulties have required adjustment. I shoot long guns left-handed, for one thing. In high school, catching the football or basketball was difficult because of my lack of depth perception. I never played football in college, although I suppose I could have tried. The ROTC rejected me at St. Olaf so I could not graduate as an officer and a gentleman, merely a gentleman. I was also ruled 4-F by the Selective Service and passed the Foreign Service Entrance Exam preparatory to beginning my chosen career, but was rejected because of the eye examination.

From the late forties I noticed what others perhaps may not have seen but which I saw each time I looked into the mirror. My right eye began drifting slightly starboard. My college yearbook pictures all show me in some sort of clowning action so I would not have to stare directly into the camera lens. As I looked directly into the eyes of anyone, I felt unsure, waiting for them to avert their gaze, which some did.

And then there was the incident sliding off the Menomonie bridge on the way back from Homer's 1957 New Year's Eve party in Eau Claire. After the crash at the end of the bridge, and starting from the bottom of the deep snow-covered ravine, Hoz and Gus somehow pulled me to the top, climbing all the way up the steep bank holding my eyeball in my hand as blood gushed out. That incident did not help matters with my eye. Fortunately, my wife accepted me as I was, and that matter never became a troublesome issue.

As I rolled through the sixties, however, the eye drifted more and more so that I became a walleyed teacher, most distracting to students whenever I would call on someone without using a name. I noticed, more frequently, students would look from side to side, wondering whom I meant.

Finally, in 1969, I asked a friend from St. Olaf, Dr. John Nilsen, by now a distinguished ophthalmologist, to adjust the muscles on my eyeball. This "strabismus process" was more or less successful and a source of great satisfaction and relief. One problem was solved, although only cosmetically.

I still bump into cupboard doors, tree branches and idiots who don't watch where they are going, and of course I occasionally fall out of apple trees. Bright light enters a pupil that is always dilated, a problem on bright days. The iris is still elevated somewhat, as I see when looking into the mirror. The onset of glaucoma has been the result of too much insult to the eye. Fortunately, I can control the pressure within the eyeball by daily instilling a drop of "timoptic."

And so it is, Hobo, that each day I have a reminder of that day in 1939 when a six-year-old had his life changed — by chance.

Argo — March 22, 1996

Peace on Earth, Good Will to All People!

Dear Donald,

I'm forwarding the Christmas card I received from Cricket in Boston, in case yours got lost in the mail trying to find you at your many known and unknown addresses.

Argo —

Dear Argo, Fabled Fubars, Family and Friends!

June and I are well and enjoying a life of refined, if not Retired, grace! Well, as much as possible in this day and time.

We bring you greetings from our aging home in Newton, Massachusetts. Also home to the former World Champion Boston Red Sox, N.E. Patriots, still 'presumptive' Celtics and, soon-to-be, Stanley-Cup-winning Bruins! Ah well, no matter, still winners, all!

We have been blessed this year with various visits to exotic places such as Gales Ferry, Connecticut (June's Grandkids); Long Beach, Palos Verdes, and Yorba Linda, California (My Grandkids); Leipzig, Germany (Choral Workshop and concerts); and Stavanger, Norway (Looking for Jarratt roots), where our picture was taken inside the humble red-brick Lutheran Cathedral, while I listened to a J.S. Bach Prelude and Fugue being practiced on its wonderful organ. Would I have been there in 1955 with Argo and the magnificent St. Olaf Choir!

June has been busy making and selling her unique jewelry; Yours Truly getting his flying memoir and first novel published, writing short stories and singing with several local organizations, including The Highland Glee Club's 'Century of Singing' celebration, having been founded in Newton Highlands in 1908. June is working on her eBay-like website and David has his web page 'on line' at www.dajarratt.com.

We had hoped to send each of you a singing email Christmas greeting, but something happened during the digital non-recording thereof that prohibits a repeat of last year's offering. We look forward to better success next year.

We trust this epistle, and the above beautiful reminder of the coming season, find you all in fine fettle. And, that you will all have a blessed, healthy and prosperous new year.

Sent with much love and God's Blessings,

— The Cricket —
David Jarratt & June Lion
19 Walsingham St.
Newton, MA 02462-1511, USA

Bottle Adventures

Dear Donald,

I have gathered a number of herb bottles, small, thick glass, with tight fitting plastic fitments on the lids so that when closed, they are both air tight and water tight. Just to make sure they will not leak, I epoxy the lids so they cannot be removed without breaking the glass with an implement — but not before I enclose a message in the bottle — a new message for each bottle.

A sample message will be: "If you're reading this, you're too close to my island." (signed, "Argo"). Other messages from you may vary in content, scope and meaning. I envision, for example, an invitation to the dance, in the event the bottle is opened by a single woman in her fifties (n.). I will let your imagination, which is unmatched by anyone living in states west of the Mississippi, take you through the multitudinous possibilities. You may choose to record your suggestions and ideas on 3" x 5" index cards for later reference.

The prepared bottles will be released into the Cannon River in Northfield behind the Carleton stadium, preferred because of its proximity to the former home of our dear friend, Rawhide. We don't know the duration of the journey for each of the bottles to its destination, where each will be found by some fortunate individual on the coast of Norway or in one of its fjords. Whatever.

We follow the course of the bottles: Cannon River, thence Mississippi River, into the Gulf of Mexico, around the Florida Peninsula on the Gulf Stream Current, eventually to the North and Norwegian Seas.

In one bottle, I will enclose an example of military occupation scrip from World War II, Asian Theater. I happen to have a quantity on hand which I had saved for some useful purpose such as this. The next bottle will contain a $1.00 bill, autographed by me. This may be called "Throwing good money after bad." I do it all the time.

Another bottle will contain your name and address together with an invitation to dine with you at your place on a good home-cooked meal of pork chops with mushroom gravy and homemade bread. The invitation will ask that the finder notify you of the approximate time of arrival in Portland or San Francisco so you can clear a place at table. I hope you approve.

A lock of my faithful Argo-the-dog's hair (i.e., fur) will be placed in another bottle together with a note inviting the finder to go on an all-expense paid pheasant hunt with Argo & Argo, somewhere in Rice County west of Dundas. Guns and ammo will be provided for use free of charge.

Of course, I cannot resist a ruse. I enclose a Powerball lottery ticket with a note informing that the ticket won $10 million US dollars and that the deadline for redeeming the ticket is January 1, 2005. The finder will likely overlook the obvious inconsistency in the information, but the motivation to believe is too strong to resist.

Some people will believe anything no matter how preposterous if they are of a mind to do so (cf. gold tablets Moroni found buried in the ground in upstate New York by Joseph Smith).

Yes, Donald, our bottle adventures will be fun.

Argo — 3/3/1997

Ytterboe is Dead

Dear Donald,

The Fubars recently had their 40th Popstand reunion and here are the collective notes we assembled when the boys rallied in Burnsville to recount the shooting of Ytterboe-the-dog on May 22, 1957. We were all there at the time, all of Fubar, and we were all involved in the historic Ytterboe event one way or another.

You will recall that I graduated from the Popstand in 1955, but then took a post graduate year in 1956-57 after selling insurance with my new red Buick the year before, so I finished the last time at 'Olaf in the spring of 1957. What a year that was. Ytterboe was probably the first major incident at St. Olaf where nearly all of the students reacted to a particular incident, and most of Carleton joined in as well.

When the Fubars were here for the 40th reunion of the class of '58, we had a great time breaking bread at Argo's round table, telling stories, and piecing together everything we could remember about the shooting of Ytterboe; we also consulted the May 1957 newspapers and magazines, but they often got it wrong. Here's what I recall about the spring of 1957 and the so-called "silent" Eisenhower era — please send your recollections.

First of all, Hobo, remember the time of the year. It was May and things always start to go funny in the month of May because we're getting to the end of the school year, the warm weather comes, the students change. In the Eisenhower years, we were called the "silent generation" because we didn't seem to have any control over our destiny when we grew to maturity in the fifties.

We had the draft to face, strict mores and standards of church and state, and all of the control in a town like Northfield rested with the "townies" — chamber of commerce, junior chamber, business clubs like Rotary and Kiwanis, and others like the VFW, American Legion, Eagles and the Elks, right out of Sinclair Lewis' Gopher Prairie.

The "townies" were mostly World War II veterans, and after the war they took over every aspect of the town, but we really didn't have any way to move around in that system, "to be somebody." It felt rigid and it felt stifling.

We may have been called the silent generation, but I don't think we were silent for very long. I recall the spring of my junior year in 1954 when we made a trip to the River Road Club in Mendota to hear the first rock-and-roll music that had just started to catch on. The same year, I wore the first pair of Bermuda shorts on campus and everybody was saying, "Wow," so I ran down to Perman's clothing store and told them, "You better order a lot of these pants with the legs cut off." Dr. Agnes Larson ("Aggie") wouldn't let me in the door of her history class wearing them, but that was all right.

Northfield in the 1950s was also affected by the beat generation — beatniks and weird people with strange new poetry and literature that college kids liked and found liberating. We had poetry readings at different places. Dylan Thomas, for example, was popular, and many others. We didn't just stick with the English classroom textbooks and reading program that was given by 'Olaf. We went far field to get into other things like Unamuno, "in search of meaning," our phrase of the day.

There was an Air Force ROTC detachment at St. Olaf in the '50s and a lot of students were involved in that, including several Fubars, and it may or may not have changed their mindsets on things, but I don't think it made them more conservative. Marty and Hoz both made full colonel and remained Fubar; Cricket too, as an Air Force pilot and Army aviator.

The country was in a Cold War with the Soviet Union in the '50s, and we had a draft law at the time so all of the guys had to go into the service after graduation unless you had a medical deferment like I had with my bad right eye or were a conscientious objector like Howard Hong in World War II.

And then came the shooting of Ytterboe on a nice spring day in May and the uproar the subsequent events had in town and at Carleton and St. Olaf. I generally got along fine with the local power brokers downtown town and with the 'Olaf administration as well, especially with president Granskou; he was an ally and we had a good friendship for many years. I didn't really fear anyone on campus, including the Dean of Men, because I knew if anything happened, Granskou would come to the rescue.

Our small group of mostly Northfielders was called "Fubar."

It was like an exclusive club that several others tried to join but couldn't because they were considered "phonies," and we hung out pretty much together. We didn't have any dues or anything like that, but we were very good friends and have remained so ever since.

There wasn't any real rebellious attitude around the campus except for some individuals who might get a little goofy from time to time, especially in the spring, and if there was some beer drinking going on.

I remember when some guys chained the entrance doors to the library and padlocked them shut so people couldn't get in or out. Then someone else cut the lights. The gals started squealing and the guys were running around trying to get out. I was there and got onto a step ladder trying to make some order out of the chaos and Lottie Bergh, one of the assistant librarians, knocked me over and said, "Get out of here."

There was another episode when some guys started up a bulldozer when they were building Boe Chapel and parked it in front of the main entrance doors of the library, then ran down the battery so it wouldn't start.

Another time, somebody hot-wired several cars in the Agnes Mellby parking lot and parked them in front of the library. I know who did it, but I'm not telling. That was in the spring of 1953 — everything happens in the spring.

As far as that dog is concerned, I never paid much attention to Ytterboe until he got shot by Percy Morris. I would see him around campus and around our house at 101 Lincoln and I gave him snacks from time to time. But I didn't have much to do with him nor did I ever pet him; I only pet faithful Argo after the hunt, which is one of the reasons he is so loyal and hunts so well.

I would see Ytterboe-the-dog from time to time, but it wasn't a particularly affectionate thing, fawning over each other and the like — he was our mascot and we both knew that was his job, his duty. Ytterboe certainly liked the students and they liked him, and he knew his way around campus — all the good spots for a choice morsel behind Ytterboe and Mohn cafeterias, and back of the Lion's Den or the Ytterboe garbage cans.

Most of the students were from out of town. The campus was home and a dog like Ytterboe became an important part of campus life, something that kept students in touch with their roots and their home.

Even now when I come down to 'Olaf with faithful Argo, students will stop to pet him and ask his name, and of course we talk: "Where are you from, did you know this dog speaks Norwegian?" Students of all eras can become attached to a campus companion like Ytterboe. I call him a companion for that is what he was, not just a "dog," and the students sensed it — even for those of us who lived at home.

The date we are concerned with, Hobo, was Wednesday, May 22, 1957 — that's when it happened, late afternoon sometime after 3:20 pm because afternoon classes finished about then. Some news reports the next day said three police officers came up to the campus in search of a dog that had supposedly bitten a young boy and was shot by Officer Percy Morris that afternoon, but the news was often wrong as we have seen.

Percy, of course, was one of Northfield's finest, one of the town's four police officers. News reports said Percy Morris shot Ytterboe in front of 50 students on the hillside by the library. Well, Ytterboe was definitely shot there by Percy, but there weren't three cops, only two — Percy Morris and Roger Robinson. Lenno Brandt, police chief since Wesley Fredenburg was fired in 1955, definitely wasn't there — he was too fat for a job like that and was probably at home taking his usual nap before supper.

Alas poor Percy, I knew him well. I went to high school with Percy; he was a year ahead of me at NHS and not the smartest at his profession — too quick on the draw, having learned from Lenno to "shoot first, then think." And there were the other Northfield patrolmen, Roger Robinson and Bill Carroll, also trained by Lenno. Robbie was a year behind me at NHS and Carroll lived across the street from us at 101 Lincoln.

But there weren't 50 students on the library hill that day, not more than a couple of dozen or so — a few guys and gals lounging around on the grass, pretending to be reading something important, looking for dates — lolling around between the library and Holland hall, the admin building where we took science classes and labs. It was a nice spring day and always a great place to watch the coed traffic — flowing crinolined skirts and long legs flighting their way up to the Ole sanctuary via the steep, long stairs by the library.

My recollection is that the patrol car came around the curve at a pretty good clip heading up the hill, then screeched and skidded to a stop by the steps just as the brakes were sharply applied. They spotted their prey right of the steep stairs a few feet above the road, apparently headed for a fire hydrant.

Percy got out of the patrol car and shot at Ytterboe but missed, then fired again with deadly double-aught buckshot from his sawed-off shotgun. Two loud blasts and that was it — over in a second — shots heard coast to coast, even in London and Oslo. Percy loaded the dog into the trunk of the patrol car with some bloody fur sticking out and took off down the Hill to tell the story in town.

Percy said there was a leash law in the month of May and that all dogs had to be tied up. I went to school with Percy and knew a lot about him. I also knew that Ytterboe had been in a garden that day across the street from 101 Lincoln. I lived across the street from officer Bill Carroll and his wife Marcella who worked at the Ole Store.

She called the police station and said Ytterboe had nipped their son's arm when the seven-year-old boy hit Ytterboe with a stick, trying to get him out of the Carroll garden where he was digging up one of his Ole Store bones. Ytterboe apparently responded to the tap on the nose by nipping at Billy and making a scrape on his arm, but it didn't break the skin. Marcella told me it wasn't a real bite, just a scratch, but it was on that basis that she called the police station and said, "Somethin's gotta be done about that dog."

The town cops knew Ytterboe didn't have a leash or a collar, and it was the month of May, so off they went looking for him that afternoon with nothing better to do on a nice spring day. They quickly nailed their prey on the Ole campus, Ytterboe's daily haunt.

Right after the shooting, I went into the library and told some people what happened. Soon more students started to come out of the dormitories to find out what was going on. That's when the Fubars sprang into action.

HozKnoz could have a car at school because he lived at home and about 4:30 or so several Fubars drove up Cedar Avenue from the Popstand to a 3.2 beer joint in Lakeville to talk about what had happened. There had to be a funeral, right? Right!

Well, we had all seen the recent movie "Julius Caesar" with Marlon Brando playing Marc Antony. Hoz had memorized Antony's funeral speech: "Friends, Romans, Countrymen, lend me your ears — we are come to bury Caesar, not to praise him..."

Hoz was the leader in this and sketched out a funeral speech, substituting "Ytterboe" for Caesar" so it would read, "...the evil that dogs do lives after them, the good is oft interred within their bones...so let it be with Ytterboe," etc.; "Percy is an honorable cop...," etc.

We talked a lot and wondered what might happen that night, that there should be a funeral the next day, and ordered another pitcher of beer. As Hoz was drafting the funeral speech from memory, substituting "Ytterboe" for "Caesar," we all agreed that the Marc Antony speech was a perfect model for Ytterboe's funeral.

It was one of those warm, fragrant nights in May when you could just feel inside you that something significant was going to happen. We had been in Lakeville nearly an hour when someone burst into the bar and said, "There's mob scene downtown Northfield over the dead dog."

We drove back to Northfield down Cedar Avenue as quickly as possible. On the way your Argo finalized the Marc Antony funeral oration with the name "Ytterboe" substituted throughout, and added a special Argo touch that brought in some humor and served to calm a potentially explosive situation. We were prepared for a 20th century mob scene Hollywood and Shakespeare would have envied.

Yes, Hobo, we were ready for big-time action when we arrived downtown at the Community Center on Division Street where the mob had assembled, Hollywood-style. People were packed in the streets, piled thick in front of the police station on Division Street where the squad car was parked, blood still on the bumper, a bit of Ytterboe's fur still sticking from the trunk.

By this time it was nearly 7:00 pm or so, and it was still light outside. All of St. Olaf and most of Carleton seemed to be in the streets — 'Olaf had about 1,750 students at the time and Carleton 750 or so, plus the local "townies." Pandemonium had broken loose, but there was no leader.

Looking at the mob scene from the Community Center where

the cop car was parked, students were crowded all the way up to the Carnegie Library hill and all the way to Telander's Drug Store; all the way past the Community Building and up beyond the First National and Northfield National banks by Bridge Square.

The streets were packed for blocks, people shouting and disorganized, but there was no leader, just a mob energized by a cop's action against a harmless dog and a wonderful spring evening in May. The crowd soon started to get noisy.

Some may have had a little beer by now, and the rowdier ones started shouting at the police chief, fat Lenno, who was a caricature of a policeman. Every Halloween, we would flip a coin to see who would be first to measure Lenno's waist, sneaking up from behind. We knew it was over 50 inches and would bet to see how much it had grown.

He was always a good sport and none of us knew at the time that he was a real hero in World War I fighting against the Germans at the Argonne Forest in France, winning the Distinguished Service Cross and Silver Star for exceptional bravery while capturing a German machine gun outpost singlehanded. Lenno never thought he would become chief, but he was the only choice after chief Wesley Fredenburg was fired for "conduct unbecoming to an officer" in August 1955.

By now the mob was getting a little out of control and started shouting, "Give us Percy! Give us Percy!" Lenno stood on the sidewalk like a brick outhouse with his hands on his hips by the patrol car and shouted back, "I ain't given' him to you." We thought Percy was probably cowering somewhere in the police station, afraid to come out, because he wasn't to be seen.

I didn't shout at Percy with the others and we began to wonder if the mob might really storm the Bastille. After a while, a few guys from Carleton started to rock the cop car back and forth, trying to tip it over but they couldn't do it, so they just rocked it vigorously and let air out of some of the tires.

By this time, the state highway patrol started to arrive in their maroon patrol cars but the streets were so packed along Division Street in front of the local police station they could get no nearer than Bridge Square.

It was absolute bedlam downtown when Mark Almli appeared. He was the St. Olaf Dean of Men, and he stood by the door at the steps of the Community Building where the police station was located and tried to get some order out of the chaos, but the mob hooted him down, booing and shouting, "Get out of here, get lost, Lumli."

He disappeared and then Merrill Jarchow, Dean of Men at Carleton, got up in front of the Community Building and tried to appeal to the combined Carleton-'Olaf mob. He was also hooted down, told to get out of there, get lost, and someone hollered, "Hey deanie — why don't you grow up and be somebody!"

Then the state troopers started inching their patrol cars northward, slowly through the mob on Division. It was like a parade by the state highway patrol — six patrol cars creeping slowly and cautiously through the crowd up the middle of Division Street, heading north toward Carleton.

They looked at the mob all around them, and the mob looked back at the troopers. The cars continued slowly to the intersection for the Second Street Bridge and were not seen again that evening — discretion served the better part of valor for the Minnesota State Highway Patrol that night — smart move.

But you could sense that it might get ugly. A lot of people were protesting and milling about by now, daring Percy to come out, and we heard afterward that a Percy effigy had been burned at Bridge Square. From the time we arrived at the Community Building shortly before 7:00 pm or so, we never left and the mob certainly did not leave — it had grown, waiting for a leader.

We had never been in a full-fledged mob scene like this before and had never thought about organizing such an event except for the "Lend me your ears" speech we had crafted. That's when HozKnoz said, "Argo, read the speech, give 'em Ytterboe's funeral oration — read the speech, Argo."

And so I prepared to speak shortly after the highway patrol went by. The mob was still there, bigger than at first and a lot angrier. Almli had had his say, Jarchow had had his say, and my fellow Fubars were standing at my side — HozKnoz (Wayne Quist), Marty (David Martinson), Stud (Paul Netland), Rawhide (Charlie Nelson), and Gus (Pete Charleston from Portland) — plus others later.

We had been together in Lakeville and were prepared for a funeral that night or the next day, or whenever, but not for a mob scene like this and only Julius Caesar as our guide.

Hoz shouted to the crowd, loudly at the top of his voice several times, "Quiet everyone! Quiet! Quiet please — lend Argo your ears — it's a speech, hear the Ytterboe speech!" The mob sensed something was about to happen and got quiet enough for me to begin.

Hobo, there's a well-publicized picture in the Northfield News of HozKnoz standing next to the Argo as Argo reads the funeral oration. We will gaze on that photo and talk about it the next time you are here, Hobo.

Well, your Argo started speaking in his loudest basso profundo — slowly, solemnly, deliberately. The opening lines were, "Friends, Oles, Countrymen — Lend me your ears! We are come to praise Ytterboe, not to bury him, for the evil that dogs do lives after them, the good is oft interred within their bones. So be the case with Ytterboe, for we so loved our faithful mascot."

It was right out of the Mark Antony speech, the crowd roared in recognition, and I continued: "The noble Percy hath told you Ytterboe was ambitious. If this were so, it were a grievous fault, and grievously hath Ytterboe answered it, shot in coldest blood on our campus; yes, grievously hath our Ytterboe answered Percy's charge — (roar from the mob). But was our noble mascot ambitious, was he a maker of trouble, had he such ambition? Percy hath told you Ytterboe was ambitious and Percy is an honorable cop."

The mob responded as if on cue, "No! No! Ytterboe, was not ambitious, it was Percy." Then I switched gears and came out with some lines that changed a potentially ugly situation. I departed from the Mark Antony speech and calmly said, "Friends and Countrymen, fellow Oles and Carls — let me tell you of Ytterboe and his magnificent lineage, where he was born, his humble education, his duties in life."

I continued, "Hear me, friends, and let it be known to all assembled on this historic day — to all people everywhere — that our beloved mascot, Ytterboe-Ole-Olaf, was born in the year nineteen hundred and forty-nine."

Then I asked, "But where was he born? — let me tell you — he was born Out of Blissful Wedlock — and where was that? — on a dusty street in Dundas."

The mob roared in good-natured laughter and I continued:

"Friends, now let me tell you the rest of Ytterboe's story." A loud roar of approval arose from the assembled mob — "Yes, tell us more." They started to cheer, for now there was a leader and a little humor had started to change the mood of the crowd.

Your Argo declaimed further, "Was Ytterboe's humble beginning from the dusty streets of Dundas — born Out of Blissful Wedlock, as it were —struggling to improve his humble place in life — Was this Ambition?" The mob roared, "No! No! Ytterboe was not ambitious!"

Argo continued, "Yes, ambition should be made of sterner stuff, like Caesar, so permit me, friends, to relate our mascot's story to you. Moving from Dundas to Northfield at an early age, Ytterboe-Ole-Olaf found meaning, truth and validity on these very streets you stand upon this evening."

The mob shouted "Tell us more," and I said, "Our mascot aspired only to become a Humble Fire Hydrant Inspector about town, with a solemn duty to inspect each and every fire hydrant, daily, on the West side of the river leading up to that college on that beloved Hill, the Popstand called St. Olaf."

Oles and Carls cheered, townies too, and I went on, "Friends and Countrymen, it has been said that our dear Inspector Mascot, as he died ingloriously today, was even planning to inspect each and every fire hydrant surrounding the campus of a school here in this town that some call Carleton!"

The mob roared in approval and the entire mood had changed, but they asked for even more. I could have given them "more" by finishing like Marc Antony and saying, "...let us move the stones of Northfield to rise and mutiny!"

But I didn't do that — the mob would have stormed the Bastille police station and tipped over the patrol car, demanding Percy Morris step forward and God knows what might have happened then.

Instead, I offered a bit of seriousness and said, "Oles and Carls, Countrymen and Friends — we know that Ytterboe was not ambitious, he was our loyal friend, our campus mascot, our faithful companion — we should now grieve for him — so sing loudly with me, 'Ytterboe is Dead' — sing like spirited boatmen on the River Volga, giving life to a simple dirge of sadness and sorrow."

I started singing the dirge with my fellow 'Olaf Choir basso profundos — "Ytterboe is Dead" — to the solemn tune of The Song of the Volga Boatmen — "Yo-Heave-Ho" — Ytterboe is Dead!

Ytterboe is Dead,

Ytterboe is Dead,

Oh-Oh-Oh-Oh,

Ytterboe is Dead.

It caught on immediately because of its simplicity and the perfect timing of a perfect tune for a magic moment — "Ytterboe is Dead, Ytterboe is Dead, Oh-Oh-Oh-Oh, Ytterboe is Dead."

The Ytterboe funeral dirge continued with hundreds, maybe a couple thousand voices eventually singing the mournful dirge to the tune of the Volga Boatmen — "Ytterboe is Dead, Ytterboe is Dead, Oh-Oh-Oh-Oh, Ytterboe is Dead."

It sounded good, it sounded big, it resounded, and it went on non-stop several dozen times or more, everyone singing as they started to disperse, small groups walking home as they sang, "Ytterboe is Dead."

What magic music, poetry can bring. How often the human condition is changed in a moment, during the course of uncertain human events, by the magic of music and poetry — that is what we learned at 'Olaf.

The mood had totally changed from possible confrontation to light springtime gaiety. Laughter and song changed the spirit of the moment. Fear of something getting out of control disappeared.

It was by now getting on into the evening, close to ten or so, maybe later, but no one watched the time except we knew it had gotten dark. When we first gathered it was still light outside, and when we finished singing the Ytterboe dirge it must have been after ten as the crowd, by now light-hearted and non-threatening, started to slowly disperse.

Another Fubar, Scuba (Leland Mebust), was also with us. Scuba was the newly elected president of the St. Olaf student body and Mark Almli had told him earlier to try to disperse the students. In between refrains, Scuba shouted to the mob in his deep bass Ole Choir voice, "Funeral for Ytterboe Friday —

Funeral at St. Olaf on Friday — Funeral for Ytterboe! — Let's go home now — see you Friday at Ytterboe's funeral."

That was a good move. Word spread quickly there was going to be a funeral for Ytterboe — not tomorrow, but on Friday. That provided time to cool off and now there was a plan everyone could accept.

The dirge continued spontaneously a few times or more and people slowly drifted away toward home, or to the Well, or Bert's Bar owned by Bert Morris, Percy's father, but that was a Carleton hangout. Fubar went home for some rest after an exciting evening because final exams were in the air; I think I got a ride with Marty.

Thursday was planning day for the funeral, but Fubar had nothing to say or do about that event — the funeral was for Scuba and the student body organization he presided over as president. The student body officers and Manitou Messenger staff called the local press, wire services, Life Magazine, Time Magazine, Minneapolis Star, Minneapolis Tribune, and St. Paul papers. They called all over the country and said there's going to be a big funeral at St. Olaf following the mob scene Wednesday night.

The Thursday papers covered some of the story from the night before and had contacts with the Northfield News and Northfield Independent. The callers lined up all of the publicity and someone even found an old black hearse.

I stood on the hillside by Holland Hall during the funeral on Friday, but early Thursday morning Mark Almli, the Dean of Men, called me at home and said, "Get up here right now." I went up to his office and he said, "Don't say anything. You think you're running this college, you think you're running this campus, don't you?" I said, "No."

Dean Almli said, "Don't say anything; if you say one word before I'm finished, and I might take 15 minutes to finish, you're out of this college. Now there's going to be a funeral, we know that. I just want to warn you that if there's anything happening at that funeral, if there's any Christian symbolism or any prayers or any cross, anything like that, you're gone, straight outta here. I'm going to hold you responsible."

I stood mute. I didn't dare speak because he was going to kick me out if I spoke, and I wasn't in charge of the funeral, so what to do?

I left and went to see Scuba and a couple other guys and told them what happened. I said, "My neck is in the noose if you guys say any prayers or do any Christian stuff or have anything that is counter-religious for a dog."

They said, "No, we're not going to do anything like that. We're just going to have a dignified reading of some poetry, some singing, a beautiful poem written by Dr. Theodore Jorgenson, the Ibsen scholar and teacher. He gave it to Didi Wilson, student editor of the Manitou Messenger.

At any rate, Jorgie was concerned and you know what — he contributed $100 to the funeral, a lot of money in 1957. He loved Ytterboe and thought the mob scene downtown was a great theatrical event.

But Mark Almli wasn't around for the funeral oration downtown, so he didn't know that my intent was never to get people agitated. Quite the opposite, my oration Wednesday night had some humor and it settled everybody down. I think I can take credit for that because the mob settled down with the Volga Boatmen dirge. The mob needed some closure and a way to get out of a mob scene, which they did with singing the dirge, but Lumli didn't know that. He thought the Ytterboe thing was going to spill over onto the campus where there already was a hole in the ground for the grave and that everything bad was going to happen with an out-of-control funeral for a dog.

I wasn't the only one to lock horns with the administration, Didi Wilson did too. The Vice President, David Johnson, took Didi in tow and brought her to President Granskou's office where Granskou said, "Keep your mouth shut when you talk to the press. Don't tell them anymore, or else." How's that for freedom of the press! Didi had been interviewed on the Dave Garroway Show from New York, so she was already on national TV and had her picture in the St. Paul press and other papers on Thursday.

Didi was a real investigative reporter and went to the city dump with friends where they found the remains of the dog, then drove to the rear of Ytterboe hall by the incinerator and garbage cans and dropped off the remains until the funeral. They didn't know what else to do and didn't want Ytterboe left in the dump.

That's when "Doc" Pete (Donald Petersen) heard about it.

"Doc" Pete was the medical doctor at the Ole health service across from the rear of Ytterboe hall. He removed the dog's head for a rabies test which the police should have done the night before.

Granskou putting the scare into Didi must have involved the upper administration at the school as well; otherwise David Johnson wouldn't have hauled her in. He was party to it, but Granskou didn't say anything to me — he knew I was a good citizen and was not going to be any trouble for the school.

The funeral took place about ten in the morning on Friday May 24th. It was a beautiful spring day and Carleton was well-represented with their president bearing a gift just by being there. We welcomed Carleton because that would bolster the crowd, and Carls had been downtown for the mob scene too. They were part of this "silent generation" happening and we wanted a big crowd for the funeral.

We wanted a big demonstration, for it was a big show on national TV and in the national press; Time and Life magazine, no less — and it was something special to do on a beautiful spring day in May. It was fun and we got bored with the other stuff, a little bit frazzled studying all night for final examinations coming up and term papers due.

I thought the funeral was tastefully and sincerely done. Scuba deserves a lot of credit and everyone appreciated it, especially when a fellow dog that knew Ytterboe came upon the scene and laid down, right in plain view like he was a brother, a special mourner choreographed for the moment. I thought that was so sweet when another dog just came and laid right down like he belonged there. That was nice — a special touch you couldn't have orchestrated.

Several people wrote songs about Ytterboe or poems for the funeral. Phil Dybdahl from the class of '59 sang and played the guitar; Dale Gilhoy sang and Ron Hendricks was there. Those people, I think, have a memory of the funeral because they participated. I have a memory of what happened downtown because I participated, but as far as the whole school is concerned everybody at that time has a general recollection or can remember the funeral.

More than that, life quickly got back to normal. The reality of papers due and final examinations coming up were hanging over everyone, but the whole thing was a lot of fun for everybody and it was a change. The spirit of the times wasn't necessarily as important as the fact that it was the month of May, for all sorts of goofy things happen then. You just have to do something because the warm weather comes out, the blood gets boiling, and you're eager to get out of school and get going into different things.

Looking back, now 40 years ago, I attach a pleasant memory to the Popstand and I think remembering Ytterboe the dog should be an important part of student lore and campus lore at St. Olaf, something that should last. The event was more than just the tragic death of a dog. It rallied two colleges and an entire town in a cause of justice, demanding fair play from the local police, and it ended peacefully without violence because of poetry and music.

That's what they taught us at St. Olaf — the liberal arts — music, poetry, history, philosophy, science. Of course the name "Ytterboe" is practically sacred at St. Olaf, not because of a dog but because of the man Ytterboe, one of the stalwarts of the first generation of founders.

The story of Ytterboe the dog was very important and remains something students know something about today. I'm sure that if I were to have lunch with students today and asked if they know anything about a dog named Ytterboe, they might say, "Well yeah, sort of. Isn't that the dog, the mascot that was killed some years ago?" And if I were to say I was there, you would have a great deal of interest because they like to hear about the old students. I've found that St. Olaf students are always respectful, always polite, and they all have perfect teeth.

I think the Northfield community was divided over Ytterboe. There was an editor for the Northfield Independent named Carl L. Weight who went on and on for half a page, trying to make some sense of the thing. The town of Northfield had a tendency to be divided between what we students called the "townies" and what they called the "college kids."

Sometimes the two were at odds with each other even though the town depended upon the colleges for what the students and the colleges spent in town. But the "townies" didn't seem to care about that. And most of the townspeople didn't like Carleton students, not because they were rich kids from the East, but more because they caused so much trouble. Many of the

'Olaf students were farm kids and small-town kids who were a lot more conservative, and many Northfield kids went to St. Olaf.

Lenno's police department tried to take a low profile afterwards, and eventually Percy moved to St. Louis Park and took a job. But he never lived it down — the shooting of Ytterboe bothered him to the end.

I didn't hold any animosity toward Percy. He did what he did and there was no sense bearing any grudge about it. He had surgery on his back that went bad, and he was confined to a wheelchair for the rest of his life. He died a few years after that and I felt sorry for him. He made a mistake in the view of some, but in the view of others the dog didn't have a tag and deserved what he got.

But why didn't somebody at St. Olaf cough up a dollar and buy a tag for the dog? I suppose they would have if they knew that they were supposed to, but they didn't know. A lot of people didn't know dogs were not supposed to be loose during the month of May because they supposedly root around in gardens. I didn't know that. No dog of mine ever rooted around in gardens in May, either in our own garden or in others. They probably just didn't want dogs mating in public, that's more like it.

Well, Donald, that's what I remember about the Ytterboe event. As soon as finals were over we got out of town as quickly as possible, and I can tell you one thing, I was going to go west again to Glacier Park. I had three months to make some money and I knew I could make more out there with a job in Glacier Park than hanging around with the "townies."

I jumped a freight train in Northfield and one of the Fubars who had helped plan the oration, Dave Martinson, and his partner were on the freight train with me. We were three on a freight headed to Spokane and ROTC summer camp, but I got off at Whitefish, Montana and went up the road for a job as a singing waiter at the Many Glacier Hotel in Glacier Park.

It was easy pickings, and we quickly forgot about poor old Ytterboe a-moldering in his Ole grave, there by the steps where he was shot toward the end of May in 1957. Yes, the memory, Ytterboe is dead.

       Argo — Midsummer solstice, 1998

A Look at the Second Amendment

Dear Donald,

People everywhere seem to have differing opinions about the law and what is meant by various ordinances, statutes, court opinions and constitutions. That is just fine with me, for I am one of the "people" and have a right to my opinions.

We appreciate the finality that comes with knowing for certain what the law says. Our first Chief Justice of the Supreme Court, the Honorable John Marshall, established that principle with a sentence in Marbury v. Madison (1803): "It is emphatically the province and duty of the judicial department to say what the law is."

I wonder what gives me the right to own a gun? I have no doubt that I enjoy that right, for I own guns and I use them. Does this right stem from the constitution? If so, where does it state that? Could it be the Ninth Amendment? "The enumeration in the constitution, of certain rights, shall not be construed to deny or disparage others retained by the people."

Or how about the Tenth Amendment: "The powers not delegated to the United States by the constitution nor prohibited by it to the states, are reserved to the States respectively, or to the people." We note the term, "the people," is used in the constitution only about five times according to my count whereas the words "person" or "persons" occur over forty times.

Let us examine how these terms are used. In the Preamble, we read "We, the People..." In that case, as in all others, the word "People" refers to a group linked by a common interest, not the individual person. The Twelfth Amendment refers to senators being elected by the people. In case of vacancies, the governor of the state may make temporary appointments until the people fill the vacancies. The word "people" also appears in the Second Amendment, as we shall see.

What about the individual? We find that in the Constitution, the individual is referred to as a person; sometimes a citizen, or, the accused. Thus, the word "people" suggests a group, or assembly, or linked by a common interest; whereas "person" is used to describe individuals. Person or persons means individual or individuals.

Now let us look at the Second Amendment: "A well-regulated militia being necessary to the security of a free state, the right of the people to keep and bear arms shall not be infringed." Note that it does not say the right of a person. If the authors of the Second Amendment wanted to write the amendment differently they could have used wording similar to that used in the First Amendment — something like this: "Congress shall make no law infringing on the right of a person to keep and bear arms."

But the authors did not write the amendment with that wording — though we know they could have — because that specific right was not intended for an individual person, rather for the people as a group linked by a common interest for the purpose of providing militia for the states to protect the people.

Use of the word "militia" confuses some persons. Article II, Section 2 [1] "The President shall be the commander in chief of the army and navy of the United States, and the militia of the several states, when called into the actual service of the United States." We understand that militia means the National Guard of a state, under the command and control of the governor.

In 1791, when the Second Amendment was passed, an assumption was made that the citizen soldier would report for duty in the militia with proper arms that were similar to those generally in use by the militiamen. Times have changed, and the militia are no longer for men only. Furthermore, it is no longer necessary for you to show up for duty with your own weapon; they issue them.

The Second Amendment has a definite meaning. It is a right held by the states, not by private citizens, and is meant to affirm individual protection — but only in the context of the maintenance of a militia or other such public force. In United States v. Miller, the Court stated, "The militia originally were composed of civilians primarily, soldiers on occasion. It was on this force that the states could rely for defense and securing of the laws."

I believe in personal gun ownership. I own guns, and I use them. But my right to own a gun does not spring from the Second Amendment. That right is reserved for the militia, necessary to the security of a free state.

Take another look at amendments nine and ten above, and see if you can arrive at a theory about a person's right to keep and bear arms as authorized in the constitution. I don't know the answer, but am certainly willing to learn.

I would like to know if my right to keep and bear arms, and yours, is authorized somewhere, and if it is, what does it say? Take a look at the Second Amendment.

    Argo —

Athletics, Northfield High School, Long Ago

Dear Donald,

As an illustrious NHS athlete and distinguished letterman, you will enjoy some of the following trivia about Northfield High School athletics of long ago.

Argo —

In 1896, Billy Benson played tackle for Northfield high. A touchdown counted 5 points, a field goal 4.

In 1898, Shattuck played their coach, Allen, and the Northfield News said: "Allen is a man from Chicago University and he is accused of playing some very dirty football, slugging and throttling intentionally on different occasions. It shows a badly depraved nature when a college man resorts to such tactics, especially against high school boys, and he should have been ruled out of the game on the first offense." Northfield vs. Hastings: Later in the game Hastings was declared offside. "Hastings refused to accept the referee's decision and withdrew, taking with them their ball."

1912: Northfield beat Farmington 77-0. Our team was "penalized 1 yard because Capt. Clyde Lee took more than one minute explaining to Farmington how to line up on the kickoff. The next play went fine, but on the second play the ball was lost in a patch of weeds on an attempted forward pass, and time had to be taken out while the players hunted for the ball."...When the score reached 50, the score keeper resigned with a headache. "... Substitutes were chased from the field by a cow who resented such intrusion into her accustomed haunts."

In a return game, Nov. 9, 1912 Northfield crushed Red Wing, 79-0.

Northfield News, Dec. 7, 1912: "Those who played football this last season 12 quarters received their "N" in chapel (Carleton's Skinner Chapel) Tuesday morning.

1920: Northfield 0 - Faribault 0. "The Northfield team punted invariably on first down and managed to keep the ball out of striking distance of the goal." It was considered a "moral victory."

Jan. 7, 1921: Northfield defeated Owatonna in basketball, 11-10 after leading 5 - 1 at intermission. Fremouw got into the game. A game with Kenyon was canceled because six of their men were ineligible.

1924 Football: Coach Joe Hutton, Hamline graduate, Basketball

1924-25, Joe Hutton, coach, Rolf Mellby played, District held at St. Olaf. Northfield 11 - Red Wing 10.

1935 - Era of spring football practice; Regional at Carleton. Finals: Faribault 18 - Northfield 15; Hutton left town.

1937 - Golf: Gene Christenson sets Northfield course record with a 31 and also wins Minnesota State High School Title by 10 strokes.

1950 - Big Nine champs in football, Dale Quist all-state halfback, one of the best all-round NHS athletes; Lars Kindem quarterback, pole-vaulter, ski-jumper.

1953 - Don Clark, top wrestler in his weight class, undefeated, always.

    Lars —

The Supreme Court of the United States

Dear Hobo,

I received this from Hoz about one of Northfield's own, Associate Justice Pierce Butler, member of the U.S. Supreme Court from 1923-1939.

Argo —

Pierce Butler was born on a farm in rural Waterford Township near Northfield, Minnesota, on March 17, 1866. He attended Northfield High School and graduated from Carleton College in 1887 with degrees in both arts and science. His father was Patrick Butler, a Waterford farmer. He moved to St. Paul and read law for one year at a law firm and was admitted to the bar in 1888.

Three years later, Butler became an assistant county attorney of Ramsey County, which embraces the city of St. Paul. In 1893, he was elected County Attorney and served until 1897. While serving as County Attorney, Butler joined a law partnership and eventually became senior partner in a successor firm.

In 1910, the Attorney General of the United States engaged Butler to represent the government in a number of antitrust cases. Butler served as a regent of the University of Minnesota from 1907 to 1924.

President Warren G. Harding nominated Butler to the Supreme Court of the United States on November 23, 1922. The Senate confirmed the appointment on December 21, 1922.

Butler served on the Supreme Court for sixteen years and died on November 16, 1939, at the age of seventy-three. Justice Butler, a Catholic, is buried in Calvary Cemetery in St. Paul, Minnesota.

Northfield Honors WWII Veterans

Many show gratitude in heartwarming remembrances, music, parades, shows, flyovers of vintage warplanes, latest news alert from Argo.

Dear Donald,

As I approached Northfield on Highway 19 today I was under attack by a blue Corsair and a silver P-47. They did not fire, no, but they let me know they were there. I sped over to the corner of Lincoln Street and 2nd, in front of Ken Wilken's place and parked, knowing they would circle and make a pass at the Old Main. They did, and I took a picture of them making a turn over the campus.

I knew this was going to be a memorable day in Northfield. As I approached downtown, I saw the two fighters buzz the Ames Park alongside the Cannon which did not fire at them, but folks assembled there sure waved a lot of handkerchiefs. I joined the crowd, some sitting on the grass, some on lawn chairs, and some walking around greeting old friends. It was good to come to Northfield this day, August 19, 1995.

There was a crowd of people there. I went first to the history office to buy a copy of the commemorative book from the two volunteers, Reverend and Mrs. Clifford Swanson of the St. Olaf family, retired. I asked Swanson if he remembered the two Northfield boys, both Oles, Marty Jensen and Stan Edwardson, two among the first from Northfield to be killed in the war. He did. He knew that Marty, who lived on the corner of Madison St. and St. Olaf Ave. was our scoutmaster at St. John's, and that Stan was a low bass in the St. Olaf Choir. Stan lived kitty corner from the Viking lunch.

The two boys had been classmates for 16 years. Stan sank a German U-boat in the Caribbean before perishing in the Pacific enroute from San Diego to Hawaii. Marty, a bugler on the South Dakota, lost his life in a battle off Savo, in the Solomons where my brother, Alf, served on the cruiser Tulsa and was wounded twice. I brought news of each death home to my mother who fainted both times. She had four sons in the service. But I digress.

So now, then, let's move on to the park adjacent to the Cannon River. All that river needs is a poet, as Edna Hong has reminded us. Some of the men in the crowd had poured themselves into their old uniforms. Most were in their seventies and wore red, white and blue ribbons — dangling gold medals commemorating this 50-year anniversary celebration honoring them, 1945-1995.

Four hundred Northfield boys and men served during World War II and fifty did not return. Those who did return and were present in Northfield August 19, 1995 were glad to be there for more than one reason. St. Olaf lost 56 alumni. This was the parade they never had, from the folks who cared enough to gather in a wondrous show of appreciation.

It was, as my brother Erling said, "...their last Hurrah." This sobered me a bit. I knew I would again be seeing my two brothers who were present. I no longer would see the two others who served and will never be present again for roll-call, but they are not forgotten. They were companions in raids on the various establishments in Rice County and even places of revelry on Lake Street and environs. No more. Too late.

The other familiar names and faces brought memories of more than fifty years ago when I had seen these men through the single remaining eye of a child who would not be able to serve — but do they really serve, those who only stand and wait?

I had heard their names and various exploits across the dinner table at home; some were athletes at the school where I also gave my heart and soul doing my best on the youth's field of honor to the glory of school, family, loyal friends and one named "Marie."

No, most of us gathered at the park will not see each other again, except perhaps for those who show up annually at Northfield's version of the Gunfight at the OK Corral, September 7, the most important date in Northfield, even greater than July 4th and the 17th of May, even though Jesse James may never have been in Northfield, according to W. W. Pye and Hoz.

The Ames Park narrator was Ken Wilkens, a navigation instructor during the war at various venues such as Shepherd Field, TX, Chanute Field, IL, Walla Walla, WA, Ardmore, OK, and McDill, FL. I was proud to see Ken up front on the stage with his script, standing in front of the orchestra. He read with stentorian intonation various speeches of the wartime era in

Dear Donald

straight unadulterated Northfield English, the kind that radio and television broadcasters throughout the United States north of the Mason Dixon Line use.

I thought, "Good grief — this man doesn't even need a microphone!" I snapped a couple of pictures of him, and he signaled back with the thumb-forefinger connected "OK" sign and a smile that meant something. I like Ken a lot, though he was never my teacher at St. Olaf.

As I returned to the midst of the crowd, I spied an Air Corps Tech Sergeant sitting in a chair looking very handsome in his complete World War II uniform. As I approached, he looked alert and ready to listen to what I had to say. I asked who he was, and how he got into his old uniform after these 50 years. He said they called him Lowell Smestad. I asked if he was related to Jim Smestad, photographer for the Viking at St. Olaf. They are cousins.

I took his hand, and said, "I am glad to see you here. You honor us by your presence." He thanked me, and I moved on to repeat the thanks and messages to others who deserved them. So now I decided to look up this man who still fits into his uniform 50 years later in the Northfield book I bought for $5.00, "To Honor and Remember, 1945-1995, Northfield." It reads like the story of Erling Kindem:

"Lowell Smestad, Tech. Sergeant, 759th Squadron, 459th Bomb Group, 15th Air Force. US Army Air Force. Lowell entered the service in March, 1943. His basic training was in Santa Ana, CA. He took additional training in Fresno, CA. He served in Sioux Falls, SD; Laredo and Eagle Pass, TX; Salt Lake City and Kearns, UT; Casper WY; Topeka, KS; Camp Henry and Newport News, VA; Camp McCoy, WI and Tampa, FL. His overseas tour of duty included North Africa and Italy. He served as a radio operator and gunner on B-24s and saw action in several combat missions in the Balkans, Central Europe, Po Valley and Rhineland. He was wounded 20,000 feet over Europe and was awarded five Battle Stars, the Air Medal with two Oak Leaf Clusters, and the Purple Heart."

The only difference, really, between this man's military experience and my brother was that Erling was not awarded the Purple Heart. Erling was in a B-24 so damaged by enemy fire that they were forced to land at one of the emergency landing fields maintained by GIs and partisans near Zara, Herzegovenia,

Yugoslavia. They landed in a silver plane but changed planes and returned to their base in Italy in a brown B-24.

Missing from brother Alf's record was his battle experience. I suppose those who wrote the book in Northfield couldn't find anyone to speak for him. That was often his misfortune. He died in 1972 but I have his New Testament, water-soaked, wherein he made entries in language which showed his limited 8th grade education. He served on the cruiser, Tulsa, and saw much action at Mortai, Savo, Leyte Gulf and Formosa. Alf was knocked out of battle after eight hours of combat, including two kamikaze hits in the Battle of Leyte. Wounded with shrapnel in one lung and knee, he spent six months in the hospital and was honorably discharged before his 18th birthday. He returned to finish Northfield High School after the war. It is safe to say that Alf saw too much of life before coming of age during the ravages of war so far away from home.

But there was a lot of fun in Ames Park that day. We saw a Marine named Lindberg of Richfield, MN who is the last living member of the group that raised the flag on Mount Suribachi, Iwo Jima. My impression was that the folks liked this man a lot. He was Grand Marshall of the parade, too. The subsequent flyovers were so impressive and well-received as to nearly boggle the mind. The first was a B-25 bomber, the noisiest two engine bomber, I am sure, in the history of the world. The old crate circled many times. Then came a tight formation of two P-51s with a P-39 in between. They were good, especially the hot dog on the starboard side who did some radical steep climbs and rolls while the crowd roared approval. They made about eight passes, waving to the crowd. It was sweet. I had visions of Claire Chenault and the flying tiger-painted craft that scared shit out of the Japanese.

I left Northfield, full of everything good, and set out for Randolph, USA, and my annual meeting with the folks at the local fundraiser put on by the Volunteer Firemen.

ANOTHER BIT OF "AMERICANA"

Randolph: Scene of the firefighters' annual chicken barbecue.

If you want to find out about what America looks like at its best, go to Randolph, out of Northfield on Highway 19, past where Rawhide lived, past the Stanton Airport, and north on Highway 56 a few miles until you see huge billows of smoke

Dear Donald

swirling skyward near the old elevator that leans to the East about five degrees. Call it the Leaning Tower of Randolph. Nearby is the tavern where some Fubars would while away the hours from time to time. But I don't go there any more, no.

There it is. There it all is. The antique locomotive, devouring logs and spewing steam through pipes into the 500 gallon cauldrons of mid America's favorite August Delight, sweet corn on the cob. "Hey you guys, blow the whistle!" I shout, "Ring the bell, there are guys here from the Cities who ain't never heard it." They gladly oblige, knowing they are in a position of power again, once a year, and that suits them fine.

The cattle watering troughs, all eight of them, with dozens of bags of red hot charcoal spew out the smoke of burning chicken fat drippings from the thousands of chicken quarters resting on grates with protruding handles for the grill men.

These sweaty, dirty tee shirt-clad men work with the precision of a drill team, hoisting and turning the screened-in chicken parts for a little doing on the other side before they are transferred, piping hot, to the serving area where folks in a two-hour line I cut in on, already have beans, a bun, coleslaw, two ears of butter-drenched corn on a paper plate. Paper plates are never large enough, so they just pile it on, and nobody complains, no. The kids love this place because there is also free pop — all they can drink. And they run about, lurching, bumping into each other and having a good time.

Up on the hill next to the huge tent with dining tables is the horseshoe pitching field, in E.B.'s back yard. E.B. is the St. Olaf cop, one of them, who has done favors for me and also goes fishing on Lake Vermilion at Charlie's with the boys. I was not even remotely tempted to enter the horseshoe pitching tournament, although I qualify as to age. These guys are too good. You can see guys throw 10-12 ringers in a row! I just sit and eat, like most, and make small talk about stuff, tell stories which cause kids to hang around to hear the real things that they have not yet experienced. Remember, most of them have been to the Cities only once or twice.

We plan the fall fishing season, the grouse hunt, and start preliminary psyching up for the deer season. This year, a pheasant hunt near Watertown, SD is on the program. Argo-the-Lab qualifies as an interstate hunting dog, no visa required. He thinks sloughs and stubble fields are the same in Dakota as in Rice and Dakota counties in Minnesota country. We'll see.

I cannot for the life of me imagine anything with more of the imprint of true "Americana" than the giant chicken barbecue at

Randolph, Minnesota, put on by the Randolph Volunteer Fire Department and attended by hundreds, perhaps thousands of folks from around there.

They even have a small flea market with homemade stuff, antiques, and Watkins products. I would go there twice a week all through the month of August if they had it. Nothing better to do. Got to go outside and smoke my pipe. The computer does not like smoke, no.

Lars, Argo, Watson, Lefse, hey you! Pappa, & Grandpa
— August 20, 1995

Kernel Dr. Martinson, BA, MA, MBA, PhD

Dear Hobo,

Here's Marty's Air Force bio, pretty impressive, two masters degrees and a PhD in Shakespeare to boot — not many make full kernel and a PhD in the same lifetime; I didn't do neither. Who named him "Dogface?" It must have been Gus.

Argo —

Colonel David J. Martinson was born in Clinton, MN, and was graduated from Central High School, Northfield, MN, in 1954. He earned a Bachelor of Arts degree from St. Olaf College, a Master of Arts degree from the University of Minnesota, and a Master of Business Administration degree from Auburn University. He has a Ph.D. in English obtained from the University of New Mexico. Colonel Martinson completed Squadron Officer School in 1962, Air Command and Staff College in 1972, and Air War College in 1977, and is a Distinguished Graduate of all three schools. He also completed the National Security Management curriculum.

Commissioned a second lieutenant through the Air Force Reserve Officer Training Corps at St. Olaf College, Colonel Martinson entered the Air Force in October 1958. While assigned to Lackland Air Force Base, TX, as an Officer Candidate School tactical officer, he was selected to attend Air Traffic Control School at Keesler Air Force Base, MS, in December 1958. In April 1959, Colonel Martinson was assigned to the 2039th Airways and Air Communications Service (AACS) Squadron, Fairchild Air Force Base, WA, as the Flight Facilities Officer. In April, 1960, he went to Sondrestrom Air Base, Greenland, where he served as Chief Controller, Military Flight Service Center, 2004th AACS Squadron.

From 1961 to 1964, Colonel Martinson was assigned to the 2179th Communications Squadron at Patrick Air Force Base, FL, supporting Project Mercury as Chief Controller of the Control Tower; then, Chief Controller of the Radar Approach Control facility; and, finally, as the Flight Facilities Officer.

Colonel Martinson's next assignment was to Lindsey Air

Station, Wiesbaden, Germany, as an air traffic control staff officer at European-African-Middle Eastern Communications Area. In July 1967, he became an Assistant Professor of Aerospace Studies at Air Force Reserve Officer Training Corps Detachment 415, University of Minnesota, where he was recognized as the outstanding Angel Flight advisor in the nation and his area's outstanding Aerospace Studies instructor.

In 1972, Colonel Martinson joined the 1964th Communications Group at Tan Son Nhut Air Base, Republic of Vietnam, as the Group Flight Facilities officer until the withdrawal of the U.S. Armed Forces troops from Vietnam in March 1973. Colonel Martinson spent the following three years as Chief, Fixed Air Traffic control Operations Division for Tactical Communications Area at Langley Air Force Base, VA.

Colonel Martinson was assigned to Headquarters, Air Force Communications Service at Richards-Gebaur Air Force Base, MO, in July 1977, as Chief, Air Traffic Control Airspace Division until the headquarters was relocated to Scott Air Force Base, IL, that September, where he worked as Chief, Air Traffic Control Support Division and as Director, Air Traffic Control Operations.

Assigned to the 1961st Communications Group, Clark Air Base, Philippines, as Deputy Commander in July 1979, and then as Commander in June 1980, he also functioned as the 13th Air Force Deputy Chief of Staff, Communications-Electronics; Director, Communications-Electronics, 3rd Tactical Fighter Wing; and Director, Communication-Electronics, 3rd Combat Support Group.

Promoted to Colonel in November 1979, Colonel Martinson remained at Clark Air Base until 4 April 1982. During his tenure as Commander, the 1961st received the Major General Harold M. McClelland Award as the most outstanding communication-electronics organization in the Air Force. His air traffic control (ATC) facilities were also recognized as the Air Force's ATC Complex of the Year.

Colonel Martinson was next assigned from April 1982 to July 1984 as the Assistant Deputy Chief of Staff for Communications-Electronics for Headquarters Pacific Air Forces and as Vice Commander of the Pacific Communications Division with collocated headquarters at Hickam Air Force Base, HI. The Division received the Billy Mitchell Award as the best Division in Air Force Communications Command during that period.

From Hawaii, he was assigned to a general officer's position in the Pentagon as the Director of Systems Management, Assistant Chief of Staff, Information Systems, Headquarters United States Air Force, Washington, DC, where he was responsible for the implementation and management of Command and Control and Support Information Systems throughout the Air Force, as well as information systems support of the National Military Command Center, the Chairman, Joint Chiefs of Staff, and the National Command Authorities.

Colonel Martinson's final assignment was from 1986 to 1988 as Chief, Policy, Plans, and Requirements Division of the Command, Control, and Communications Systems Directorate, Headquarters United States European Command (USEUCOM), Stuttgart, Germany. He was responsible for assuring responsive, survivable, and enduring systems in support of USCINCEUR command and control requirements throughout the USEUCOM theater of operations and representing the United States on various NATO command and control forums.

Colonel Martinson's military awards include the Defense Superior Service Medal, the Legion of Merit with one oak leaf cluster, the Bronze Star, The Meritorious Service Medal with two oak leaf clusters, the Air Force Commendation Medal with one oak leaf cluster, the National Defense Service Medal, the Vietnam Service Medal with one bronze service star, the Vietnam Air Service Medal, Honor Class, the Vietnam Gallantry Cross with Palm, and the Vietnam Campaign Medal. Colonel and Mrs. Martinson, the former JoAnn Nelson of Soap Lake, WA, have two children, Stacy and David, and currently reside at 6315 La Plata Peak Drive, Colorado Springs, CO 80922.

P.S. Then the Kernel got a PhD in Shakespeare and was awarded the Fubar Cross and Knight of the Holy Grail with multiple battle scars and ribbonry for services far above and beyond the call of duty throughout many parts of Rice County, Dundas, Glacier Park, Corpus Chrasti, and Nuevo Laredo.

      Argo—

Brother Erling's Birthday

Dear Donald,

As you requested, here is the list of Northfield High School teachers that Erling and I assembled on his birthday:

Paul Jorgenson and Tor Faxvog - Algebra, Plain Geometry, Solid Geometry
Ruth Labbitt, Latin
Graham Frear and Miss Moynihan - English
Clarence Sandburg, History
Ken Heacock - Chemistry, wrestling coach, K&M drive-in
Elton Lien, Physics
Casey Hero, Speech and Drama
Ed Byhre, Ozzie Simonich, Ken Heacock, Loyal Burmeister - coaches
Wes Westerlund, boys' Phy-Ed
Victorine McCartney, Jr. High Math, English VIII
Katherine Zimmerman, Jr. High English
Mary Champlin, English X
Emma Overvaag, English XI
Celestine Magner, American History
Loyal Burmeister, Social Science, Baseball Coach
Donald Benschoter, Business & Law
Katherine Wulfsberg, Jr. High Social Studies
Esther Engebretson, Biology & German
Bud Nelson, General Science, Athletic Director
Chauncey Larson, Ruben Hovland, Paul Duba, Agriculture
Homer Mason, Industrial Arts
Paul Stoughton, Music
Marvel Rettmann, girls' Phy-Ed
Eva Lou Russell, Art
Nellie Conarroe, Nurse
More than that, I cannot remember.

Argo—March 2, 1996

Cues, Miscues, and Choir Memories

Dear Donald,

You have frequently inquired about the St. Olaf Choir. Well, let me tell you, it happened only twice that the Choir screwed up during my time. The first miscue was 1953 in Duluth, and the only other time was on tour in 1955.

Argo —

We developed a system of Choir cues that we would use to spot and affirm the best "babes" in an audience. It went like this, as we lined up to sing, and for use in between numbers:

Scan the audience and find a prime target.

Signal the guy next to you by squeezing his hand.

One squeeze, look at the audience on the left side; two squeezes, look at the audience on the right side.

Pause, then one squeeze per row, starting from the front.

Pause again, one squeeze for each person, starting in from the center aisle.

There she was beaming and beautiful!

Response from your cohort — one squeeze means "No-No-No;" two is "OK;" three means "Very Nice;" four is Wow!

It was in Duluth and we were singing "Ascendit Deus" by Gallus. The sopranos started a theme followed by the altos who missed a beat in the fugue — then the tenors didn't know where to come in and they were hopelessly lost. It was chaotic, so Olaf waved us off, stepped off the podium with a stern look as only he could muster, and we started over and did it right, the Olaf way. Our 1955 miscue happened when we were doing a piece by Jean Berger called "Vision of Peace," a number that I believe started like a thunderclap in the key of A. One of the guys had asked to give the pitch which we would hum during the applause for the preceding number and that way get a running start for the next number. Well, he gave the wrong pitch, up about a fourth, and we all knew it was wrong. Olaf's rule was a standing order, "Don't sing if you are not sure what is going on." When Olaf strode out to the podium following the applause, he bowed to the audience and confidently gave us the attack beat, but nothing happened. He quickly gave it again, vigorously, and a third time, demanding — but not a sound! Olaf exhaled with a hiss through his pursed lips, stepped down, approached the choir and whispered, "What is the pitch?" Someone gave the right one, and this time we really hit it hard with, "Let all the nations be gathered together!" No big deal, but no one ever admitted giving the wrong pitch.

Hobo, you have perfect pitch for a southpaw. I know this to be true from playing baseball and softball with you — but why has no one from Northfield ever been picked up by the New York Yankees for perfect pitch? Squint Hower had perfect pitch with a pitchfork until he lost an eye haying, but in Norway everyone has perfect pitch, just like the perfect teeth St. Olaf students have today, without braces or cavities. In the old country, when a Norwegian choir sings, the director uses a tuning fork and passes the starting notes to each section of the choir. It sounds like perfect pitch, but we always did them one better when we sang in Norway. We would sneak in the pitch during the applause and continue to hum the pitch for the next song so we could hear it, but the audience could not. Several reviewers marveled at this fantastic Norwegian-American choir from St. Olaf College in which everyone, every member of the choir, had perfect pitch — for no matter what song they sang and in whatever key, the choir would start without any help on the pitch. We called it perfect "Ole" pitch.

P.G. Schmidt was our low bass and former manager but he had to sit out the 1953 Christmas Festival. His wife had been seriously ill and P.G needed to be with her. He was able to get to one Christmas concert and we were pleased to see him. I went to him after the concert and asked, "Well, P.G., what do you think about the choir this year? He replied, "Pretty good, but I have nothing to compare it with for I have never heard it before. This is the first time I have heard the choir in concert since we started in 1903."

When we visited Louisville in 1954, the entire school system turned out for our concerts, of which there were three that day. The mayor apparently liked St. Olaf and his son enrolled the next year. Naturally, school children enjoy collecting autographs and we were happy to oblige. We signed dozens, with names such as Enrico Caruso, George Mikan, and other famous people.

Then I made a mistake and signed "Bing Crosby." The kid looked at me in disbelief and said, "Aw c'mon, you're not Bing Crosby!" I replied, "I have to go now," and disappeared into the auditorium, busted.

Donald, you always asked about tryouts to get in the choir. Well, every person who tried out got an individual audition, which for some was a very frightening occasion. Olaf Christiansen could be the scariest looking person in the world. After all candidates had auditioned, a recall list was posted for the final tryouts which were held one section at a time in Steensland Hall where the choir held rehearsals. I was a sophomore, and after one year of voice lessons, was prepared. I sang first with the baritones, then alternated with the basses. Olaf had the men sign up after they were selected, but something went wrong — I was left out. So I went over to the music hall to tell my voice teacher, Ella Hjertaas Roe. I told her I thought Christiansen had a tin ear. She said, "There must be a mistake; you should be in the choir." She wept. I felt like doing so and went home to our house on Lincoln Street below the Old Main. There was my mom and another lady, so I had to watch my tongue. But I was really angry, and I told my mom there had been a foul up, that Christiansen had made a mistake. "There he is now!" she said, pointing out the picture window. He banged on the door. I opened it and said, "What do you want?" He said, "I forgot you, Lars; do you want to sing in the St. Olaf Choir?" I said, "Yes, of course!" He grabbed me by the back of the neck and said, "Come on, then, let's practice." Wow, what a tryout.

So there we were, the new choir, assembled in Steensland Hall for our first rehearsal. I took a seat in back with some guys I knew. Then Olaf burst in the door, struck a chord on the piano for Bach's "Sing ye to the Lord" and we were off to the races so fast I did not have time to open my music folder. I thought I had died and gone to heaven! The joy was almost more than I could bear and I said to myself, afterward, "Thank you, God. Thank you, God. Thank you, God." And the tears came.

I suppose anyone who ever sang in the St. Olaf Choir can tell of the first time they heard the Choir sing. I can. I was late for Sunday School at St. John's in Northfield my junior year in high school. There was a sign on the classroom door indicating we were to attend the main service. In those days, the St. Olaf Choir was the church choir, I guess, since there was no student congregation on campus. I opened the door in front a crack to see if I could sneak in and find a seat. Just then, the Choir started out with the anthem, "Die mit Tränen säen." I was not able to move — only stand and listen to the most beautiful sounds I had ever heard.

In Northfield, we had a fine music program in the public schools. Naturally, we got student teachers from St. Olaf, music majors. One such person was a tall, handsome bass soloist in the St. Olaf Choir named Gene Nelson. I told him I wanted to sing with the St. Olaf Choir someday and asked for suggestions as to preparation. He told me 90% of male voices are baritone, 5% are high tenors, and 5% are low basses. He told me I should work toward developing a low bass range by cutting short my breath while exhaling, at the same time saying, "Ah! Ah!" as low as I could. He told me whenever I was alone I should do this, as often as possible. It worked fairly well, I think, and coupled with other normal activities, enabled me to do OK in the lower range. There is nothing a bass desires more than cranking a good solid low note from time to time, especially if the music calls for it. It's fun to do even if the score doesn't indicate it.

It is quite an experience for Minnesota people who have never been south of Iowa to take a tour of the Deep South in winter. It is not just wading in the ocean for the first time off the coast of Florida, but catching sun and seeing flowers and green grass in February. But there can be a dark side, too. When we went to Macon, Georgia in 1954, we found ourselves in a segregated city. We were shocked to see at the railroad station drinking fountains labeled "Whites Only" and "Colored," and the restrooms: "White Ladies Only," "White Gentlemen Only," and "Colored." We did not dare to provoke either group by making a choice that could result in a confrontation that could prove hazardous, so we just walked on, disturbed by what we had seen.

In the Baptist Church of Macon, Georgia where we sang, there was something new for us, a real baptismal tank right in front and directly behind where we placed our riser platform. Wow, holy moly, pudding n' pie! It's fair to say we jostled each other in a half-hearted attempt to cause someone to fall into the dipping tank. Fortunately, this did not happen, but just before we were to begin our concert, the local preacher got up again and intoned a loud, heartfelt prayer that started out something like this, "Brothers and sisters, we are pleased to welcome the famous St. Olaf Choir into our church," and a voice in the congregation almost on cue proclaimed very loudly and in a long stretching way, "Halle -l-u-u-u-u-jah!" The local preacher then said, "And we believe this is the finest St. Olaf Choir, ever in the world." The bass next to me said, "Amen, Brother, Amen." But we dared not laugh, just smiled as we gathered on their river, saying there shall we anoint thee, but first come to ours, froze o'er the River Cannon.

During the intermission, while we recovered in the basement, one of the boys, a playful goofy tenor, picked up a pie tin and smuggled it into the chancel under his choir robe. This was passed from singer to singer in the third row until it got to the baritone section where our soloist, a no-nonsense guy, refused to take it and pass it on. The pie tin fell to the floor with not only a big loud bang, but with a boing–boing–boing. Man, did we get scared! But Olaf did not bat an eye. He never did — if he saw or heard something he wasn't supposed to see or hear, he just ignored it; that is, most of the time. The only time I saw Olaf get distracted during a performance was when we sang an outdoor concert at the Maihaugen Museum in Lillehammer, Norway. It wasn't the people wandering in and out of the area. It was a walk-in concert with no seats and there were moths and bugs flying around because of the lights, just like the Rice county fair. A bug flew into the right ear of a soprano standing at the end. She immediately whipped her arm and hand up to her ear like a good Minnesotan, right in the middle of the "Carol of the Drum," with such a flourish that the white silk on the end of her sleeve made the gesture quite probable and noticeable. Olaf gave her a glare that could melt a stone statue, but continued, saying only "Uff Da!"

In the spring of 1955, Olaf announced that we were taking on an assistant conductor, Kenneth Jennings. We all knew him, for he was conductor of the Chapel Choir and the Manitou Singers. The first time he walked into Steensland alone and without Olaf he said, "Let us sing 'Our Father.'" This number is arguably the most religious and most holy of all the songs in the St. Olaf Choir repertoire, was also the absolute favorite of the bass section because we got to rumble way down low, and it was a challenge to really crank out the bass. From the first phrase, he had us where we all wanted to be. He set the mood, the tempo, and his timing and phrasing were superb. He had control of every nuance and drove us hard where it was needed. We gave him a cheer and a clap and he knew we liked him very much. And we truly did. Olaf was a genius at conducting, and Jennings at that point, was not far behind.

In June 1955, enroute to Norway, we had three days in New York City before sailing. We stayed at the Taft Hotel. I noted there were some rather large phone books in our room so I looked in one for the name "Alexander Gretchaninoff," the Russian composer who wrote "Our Father," one of the anthems on our program. I found his number and phoned him. Gretchaninoff answered on the first ring or two. I said, "Gretchaninoff, this is Kindem calling." I told him I was a member of the St. Olaf Choir and that we were going to sing a concert that evening at the Brooklyn Academy of Music and that his composition "Our Father" was on the program. I told him that Jean Berger, another composer of note, was going to be present, and possibly others. Would he like to join us? "I can't, Kindem," he said, "I am too old. I can't leave my apartment, and I have no way to get there. But I am honored that you are going to sing one of my compositions, and you honor me by inviting me; but I am 90 years old and can't get around very well. Where do you go from here?" I told him we were sailing for Europe the next day. He then said, "Wonderful! I hope you have a very successful tour. Thank you for calling. Goodbye." Gretchaninoff died the following January. I was at least able to speak with the old man whom we admired so much, but I will always regret not doing whatever was necessary to get him to our concert, but there was no chance as far as I could tell. Sad.

This is the night the lights went out because of a storm and power outage. But Olaf did not miss a beat, pulling out a hankie from his breast pocket and we kept on. Eventually, after we sang some more, a floor lamp was set up beside me on the end. After the concert we had the pleasure of meeting the composer of two of our anthems, Jean Berger, who was at that time a professor at Middleburg College. "[_____], (expletive) he said, "I wish I had a performing medium like this!" I thanked him and that was that.

The Norwegian-America Line's grand old 13,500 ton Stavangerfjord, built in 1917, set a trans-Atlantic crossing record of five days in 1923 while carrying Norwegian immigrants to the United States. This was the Choir's vessel for its trip to Europe in 1955. The crossing this time, however, was scheduled to take ten days, and the cost per ticket for the tourist class Choir passengers was $195 one way. Olaf Christiansen and his wife Ellen were first class passengers on this voyage, along with Fred Schmidt, Choir Manager, and his wife Lenore; Kenneth Jennings, Assistant Director; and Elida "Inky" Engebretson, Nurse. In addition to the Choir members traveling tourist class were over 150 Oslo Summer School students, mostly collegians, who contributed to the rather lively atmosphere during the crossing. Passengers from first and cabin classes visited the tourist class lounge and dance hall regularly in the evening because that was where all the lively action was taking place. Regular rehearsals for the Choir were scheduled in the tourist class dining room in between meal times. The crew members often paused in their duties to listen to the Choir practices, so it was decided to give the crew a command performance. The crew assembled and the Choir began with "The Star Spangled Banner" followed by the Norwegian national anthem, "Ja, Vi Elsker." The crew members stood at attention, hatless, as we sang "Ja Vi Elsker" with fervor and dramatic impact that was most impressive. There was not a single dry eye among the crew; and when the Choir sang the emotional tribute, "Til Norge" (to Norway) that begins in Norwegian with "You are my mother, I love you, that says it all," some of the crew wept openly. After the concert, the crew mingled with members of the Choir, clasping hands warmly and expressing appreciation that was as rewarding to the Choir as any we ever experienced by then.

As we traveled along the beautiful Sognefjord toward Förde, Sogn, we noticed a huge crowd by the side of the road in a small village. We got out as instructed and marched up to the steps of the town hall for a "command" performance of a few songs. This we did and were treated to a fine luncheon which our hosts had prepared. We then continued on to our destination.

Our concert in the Nidaros Cathedral in Trondheim was a most impressive experience. In 1930 the Choir had participated in the festivities surrounding the 900th anniversary of the Christianization of Norway by Saint Olaf (Olaf Haraldsson, patron saint of Norway) who is buried beneath the alter of the cathedral. This was our first concert in an ancient Gothic cathedral and the lengthy echoes were something to which we had not been accustomed. Of course, the concert was sold out, as usual. After the concert we located, just outside the cathedral, the grave of the founder of St. Olaf College, Bernt Julius Muus (1832-1900). The monument was about six feet tall, a marble pillar. We thought it odd that there was a monument to Muus in Norway, but none at the college he founded in 1874.

On July 28, 1955 we were to leave Hanover by bus for Gottingen, Germany. I remembered having seen a large poster in downtown Hanover advertising the St. Olaf Choir. So I rushed through breakfast, put my Seagram's 7 cardboard luggage box on the bus, and ran downtown. The poster was still there, and it was now one day past the concert date, so I took it as a souvenir. I made the bus just in time and my roommate asked where I had been. I unfolded the poster to show him my prize and in doing so coined a term never before used in the English language: "I ripped it off a pillar downtown!" I gave the poster to the St. Olaf Choir in 1994 for the rehearsal room to forever enshrine the term, "ripped off" as verbiage, but failed to copyright the "rip off" noun.

We usually travelled by two buses — one for smokers, the other for non-smokers. On the long trip on the autobahn from Gottingen to Munich we had two short stops scheduled, one in Wurzburg, another in Nurnberg. I was riding on the "smoker" bus with Kenneth Jennings in charge and there was only one tenor on board. The other bus broke down, and there was some panic, because the concert in Munich's Lucaskirche was scheduled for 8:00 pm that evening, and it became painfully obvious that not even our lead bus would arrive on time. In the rush toward Munich we were met along the way at one point by people who furnished sandwiches which we ate on the bus as we continued on, hoping the other bus would catch up. When we in the lead bus arrived about a half hour after scheduled concert time, we found a full house waiting. It was decided we would go forward with what we had, and start the concert, with Kenneth Jennings, director, and half the Choir, including only one tenor. Jennings asked me to go over to the tenor section since I assured him I knew the tenor parts too. There were many U.S. military personnel in the audience, and when the sopranos filed onto the risers, they let out a whoop and a cheer that startled the German audience. The Germans came out with a "Shh! Shh!" indicating a church was no place for cheering and hollering. Our first number, of the lighter numbers we decided to do for starters, was "Carol of the Drum." The tenor's job was to follow the bass "Prum" with a "Pappa" and so it went, nervously. Again the GIs cheered, and again the Germans said, "Shh! Shh!" After a few numbers, we took an intermission. Still, no one in the audience had walked out. Then, about 11:00 or 11:30, the rest of the Choir showed up, and this time we all went up on the risers, Olaf in tux and on the podium, and the American servicemen really let out a cheer! We finished the concert after midnight and later found that only four people had asked for a ticket refund.

As we departed Stuttgart, Germany, our bus driver, who had been a 15-year old German fighter pilot near the end of World War II, pointed out the largest mountain near the city. He told us the mountain was created from the rubble of bombed-out Stuttgart.

On tour, the Choir enjoyed a fragrance-free atmosphere on the risers. That is, unless some members took dinner that evening at an Italian restaurant and consumed lots of garlic bread. On those occasions, the garlic breath was nearly overpowering, certainly bothersome, for those who stuck to meat and potatoes. Olaf encouraged Choir members on tour to avoid heavy meats such as pork for the dinner meal. It was his contention that dinners that were easily digestible would allow for better performances, with an empty stomach providing to some degree better resonating for tone production. He also believed that hard-soled shoes were better than rubber soles for resonance. Pocket change and keys that could make distracting noises were also to be avoided. Oatmeal for breakfast was recommended. If one could not suppress a cough, it was better to cough into the back of someone's head than to raise a hand to cover your mouth or stifle it. So much for manners learned at home. Naturally, colds could spread rapidly on tour. That's one reason we had a nurse, Elida "Inky" Engebretson, traveling with us. The only cough depressant she dispensed was very rarely passed out, for it was codeine syrup, served in miniature paper cups. One time, in Mason City, Iowa, where we were housed in private homes by twos, our host said to us, "Well, boys, I'm not going to be at your concert tonight, but I'll be here when you get back. What'll it be — beer, wine or whiskey?" My roommate said, "Yes."

In Hanover, Germany, our host at a very fine reception was Bishop Hans Lilje. He said, "To put German Lutheranism in perspective for you, there are more Evangelical Lutherans in my Bishopric than there are in all of North America." Inasmuch as Germans are noted for their beer drinking, it came as no surprise that there was an ample supply of beer at the reception. We thought this was going to be enjoyable — that is, until our manager, Fred Schmidt, sized up the situation. Fred politely, discreetly, and emphatically whispered to as many as he could, that there would be no beer drinking at that reception by members of the St. Olaf Choir! When asked why not, he told a couple of us that there is a very real danger that word would get back to St. Olaf about it, and by the time the story was told, the evening would have been characterized as a drunken celebration. We had a responsibility for our image, and our conduct must be beyond reproach. The Bishop caught on and understood. His second offer, that of a fine cigar, came directly to me as he extended a box of Havana cigars toward me. I said, "No thanks your honor," not knowing how to address a real live Bishop. He laughed and said, lighting up, "You know, liberal theologians smoke pipes; conservatives smoke cigars. Those who do not smoke are not theologians." I surely would have enjoyed becoming a conservative theologian that evening.

Fred Schmidt was greatly admired as our manager and sometime father figure. He provided much wisdom and stability as we traveled on tour. He was a real pro. About half a dozen of us, from the experience of singing under Fred in oratorio and operetta as well as church performances, knew he was fully capable of directing the St. Olaf Choir should an emergency arise. He always called out, "Um Ya!" when it was time to line up for concerts, buses, or anything. If he were in charge, all railroads and buses and airplanes would run on time. The boys on the riser crew were paid $75 per tour for loading, unloading and setting up the risers and Choir wardrobe cases. Fred always seemed to know his way around. He got a big charge out of whenever we were unloading at a "union shop" concert hall where we could stand around and watch union stagehands do the work.

You may wonder what Choir members wear under their robes. Well, there is a great variety. The only items that show are shoes, pant legs and nylons. I wore the same black bell-bottom sailor pants for the more than 150 concerts over a three-year period. They were never cleaned. My T-shirt, the other garment under the robe, was usually clean at the beginning of the tour. The rule was, throw it into the corner, if it stands up, wash it. Seriously, there were many times when we had to wash out socks and underwear on tour. Some found the simple solution for soap needs was to bring along a bar of Fels Naptha soap. It seemed to be good for getting things cleaned and it would last the entire tour. Trousers that needed a crease were placed carefully between the mattress and box spring overnight. Of course, when we stayed in private homes, we had access to an ironing board. In the fifties, there were no wash and wear items such as we have now; except the early nylon dress shirts which did not breathe and were very uncomfortable.

Up until our 1954 southern tour, we were known as the "St. Olaf Lutheran Choir." Then the name used was "St. Olaf A Capella Choir" for the southern tour and our European tour in 1955. The name "St. Olaf Lutheran Choir" was resumed in 1956 and then the word "Lutheran" was dropped a couple of years later to make it just the St. Olaf Choir, which it is today.

We published, from time to time, a Choir paper while on tour. Whenever we had access to a mimeograph machine in a church, we published a sheet. It did not seem worthwhile saving at the time, but I know one who has a copy or two.

The last night of the Choir tour was an occasion usually accompanied by some sort of high jinks. The guys would go off the deep end and smoke cigars; the gals would stock up on cheap perfume and douse the guys. One such memorable event happened on a train ride back to Northfield. We had two Pullman sleeping cars with curtains along the aisles to provide privacy for the double bunks. Each of the guys went out and bought a cheap cigar, usually a "King Edward" for a nickel. Then the idea was to find the smallest possible room for our smoke-in. This was determined to be the men's restroom in our Pullman. Inspired, I ran to the restroom to get the choice seat for an obvious reason: the flush handle opened the toilet trapdoor, allowing fresh air to enter the room and thus prevent my asphyxiation. We all squeezed in, about thirty of us in all. At someone's command we all lit up and I flushed the toilet. This was followed by another command: "Take five puffs," then another, then another, until it became obvious that we would die, or worse, might not. So we quit and ran back to our bunks to wait for the inevitable raid by the gals who would run through the car in their pajamas and douse us with cheap perfume. But we were ready for them. One of the guys suggested a neat trick would be to have a paper cupful of water and return the fire. The gals sneaked in, took their positions, then on command threw open our curtains and doused us with the cheapest perfume in the world. Our counter attack was more successful than we imagined, for when the gals in pajamas were splashed with water in the front, the result became obvious. They were out of there in a hurry.

After a night in the Pullman, we sat in the lounge car to await the breakfast call. I sat next to Olaf; Tom Twaiten sat across from us. Tom and I lit up cigarettes. Olaf said, "Tom, you are a tenor with a delicate voice. Smoking isn't good for it. You, Lars, are a raucous bass; it doesn't matter with you." Then Olaf said to Tom, "You know, I didn't realize how good food tasted until I quit smoking." Tom replied, "I didn't know how good cigarettes tasted until I started smoking." I put out my cigarette and got out of there.

There is no doubt that Saint Olaf Choir members give the best back rubs in the world! One of the characteristics of the Choir singer, especially on tour, is that he or she always has some sort of back pain. Some discomfort is the result of all the standing under tension in concert. Then there are the long bus rides, strange beds each night, and heavy luggage to cart around. So the solution to the problem is to get to know the best "hands" and stick by them on tour. We had "trains" where each would rub the back and neck of the one in front, then turn around. This was more complicated on the bus, for the last one in line got no treatment without moving up in the line. We did back rubs most commonly during intermissions or after a long bus ride. There were other illnesses that plagued singers on tour. Cold viruses circulated rather freely because of the close contact, and there really was no practical way to avoid it and stay with the Choir. One year, in advance of the tour, we all got "cold shots" from the health service at the St. Olaf hospital. No one knows what the shots were or if they had any effect, but we all had to get the shot. Sometimes a singer would faint in concert but usually, however, if a singer felt faint, he or she would sit down on the risers and those on either side would "close ranks" until the person had recovered or the end of the group of songs was reached. To promote good physical conditioning, we always had lots of exercises before the concerts. Several times Olaf asked me to lead the singers on a long hike, either in the neighborhood or up and down the hotel stairs if the weather was bad. Sometimes we went for a swim if a pool could be found. There was, and is, a pronounced improvement in breathing and singing if one takes some good physical exercise an hour or two prior to performance. One concern we had was the very dry air found in hotel rooms during the heating season. We knew that humidity was an important factor in the air we breathed. So the first thing my roommate and I would do was to run the shower hot, or fill the tub with hot water and drape some water-soaked towels on the radiators at night before we went to bed. The cry, "Humidity!" was loudly voiced as soon as we entered a hotel room, "Give us Humidity!"

Fred Schmidt was very much like his father, P.G., in his conviction that Choir tours should be learning experiences. I used to enjoy very much sitting with either of them because they knew so much about areas through which we traveled. Fred scheduled "field trips" and stops wherever possible so we could enjoy seeing whatever sights and monuments were available. We visited the Oak Ridge, Tennessee atomic facility; a racetrack for thoroughbreds in Keeneland, Kentucky; Magnolia gardens in South Carolina; a cigarette factory in Winston-Salem, North Carolina; Civil War battlefield sites; the home of Jesse James in Missouri; the whispering wall in Pennsylvania's state capitol; an old plantation in the South; and many more sites. The problem, of course, was finding worthwhile sites to visit, time and distance permitting.

We had two bus drivers who looked for good sites for us to visit. They would scout out the town during the concert, then afterward drop us off at the hotel. Some would go in one door, through the lobby, then out another door to the waiting bus. One such evening (and there were not many), we went out on the town someplace in Michigan, I think Saginaw. They found a bar empty of customers when we entered. We had a beer and then someone found a fully equipped bandstand with mike, drums, piano, string bass, banjo, and whatever. Soon we started jammin' with some real fine popular tunes, taking turns at the piano, doing vocals, and so on. Gradually, a rather sizable crowd was assembled, and before long it was four-deep standing room only at the bar. The bartender was ecstatic and sent over free beers for us. Someone asked who we were, and we replied we were just some college folks passing through town.

I met my cousin when we were in Oslo, Norway, and it was determined I should leave most of my stuff there while I continued on with our tour in Germany. I was going to return to Oslo and not fly back to the U.S. from Amsterdam with the Choir. Well, I left my passport in Oslo. On the train from Oslo to Lund, Sweden, the Swedish passport control went among the passengers, checking papers. Since I had left my passport in Oslo, they stopped the train at the Swedish border and put me off the train. It was a place called "Hornsjo" with a population of about five. I went to a farmhouse and explained my predicament and asked to use the phone. How glad I was to be able to speak Norwegian for they knew no English! I called my cousin and asked if she could send my passport with the next train. She did, but the conductor did not stop the train. I phoned the stationmaster at Lund, Sweden, and asked him to get my passport from the train conductor and send it back to Hornsjo. He said he would, and he did. I caught up with the Choir a day later in Copenhagen and apparently no one had missed me. I found out that one of the gals had missed the train in Oslo and she also caught up with the Choir later. Whew!

On Choir tours we frequently had supper in the churches where the evening concert was to be held. Scalloped potatoes with ham was the most frequently served meal. Before dinner, we always sang grace; after dinner, we always sang a "thank you" to the ladies of the church who served the supper. From time to time, one of us would tap a glass with a spoon to get attention, signaling a "takk for maten" or "thank you" speech was in order. My roommate always started out with the same introduction: "I have traveled many parts of Wisconsin, and many parts of Trempleau County, and in my vast travels I have never been so astounded as I am now. What would follow could be just about anything; always impromptu, such as calling on some unsuspecting Choir member to make some sort of a speech. Some of the speeches made no sense at all, so we had a good laugh at someone's embarrassed expense.

In Norway, we always sang to a full house, sometimes in very large cathedrals. But the most unusual was in Sandnes, near Stavanger. The church held 1,200 people, but 1,800 tickets were sold. The overflow were seated outside, in the cemetery, with loudspeakers set up to broadcast the concert to them. The next day we visited the famous porcelain factory where each of us was presented with a Sandnes "gauk" (cuckoo) and porcelain bird whistle with "St. Olaf Choir 1955" painted on one side, and Sandnes on the other. We were not to use the cuckoo as a pitch pipe for concerts.

Four of us men had a barbershop quartette which would give impromptu performances on street corners or whenever, at the most unexpected times. No one threw coins.

Everyone who attends a St. Olaf Choir concert knows the gals all hold hands, but the guys do not. No one knows why the gals do this. One theory is to be able to signal if the person next to you is off key. Well, one time a gal was off key, so her partner squeezed her hand. Gal #1 did not realize that gal #2 thought she was off key, because she never would be as far as she was concerned. So #1 and #2 kept squeezing harder and harder, back and forth, so that #1 who was off key became convinced #2 was going to faint and needed help. They eventually led each other off the stage in the middle of a lullaby and when they got back stage and realized their mistake, one of them shrieked aloud which we all heard.

Members of the Choir had to return to St. Olaf right after Christmas for intensive rehearsals lasting about a week. We rehearsed two hours in the morning, two hours in the afternoon, and two in the evening. We really got in shape, and at the evening rehearsals our singing was particularly well done. One of the evenings was designated as a Christmas party evening at Olaf's house. It was then that we conducted the initiations of new members. These were silly, but fun.

One of our soloists was pestered by the gals when she bowed. Sometimes a bra strap was snapped, and once she was jabbed in the rear with the point of a safety pin. She let out an involuntary "Yipe" and jumped straight up. From then on, before bowing she would take a full stride forward, then bow. No more problems.

Olaf was forever comparing tones of pitch pipes and was rarely satisfied. Some were affected by the warmth of a hand or pocket, some by being in a cold suitcase. One day, a cocky senior said to him, "You don't need those things; I can give you the pitch." So Olaf tested him, calling for various pitches at random. He got them all correctly, and was given the assignment of humming the pitch with his Perfect Pitch.

A good roommate on tour is a joy forever. There are many considerations before one proposes to another that they room together on tour. Some difficulties are unforeseen, however. First of all, non-smokers will not enjoy a roommate who smokes. That's an easy problem to avoid. Snoring loudly comes on as a rude awakening, and this delicate situation is a tough one to handle. I have no solution other than avoidance. My roommate for two years had a habit of chewing hard candy after he got to bed, cracking the candy loudly until he drifted off to sleep. After he got to sleep, he ground his teeth. Usually I did not care at all because we were so tired anyway that it didn't matter. The roommate is many things: friend, confidant, adviser, companion, nursemaid, and usually a lifelong friend. There is a bonding effect that characterizes all St. Olaf Choirs. Those who have shared common experiences on tours need to be compatible with others. Understanding the foibles and behaviors of others is an important factor. The shared experience reinforces friendships and has a tendency to make them long-lasting, just as those friendships developed among team sport participants and neighbors often abide for life. Hobo, these are my stories about the St. Olaf Choir, many of which you have heard before — what roommates in life we have been, and what shared experiences — you can room with me anytime!

    Argo —

The Navy's March of Dimes

Dear Donald,

You weren't around during the war years, but I hit a goldmine when the Navy took over Ytterboe and Mohn Hall in 1943 at St. Olaf. The first Navy contingent of 200 Navy cadets arrived in January. I was ten years old at the time and made a killing in dimes shining shoes for the cadets and selling apples I would swipe from Marie Malmin Meyer's trees at the base of the Hill on the corner of 'Olaf and Lincoln. By modern accounting my profit margins were fantastic if not excessive, and it was so much fun.

During the war, there were three contingents of 200 cadets for three-months at a time year-round in the Navy Pre-Flight Training program at St. Olaf. The Navy housed four men per room in Mohn Hall and Ytterboe Hall, which were named "U.S.S. Lexington" and "U.S.S. Enterprise." Classes and evening study periods were held in Old Main and marching drill was in the gymnasium. The Navy also took over the women's physical education department facilities in the gym.

Teachers were recruited from the 'Olaf faculty in addition to those provided by the Navy. The curriculum consisted of military discipline, marching, theory of flight, basic navigation, dead reckoning, celestial navigation, and Morse Code at Steensland Hall. The Navy's "Bluejacket's Manual" was the bible for those guys to learn how to salute, the new Navy lingo, and Navy etiquette. Classes for the regular students were held in Holland Hall and the library. The Navy program lasted until 1945 with a constant change of new cadets. When one battalion of 200 completed its three-month course, it left for real flying training in Iowa and was replaced by a rookie battalion of 200 new cadets. I quickly learned how to cash in on the new crop when they arrived.

One of the oldest and most consistent rumors cropped up again and again when I was shining Navy shoes for a dime at Ytterboe. I started at a nickel a pair but quickly realized a dime was just as easy to get from the new guys if you clarified the price by saying innocently, like David Copperfield: "It's really just a nickel a shoe, Sir." I always pushed the limit and almost got thrown out of Ytterboe when this Navy guy asked my price and I sang out, sorta smart-alecky: "A dime a shoe, a quarter for two."

I quickly realized there was a limit to pricing, as in everything in life, which was a good lesson. Well, I made up the difference by installing a second shoe-shine chair, so I could do two cadets at a time: "Four shoes at a time, a pair for a dime." That was the road to riches and I was good at my work. The cadets loved it and I would amuse them with Norwegian songs my mother taught me and that some of them knew.

But there was always the persistent rumor that the cadets talked about at the shoeshine stand. Donald, as a former Marine Corps sergeant you would understand the circumstance and perplexity of this rumor. Was it in the mashed potatoes, or was it sprinkled on top of everything? That was the mystery of the rumor.

Every shoe I shined at Ytterboe involved a lively conversation that usually started with, "Hi kid, where'ya from, how much for a shine," and I'd say, "A dime a shoe or a quarter for two." I always got the job, usually for a dime with a nickel tip, sometimes a jackpot quarter. When I made a buck, I went downtown. The conversation inevitably involved those things we weren't supposed to know anything about, like the rubber deals they sold in the Ytterboe Navy exchange, along with Lucky Strikes, Old Golds, and Wings. And the cadets would inevitably bring up the issue of food at the Mohn hall cafeteria: "Did'ja ever eat there, kid, how'd you feel afterwards – can you still get a big one on?"

I didn't know what they meant, but here's the rumor, which I finally figured out sometime later. It was the contention of the Navy cadets that the cooks in the Mohn Hall cafeteria put saltpeter in the food to reduce their sex drive. Maybe it was in the mashed potatoes or maybe it was sprinkled on top of everything, no one knew for sure. I asked the cadets what it tasted like and they said it was pretty darn good, but no one ever saw it done or had any real proof, and they all swore someone who really knows told them saltpeter was definitely in the food. No question about it.

There usually followed the inevitable conclusion, based on jealousy the cadets felt about preferential treatment given to the fourteen Navy officers who presided at St. Olaf, that saltpeter was definitely not added to the officers' food, for everyone knew what those primadonnas were up to when they went downtown. After being discussed at every meal, most cadets decided that if they were really adding saltpeter to the food and whether or not it was in the mashed potatoes, it wasn't going to make any difference anyway, considering where they were going after they completed flying training. But those St. Olaf gals sure looked good even if the saltpeter prevented the ability to do anything about it (I loved spreading the rumor to the new cadets when they arrived).

So, between the Navy Commandant's no-fraternization policy with the Ole coeds and constant rumors that saltpeter was definitely in the cafeteria food, the Navy cadets said they were in a constant state of anguish and conflict. But not me and my march of dimes; I was happy as a lark: "A dime a shoe or a quarter for two." And I finally figured out a little later what that saltpeter business was all about and what they were selling beside cigarettes in the Ytterboe Naval Exchange.

     Argo –

Chapel

Dear Donald,

The new school year at St. Olaf begins today, and this pleases me greatly, for now I can listen to chapel services on a daily basis. Although chapel is at 11:05 M-W-F, and T-TH at 10:05, the services are broadcast on WCAL at 11:05.

They opened with the hymn, "My God How Wonderful Thou Art" (thy majesty how bright), and I was moved, not only by the greatness of the hymn, its text and tune, but the way they sang it. It brought warm memories back from my first year in the St. Olaf Choir, when we rehearsed T-TH at 8:50 in the Radio Building.

One day Olaf Christiansen said, "Well, I suppose we ought to sing in chapel today." We opened the hymnals to the hymn, "My God..." We ran through the song twice, walked over to the gym, sat on the side bleachers, and opened the chapel service the way it should be opened, with power, majesty and the glory of that hymn.

I remember we sang it in E-flat, and the bass section never sounded better at the end. It was solid, just like an organ. I reached my hand to the guy next to me, Rolf Charlston. We shook hands, and I said, "You're a good bass." He smiled and said, "You're not bad yourself." That made my day. My whole week!

I spoke with the college pastor a couple of days ago over coffee in the Lion's Cage, and mentioned that I heard chapel attendance is not very good. In fact, no one goes any more, students or faculty, and most of the faculty do not live in Northfield but commute from the Cities, so certain connections we knew in our time have been lost. Yes, he agreed, it's a concern, and they don't have an answer. I told him I listen daily during the school year, and that I think he is a good preacher.

Knowing what I know now, I would beat the door down to get into chapel at St. Olaf, were I a student. I always liked chapel. I found the hymn singing led by Olaf Christiansen on Wednesdays particularly fun. But to hear an entire congregation sing out the way they did at 'Olaf was truly an experience, and it was one I will always remember with fondness. Just think, I now get that treat five times a week!

At the end of the school year last May, the final chapel service was concluded with the unforgettable Widor "Toccata" played by the organist, Dr. Ferguson. It was wild. He pulled out all the stops, as they say. At the end there was not just applause, but a roar and sustained cheering by the students. I was cheering too, for I knew I had just heard an unforgettable performance of great music. Is it possible that some were cheering partly because it was all over for the year, for four years, perhaps? They will never again have it so good.

Forgive me for intruding on your busy schedule, Donald, but it is all right for you to get a reminder, from time to time, of where you come from, and what a great place St. Olaf and Northfield were, and are, and shall be always.

As we discussed during your last visit, I completed the deal at Oaklawn Cemetery on behalf of you, Donald, and for your neighbor — I purchased deeds for our two plots, one for each of us, side-by-side, right up front in the St. Olaf section. Our neighbors are names we both know well: Huggenvik, Søvik, Flaten, Granskou, L.W. Boe.

I like that a lot, and I know you do too. We ought to lie on our sides in our lots, Hobo, you on your left side, me on my right, face-to-face, so we can converse for eternity, or at least until the Ascension. I know that you, Donald, are a fine christian conversationalist and will excel under the prescribed format.*

Lars —

*Memo for the Record: Donald M. Clark, aka Hobo, passed away April 26, 2000 and pulled a fast one before he died by making claim as the designated Cannon River poet. Hobo had his marker in the Northfield cemetery engraved in bronze: "Donald M. Clark, Sgt., U.S. Marine Corps, POET." I had the dates 1935-2000 added after learning of Hobo's death. He and I will meet again sometime soon and talk about it, I'm sure. Argo —

Afterword

Remembering Argo

Lars G. Kindem 1933 – 2013

Memorial remarks by B. Wayne Quist – St. John's Lutheran Church, Northfield, Minnesota, February 9, 2013

We are assembled today at St. John's to honor the memory of our friend Lars Kindem, pay respects to his family and loved ones, his brothers and sisters, his children and their mother, his grandchildren. We did so, for it was appropriate to gather at St. John's, Lars' home — founded by Bernt Julius Muus, the Norwegian immigrant who founded St. Olaf College. Lars knew the Muus story well and sang bass in the St. John's Choir, and basso profundo with the St. Olaf Choir for many years.

Throughout his life, Lars adored telling humorous stories about growing up in Northfield and the College on the Hill he loved so much. Whether skiing or singing or telling amusing stories, Lars loved life and he has left us, the living, an indelible legacy of precious memories to cherish. Lars was wedded to St. Olaf and especially to the Choir, for it had a central place in his life, and the sanctity of the names woven into the Choir robes was important to him. Lars would be pleased with the following email Peter Charlston ("Gus") received from Anton Armstrong, Conductor of the St. Olaf Choir during their 2013 winter tour out west:

Peter,

Thank you for your e-mail about Lars Kindem. As we arrived in Seattle two days ago, I was saddened to learn of Lars' death. Over the years I was delighted when Lars would visit campus and sit in on an Ole Choir rehearsal. He shared with me many of the stories of his years in the St. Olaf Choir and the time he spent as a care-taker for F. Melius Christiansen during that final year of Christy's life. Lars was a good man filled with so much affection and gratitude for what the St. Olaf Choir meant to him. I am personally grateful for the support and encouragement he showed me since assuming leadership of the St. Olaf Choir in 1990. What I could do to remember and pay tribute to Lars, is to dedicate our performance of the Rachmaninoff All-Night Vigil at our Home Concert in Boe Memorial Chapel on Sunday afternoon, February 17, in his memory.

Anton Armstrong

Lars passed away peacefully Saturday morning, January 26, 2013. Noel Ness ("Gunder") and I were with Lars a few hours before he departed, and he remains with us in spirit, singing loudly from the great Choir in the sky. That last day we brought Lars a copy of Joe Shaw's biography of B. J. Muus Lars so admired, and the picture on the cover may have been the last image he saw, his last remaining image, St. Olaf.

Lars was born and grew up in Northfield at the foot of Manitou Heights at 101 South Lincoln, directly below the Old Main hill where he first learned to ski. His parents, Ingvald and Anna Kindem, came to Northfield from Norway in 1925 and each became institutions at St. Olaf in their own right. Three of Lars' siblings were born in Norway and the Kindem children grew up fluent in the Norwegian language and all things Nordic.

Four Kindem brothers served in World War II — Olaf and Halvor in the Army, Erling in the Air Corps shot down flying B-24s in Europe, and Alf in the Navy, twice severely wounded in the Pacific. Anna Kindem had a red-bordered flag with four blue stars in the living room window and Lars shined shoes for Navy cadets at Ytterboe Hall, starting his repertory of stories as a youth.

At home, Lars was tutored in Norwegian by a witty father and wise Norwegian mother who was also a master cook, and he learned to make lefse and other Norwegian specialties from her. Friends remember the delicious bread Lars baked daily, and delivered to appreciative Kierkegaard scholars and others in Northfield, and his 5-star round-table dinners were always memorable feasts.

Lars attended Longfellow Elementary, graduated from Northfield High School in 1951, and St. Olaf in 1955. He earned a Master's Degree at the University of Minnesota where he co-wrote a Norwegian dictionary. For many years after he retired, Lars served as president of Howard Hong's Kierkegaard House Foundation, working closely with Howard and Gordon Marino in promoting the Kierkegaard Library, a crown jewel of the College, second only to the Choir.

In grade school and high school it's no surprise that Lars was called "Lefse." He was a talented athlete and loved outdoor sports, especially Nordic skiing. He was launched off the St. Olaf ski jump at an early age by his older brothers, and he excelled in virtually everything in high school — class president, choir, student council president, track and football, single wing quarterback on Northfield's undefeated 1950 football team, scoring the winning touchdown with a spectacular diving catch from Dale Quist in the super bowl of high school football against Faribault, Northfield's hated rival. At St. Olaf, Lars pole vaulted and proudly wore his St. Olaf letterman's jacket his entire life; as for fishing, Lars still holds the Minnesota state record for the largest Kokanee salmon ever caught in the state.

And it was at St. Olaf where Lars met Jean Mattson. They married and had five children, three boys and two girls, proud of their Norwegian heritage; sadly, their youngest daughter Sonja preceded Lars in death. In the early 1960s Lars won a Fulbright scholarship and taught in Norway where their daughter Nina was born. Returning home, Lars and his growing family lived in Burnsville. He coached and taught Norwegian and American history for three decades at North High School and Roosevelt High in Minneapolis. He became well known as an innovative, creative, and caring teacher, and his impressive coaching record remains unmatched to this day.

Lars was awarded the title "Dean of Coaches" and in 2004 was inducted into the Nordic Ski Coach Hall of Fame as "the most highly successful and groundbreaking coach in the history of the Minneapolis high school system." His teams collected three state championships and Lars started the first girl's high school ski team in Minnesota. Within two years, there were 75 girl's ski teams in Minnesota, and when Lars left North for Roosevelt, his North teams had amassed an undefeated dual meet record of 69 wins and no defeats. His combined teams at North and Roosevelt won 17 Minneapolis city titles, 119 dual meets, and 16 district titles — a record unmatched yet today.

Lars was also a long-time member of the United States Ski Association (USSA), on the National Board of Directors, President of the Central Division, Vice President of the Nordic Division, U.S. Ski Team Board, Trustee of the U.S. Ski Educational Foundation, and U.S. Olympic Ski Games Committee. He traveled frequently to Norway and Finland to prepare for the 1980 Olympic Games as Chief Timekeeper and Winter Olympics Stadium Chief. Stories abound how Chief Timekeeper Kindem maintained order and amused King Carl Gustav of Sweden with witty tales about Norwegians and Swedes at the Lake Placid Winter Olympics in 1980. The list of accolades goes on, but Lars is best remembered as a devoted father and exceptional friend. He touched thousands of lives and was a uniquely gifted individual who truly made a difference, making the world a better place. Lars is sadly missed but fondly remembered by his many friends, companions, and admirers, and especially his brothers and sisters, his children and their mother, and his grandchildren.

Sitting as we are today, remembering Lars along the snowy trails of life's long winter, in thoughts alone we now recite what Lars would say to us —

"Do not go gentle into that good night;
Rage, rage against the dying of the light!"
Thus do we implore –
We, the old ones aging more,
Waving last goodbyes,
Distilled with life,
Our dreams yet now abounding,
Transcending all we know or ever feel,
Forever, as in the definition of a friend,
Here at Lars' home,
In this our last goodbye, together.
Proclaiming, through our hosts,
His family, and his friends,
That "in our sleep...comes wisdom through the awful grace of God."
Thus say we now for Lars —
(Lars loved to quote Henry V's St. Crispin's Day speech)

"He who outlives this day,
And comes safely home to an older age,
Will stand a tip-toe when this day is named,
Rousing in him at the name of Friendship,
Will they yearly on the vigil
Feast their neighbors, and say to them..." —
'That day, that memorial day at St. John's,
That was Argo's Day.'
"And though old men like us might forget;
Yet all shall never be forgot,
And they will remember, with advantage too...."
What feats Lars did... "for then shall his name,
Familiar in our mouths as household words —
Be in their flowing cups, freshly now remembered.

This story shall the good man teach his son;
For from this day, to the ending of the world,
We few, we happy few, we Band of Brothers...,"
So say we this, to all of you —
"Think when men's glory must begin and end;
And say our glory was, that we had such a friend."

- Hoz

Argo at the Burnsville Roundtable, 2006

Tribute to Lars Kindem

By Peter F. Charlston ("Gus") - St. Olaf College 1958

Lars Kindem was a legend on the campus when I arrived as a freshman at St. Olaf in the fall of 1954. He had already established his reputation as one of the more memorable rascals of Rice County and as a merry prankster on Manitou Heights. What outrageous actions sprang from his wild imagination!

Who else would have had the courage to climb the WCAL radio tower? Who else would have activated his own claim by walking blindfolded from Dundas to the college campus, leading a trusting band of blindfolded Oles, though only a few were able to successfully complete the journey. Who else, during a sweeping outdoor panoramic photo of the student body and faculty, would have sprinted from the end of a standing back row to the other end in time to appear twice in the same picture? And who else would have or could have dashed from a singing engagement with the St. Olaf Choir in Minneapolis to a cross-town college track meet just in time to win the pole vault competition -- in concert attire!

Lars was a ubiquitous presence on the St. Olaf campus. He grew up at the foot of The Hill at 101 Lincoln with the curiosity of a Nordic explorer that led to a thorough knowledge of the college's structural complex. His courage and curiosity not only took him to the highest point on the campus (top of the radio tower) but to destinations underground as well; he became acquainted with the college's secret tunnel system and explored its entire network. His reputation often preceded him, which is why he was blamed for or credited with turning off the power (all the lights) and turning loose a greased pig one evening in the college library. He refused to accept credit for that prank and the ensuing pandemonium though some still believe he was the mastermind behind it.

Lars was full of mischief, but he was much more than a prankster. He was a bright student, particularly interested in history and, for three years, he was a proud basso in the St. Olaf Choir. After his graduation, he enjoyed an outstanding career in high school teaching and coaching. He was inducted into the

Minnesota Nordic Ski Coaches Association Hall of Fame and was a meet organizer and chief timekeeper on the U.S. Olympic Ski Committee.

His parents, Ingvold and Anna Kindem, were born in Norway. Their five boys and two girls were raised in their Northfield home where Norwegian was spoken as much or more than English. Consequently, Lars's fluency in Norwegian and familiarity with Nordic history and culture turned out to be beneficial for the choir on its '55 summer tour of Norway.

As a student, Lars took voice lessons from my aunt, Ella Hjertaas Roe (another legend on The Hill), who, one fine day, helped him rehearse a song in her studio. She was so thrilled with his progress that she turned to him and urgently encouraged him to go home at once: "Sing it to your mother, Lars, sing it to your mother!" And he did. He dashed down The Hill and sang with a joyful heart to his loving and receptive mother, Anna Kindem, the most famous lefse maker in Rice County.

Throughout his entire life, Lars remained a proud and loyal Ole. He was a frequent visitor to the St. Olaf campus and was one of the college's most generous supporters and dedicated alums. More than anything, Lars loved the St. Olaf Choir. He loved the experience of singing in the choir under the direction of Olaf Christiansen, son of the choir's founder, F. Melius Christiansen. He loved the camaraderie of singing with his friends in the bass section, and, as a basso, he had a particular fondness for the great Russian composers, Gretchaninoff and Tschesnokoff, and the thrill of "cranking out a low C" in Our Father or Salvation is Created.

Many summers ago, Lars and Nini and their five children left their Minnesota home in their station wagon and trailing boat with the Ole Evinrude motor and drove 2,000 miles to the Far West to join Vicky and me and our two young children for a vacation at a place called Happy Camp at Netarts Bay on the Oregon coast. We stayed in cabins that had been built during the Great Depression. Eleven of us stayed in those cabins for $80 for a week, and we had a wonderful time. Lars and I motored out in his boat every day, crabbing for all the Dungeness we could pull up in the big rings, and when we came in with our catch, we'd throw the crabs into the boiling barrel-pot next to the cabins. The kids raced and turned cartwheels on the beach, and we all feasted on fresh crab, and Lars would proclaim in a resonant bass voice filled with dramatic intensity, "We are at one with the universe!"

Three weeks ago, I called Lars. We sang a song in Norwegian that he taught me many years ago, a humorous song about mice dancing on a drum. He was in good voice and good spirit. It was our last reunion. His magnanimous spirit is now and always will be transcendently glorious.

"Whence comes such another?!"

Donald McCornack Clark

Born February 9, 1935—Died April 26, 2000

Donald M. Clark, 65, died on April 26, 2000 in Carson City, Nevada after a lingering illness. He was born in Mitchell, SD in 1935 and was preceded in death by his parents, Dr. Francis Clark and Bernice Clark.

His family moved to Northfield in 1947 when his father became a professor of Psychology and Education at St. Olaf College. Clark was married to Linda Ruberg of Staten Island, NY in 1958 and Glenda Holmes of Newcastle, England in 1978. Donald and Linda had four children. Clark is survived by three sons: Sam, Russell, and Steven; daughter, Jennifer Clark Mattucci in Pittsburg; and six grandchildren. A sister, Judith Clark Murashige resides in Illinois.

Following high school in Northfield, Clark served proudly as a Sergeant in the United States Marine Corps air wing in the Far East during the Korean conflict. He returned to Northfield and graduated from St. Olaf College in 1959 where he became a lifelong member of Fubar, a fraternal band of brothers seeking meaning and truth in the absurdities of life.

Upon graduation from St. Olaf, Clark became a parole officer in New York City. After retiring, he held various positions in the social work field in Virginia. Clark attended graduate school at New York University and Gallaudet University for the hearing impaired in Washington, DC. During retirement, he lived in Silver Spring, Maryland; Portland, Oregon; and Carson City, Nevada.

Clark was an outstanding high school and college wrestler in the 145-165 pound classes; his opponents were "unworthy foes" according to the 1958 St. Olaf yearbook, and he had the honor of being the top wrestler in the history of Northfield High School. Clark was an avid reader and collector of firearms as well as a large and whimsical collector of other memorabilia and non-memorabilia.

He was cremated and his memory is etched on a bronze marker next to Lars Kindem's in the St. Olaf section of Oaklawn Cemetery in Northfield that reads:

DONALD M. CLARK
SGT USMC
1935 ✝ 2000
POET

The First Fubar to Fall

*By Peter F. Charlston "Gus," St. Olaf '58,
in memory of Donald M. Clark ("Hobo")*

Grieved but not surprised to hear about Hobo. News of the first Fubar to fall came via the internet from Argo while we were, as fate would have it, in the Argolid. A mere decade ago, my old friend from Rice County, Donny Clark, alias Hobo, came to visit us at 3040 in Portland for two weeks — and stayed for three years. He had some annoying habits, but he became a member of the family anyway. The grandchildren, in particular, expected him to be with us for family dinners and other special events. They enjoyed his familiar presence; he certainly took a liking to them.

Hobo shared the festive board with us at 3040 for Thanksgiving, Christmas, Easter, Greek Easter and birthdays. He also joined us for picnics in the park (Mt. Tabor). We made the rounds. At least twice a week we went to the bank, post office and Freddy's one-stop-shopping center. We even occasionally sallied forth on more adventurous excursions — from the Columbia River Gorge to the Oregon Coast, Vancouver Barracks to Autzen stadium in Eugene (U of O football.)

With a little encouragement, he worked some physical exercise into his daily routine: swimming with Gus and the girls at Grant Park, Montavilla Park and the Sandy River and biking around the neighborhood on his Italian racer — Campione del Mundi (Champion of the World). He also had spasmodic fits of creativity. Like Churchill, he enjoyed painting as a pastime and would bestow his artistic gifts upon the girls and rest of the family. He always remembered birthdays with cards and gifts, a surprisingly generous side of his character.

As Argo hath so accurately said in the obituary he assembled for Donald, he was a "collector of memorabilia and non-memorabilia." He never saw a yard sale he didn't like, and we made frequent pilgrimages to Goodwill and to Bwana Junction (Joe's Gun Shop). The Jehovah's Witnesses have made door-to-door visits on Saturday mornings for many years. They are often reluctant to leave the premises until they have made their statement. Three elderly black ladies with the latest news from

Armageddon had the run of the neighborhood while Donny was living at 3040.

But instead of telling them to get out of his ears and off the porch, he would trade information with them and engage them in a new and different sort of proselytizing with some startling philosophical insights. They would finally have to excuse themselves from his eclectic diatribe so that they could get on with their business.

However, they must have enjoyed this experience and agreed among themselves that he was the most unusual character they had ever met because after he moved from 3040 to the Hancock House, they would come to the door and enthusiastically ask for Donald.

They were disappointed when I told them he no longer lived here. Donny lived off and on in the Hancock House for six years, but during this time, he continued to be a frequent guest at 3040. He never failed to entertain our other guests with a maze of tales, slow-motion yarns of eccentric characters in action, stories that often tested their willing suspension of disbelief.

The last time Donny came to Portland from his new home in Nevada was with his friend John and a U-Haul trailer in order to retrieve his possessions from the Hancock House. They stayed for Christmas and another trip up the Gorge but Donny did not look well; he lacked the spark and spunk we had come to know so well. He was not always in great health when he lived in Portland as I took him more than once to the VA on the hill. Yet he always rallied. His decision to move to Nevada was, as it is for many, a gamble and was, as it turned out, the beginning of the end. Trying to get through the winter in a house without a working furnace didn't increase his odds for survival.

Some of us like to remember the tough young Marine who shocked the innocent young coeds when he first appeared on Manitou Heights in tight Levis, kick-ass boots, and a T-shirt rolled up to the shoulders exposing USMC tattoos on his biceps. These sheltered young women would look at each other in wide-eyed amazement and ask each other in unison, "Is he really the son of Dr. Clark?" And we remember his strength and quickness on the wrestling mat at St. Olaf and on the fighting floor of the 3-D in Dundas. We all knew that he could end a match in a hurry. And we remember his bold and colorful presence at the Well and the Hurry Back, the Carleton Arboretum and the Union Lake

Floating Keg Blast. He was, after all, a charter member of Fubar.

As the Hobo, he was, for much of his life, a man of the road. Since he admired the songs of Roger Miller, he could even be the king of the road. After working for the Parole Board in New York and after a couple of marriages without an excess of bliss, he was ready to return to the road, depending not so much on the kindness of strangers as on the willingness of friends. His UPS boxes usually preceded a cross-country move.

Then the call would come — not from the Greyhound Bus station but from the Green Tortoise Bus stop. The Green Tortoise is an alternative adventure in travel where passengers sleep in aisle beds and are allowed to smoke grass but not conventional cigarettes. Thus, one may travel with people who don't need cell phones to be happy. Hobo fit in nicely on the Green Tortoise since he was always looking for the alternative anyway, an escape from the ordinary. That was his distinctive style.

Sometimes he talked about his family. He frequently made long distance phone calls and occasionally visited his parents in Florida (his "dear old mom and dear old dad"), sister in Missouri, daughter in Pennsylvania and his second wife in California. Once in a long while he would get a long distance call from one of his boys.

There was unquestionably one person in his life who had more impact on him than anyone else — in or out of his family: the friend of his energetic youth in Northfield, the young teenager who became his mentor, the man whom he greatly admired and whose name he would cite and whose anecdotes he would relate in social gatherings at 3040, or Powell's Book Store, or Stanich's Ten Till One, or to sidewalk strangers with whom he felt a sudden need to communicate. In Donny's mind, the man's words were gospel, right up there with Matthew, Mark, Luke and John. Lars was the main man in his life, the voice of humor and wisdom, the one who gave him a serious belief in the absurd.

It could easily be said that Donald didn't have much of a religious life. In a conventional sense that is true. He was encouraged to hike around the corner from the Hancock House to Central Lutheran for a morning worship service and once in a while he would. He enjoyed talking with the pastor in the fellowship hall after the service, especially if there was food. He rarely showed up for the Eucharist, but he did have an appetite for moral philosophy and observations regarding the human condition.

In particular, Hobo and I shared a certain admiration for that mischievous man from Missouri, that inquisitive individual with a penchant for humorous perspective and candid advice. When Hal Holbrook brought his "Mark Twain Tonight" to Portland, we were there. We had memorized the recording years ago and would often recite our favorite passages for each other's edification: "I was born modest, but it wore off." "It's not easy to be eccentric." "Always do right. It will gratify some and astonish the rest." "If you can't reach 70 by a comfortable road, don't go." Hobo didn't, but he is well-remembered — as a friend, comrade, rantipole miscreant. Fubar remembers!

 Abyssynia, Hobo — Gus

Hobo Reminiscences

By David A. Jarratt, "Cricket" 1936-2012—St. Olaf, '58

Gus reminded me of a few stories of my own. I had not heard from Donny for years, nor did I realize he was in Portland for such a lengthy stay. He was lucky to have his Fubar brother's extended 'Greek Family' so close since his own had in fact abandoned him. Unfortunately, his uniqueness caused a sometime disconnect, even with his friends. Personally, my patience with his idiosyncrasies was too often short in coming; his new Portland family on the other hand, obviously paid great dividends in his life. Having a connection as we age is paramount. Why else would he revel in the Saturday morning visits from his Jehovah Witness 'friends?'

In the late '60s I lived in North Bergen, NJ. My ex, Karolyn, used to arm wrestle for beers at her local hangouts; she always won! I recall Donny's disbelief when she bragged after a few 'pops,' "No one has ever put my arm down." So he challenged her in the middle of his living room floor when we were visiting with Candle and her Brood on Staten Island. And as strong as Hobo still was, he did NOT succeed! Karolyn didn't put him down either, of course; she hadn't said she would, but Hobo could not get her arm past the upright position. He was amazed! The only person ever to put Karolyn down was The Cricket, and that obviously had some husband-wife reason behind it.

Donny was always asking friends to retrieve his belongings from various locations around the USA. His arrival in Portland with a U-Haul reminded me of when I lived in northern New Jersey in the early 70s. Don had stored some fishing gear, a cycle —perhaps the same one Gus mentioned, plus assorted boxes at a cabin near Middletown, NY. The old Cricket was instructing at Stewart AFB, an airfield not far from there.

After several calls to get the proper coordinates, I signed out a US Army helicopter for some cross-country 'training,' flew to Middletown to find Hobo standing in a small clearing near the cabin, displaying well-learned Marine Corps helicopter landing signals.

We had a time figuring out how to put all his 'stuff' in the back seat of a four-place observation helicopter--it was a perfect fit, by the way! I tossed the Hobo a spare flight suit and helmet so he wouldn't look out of place, and we headed off to Dulles International Airport near Washington, DC. There we were met by not one but two Lieutenant Colonels, one Air Force — known to us all as Hoz — and one Army! Thank you Hoz, for persuading them NOT to report me after we unloaded all that gear! After refueling, I sped back to Newburgh at 7,500 feet dodging cumulous rain clouds and getting two days' pay for my efforts. It was a complete blast!

When I moved to San Francisco a few years later, who was there with his new British Bride Glenda Mae Holmes, "The Lady Glenda," but the Hobo himself. How I discovered that, I don't recall. Perhaps he sought me out; I believe he was there before me. Every Memorial Day weekend I would head out to climb a mountain or explore California in some way.

During the last two years ('80 and '81), Hobo came with me. I have some pictures of the Fubars at the top of a snow-covered Mt. Lassen and camping beside the Trinity River. Of course, Hobo brought no extra clothing for climbing Lassen and, after glissading back to the car in record time, we had to build a bonfire to dry out. I'll never forget it!

The following year we used Don's van to cart the German Klepper — a two-person kayak that travels in two trunk-sized pieces. He had 'traded' from someone in a fashion known only to him, up to the Trinity River near Red Bluff. He was adamant that we keep a flag on the stern with Glenda's initials printed on it. In his inimitable way, Hobo wanted to 'raft' down river, but I knew we should paddle faster than the current.

Half way down the river in some rapids, we ran into a downed tree whose branches extended well into the river. Need I tell you that the flag snagged the branches? In our attempt to get untangled, the Klepper was overturned and once again the dynamic duo ended-up soaked to the skin! Luckily, the river wasn't that deep and all our gear was in watertight bundles. After pulling the Klepper to shore, we built another huge fire and commenced to dry our clothes. Once again, the Hobo had neglected to pack a second set of clothing! Cricket to the rescue for the second time!

As I said, my patience sometimes wore thin, no doubt the reason I didn't pursue him after I left San Fran for my present location in Boston. I lost track, although we did talk on the phone when he was with Gunder; and I did visit his tiny trailer in Tavares, Florida, when singing a concert in Winter Haven, at least during two Decembers. He even let me buy his favorite Colt Commander when he was in need of a few extra bucks. It was like an old friend for him. I wish I could say I still had it, but I was forced to sell it a few years ago for the same reasons.

Nevertheless, my memories are good ones. My favorite? His enthusiastic need to learn fencing from me, still the novice, while at St. Olaf, after I had spent a summer with the Temple University coach. As with anything physical, he would have made a great Epee or Saber competitor. It's too bad they didn't have a fencing program at St. Olaf. The Fubars could have made an additional pointed history on campus.

In order to make restitution for my neglect, I sent a card to Reno when I read about his latest illness. He picked one of my favorite places, even if for the wrong reasons; Reno is where I learned to fly helicopters at Stead AFB. Feeling guilty I hadn't kept up, I was hoping to share another experience this summer when I expect to drive The Pony Express Trail, Nevada Route 50, and see the Reno Air Races at Stead. It would have been fun to share them both with Donny. I trust he knows this!

I was always amazed at his knowledge of such diverse subjects. I remember sitting in his 'easy' chair in the trailer, surrounded by his worldly goods, piled on every surface to the ceiling, drinking instant ice tea — he had quit drinking booze, listening, amazed.

Could his tales be his legacy? Hopefully he was able to share some of his unique insights with his own kids. I'll miss that uniqueness and always remember these unique moments. Perhaps in another life — "En Guarde, Hobo!"

— Cricket

Remembering Cricket
September 23, 1936 — March 22, 2012

David, you were our Cricket, with a legacy of theater and everlasting song — from the Ole Choir to a master of SMU music, to Broadway and The Robert Shaw Chorale — liturgical and operetta to grand opera, you sang loudly and clearly at your cue, and even yet today you ring boldly and strong in memories; aviator and marksman, you danced through life and flew with grace on the wind — the music of your Ole roots survives, your heart and legacy, your "Popstand" soul resides, deeply felt laughter and ever-bouncing ways remain, flying and soaring new, and now again, we love you ever more, not forgotten, always well-sustained, our friend and our Cricket.

    HozKnoz —

Hobo and Friends

L-R: Marty, Argo, Scuba, Gus, Cricket – Oaklawn Cemetery, Northfield, Minnesota, 2003

In Memorium Fubar
Fidelis Usque Ad Mortem

Donald M. Clark, "Hobo" – 1935-2000
Paul A. Netland, "Stud" – 1936-2011
David A. Jarratt, "Cricket" – 1936-2012
Lars G. Kindem, "Argo" – 1933-2013
Homer C. Mittlestadt, "Sahatchi" – 1936-2013
Charles A. Nelson, "Rawhide" – 1936-2015

Peter F. Charlston – "Gus"
A. Malcolm Gimse – "Maximus"
David J. Martinson – "Dogface"
Wendell D. Miller – "Shylock"
J. Leland Mebust – "Scuba"
Noel D. Ness – "Gunder"
B. Wayne Quist – "HozKnoz"

Mike & Al's in Dundas, Minnesota - August 2010

L-R: Gus, Argo, Cricket, Rawhide, Hoz, Stud, Marty

The Last Rally

L-R: Gunder, Stud, Hoz (standing), Marty, Argo, Gus, Rawhide, Cricket – Northfield Country Club, August 2010

Made in the USA
Monee, IL
18 January 2021